GHOST FISHING

Ghost

Fishing

AN ECO-JUSTICE POETRY ANTHOLOGY

MELISSA TUCKEY, EDITOR

The University of Georgia Press ✦ Athens

© 2018 by the University of Georgia Press
Athens, Georgia 30602
www.ugapress.org
All rights reserved
Set in Minion Pro and Myriad Pro by Graphic Composition, Inc., Bogart, Georgia

Most University of Georgia Press titles are
available from popular e-book vendors.

Printed digitally

Library of Congress Cataloging-in-Publication Data
Names: Tuckey, Melissa, editor.
Title: Ghost fishing : an eco-justice poetry anthology / Melissa Tuckey, editor.
Description: Athens : The University of Georgia Press, [2018]
Identifiers: LCCN 2017037410 | ISBN 9780820353159 (pbk. : alk. paper)
Subjects: LCSH: Social problems—Poetry. | Environmental justice—Poetry. | American
    poetry—Minority authors. | Nature—Poetry. | Ecology—Poetry.
Classification: LCC PS595.875 G48 2018 | DDC 811.008/03556—dc23 LC record available at
    https://lccn.loc.gov/2017037410

A Small Needful Fact

ROSS GAY

Is that Eric Garner worked
for some time for the Parks and Rec.
Horticultural Department, which means,
perhaps, that with his very large hands,
perhaps, in all likelihood,
he put gently into the earth
some plants which, most likely,
some of them, in all likelihood,
continue to grow, continue
to do what such plants do, like house
and feed small and necessary creatures,
like being pleasant to touch and smell,
like converting sunlight
into food, like making it easier
for us to breathe.

❧ ❧ ❧

CONTENTS

IIIIIIIIIIIIIIIIIIIIIIIIIIIIIIIIIIIIIIIIIIIIIIIIIIIIIIIIIIIIIIIIIIIIIIIIIIIIIIIIIIIIIIIIIIIIIIIIIIIIIIIIIIIIIIIIIIIIIIIIII

Section IV. Tell the Birds: Human-Animal Relations   155

Section V. Unquiet Air: Resource Extraction   199

Section VII. Taking Root: Resistance, Resilience, and Resurgence   293

THE NATURE OF NATURE IS TO DEFINE OUR NATURE, OR WHAT ECO-JUSTICE POETRY MIGHT MEAN

||||||||||||||||||||||||||||||||||||||||||||||||||||||||||||||||||||||||||||||||||||||||||||||||||||||||||||||||||||||||||||||||||||||||||||||||||||

A Foreword

Our word *eco* is derived from the Greek *oikos*, meaning *house*. In the context of this collection of eco-justice poetry, that *house* is pulled from something larger, from the word *ecology*, which has come to mean the relationship between living entities and their environments. In turn, *environment* suggests for us a natural world—and also the conditions that affect the lives within that world. Inside every environment, according to these definitions, is some living being's house. What an intimate way this is of thinking about the living world. True justice implies fair treatment toward survival, and one's position in the world is perilous if one is not allowed to survive in one's own house. How dependent these definitions are, not just on life, but on how and where those lives are lived is certain.

We get our word *poet* from a word meaning *maker*, and one of the things a poet makes is an opportunity for the communication of deeply felt ideas. If our word *idea* comes to us from a word that means *to see*, then the act of making a poem that communicates ideas is an act of constructing language in such a way that one person can more tangibly see the thoughts and feelings of another. In her poem "Downriver, Río Grande Ghazalion," Emmy Pérez writes, "eyes are love. Yes. Remember" and, in this light, I understand the reading and the writing of poetry to be activities designed to construct avenues toward connection, toward seeing new ways to articulate the necessity of love in and for this world.

To borrow the title of an Ed Roberson poem collected here, carefully constructed language such as we use in poetry may helps us "To See the Earth before the End of the World." Language is how we shape our imagination, how we shape perspectives. Language is how we reach toward empathy. Language is how we learn about our history, our place in the now, and the possibilities for our future, a future where, as so many of the poems in this collection remind us, there may be fewer bats, fewer beavers, fewer bees, fewer micronesian kingfishers, fewer languages that might describe the world in different words than those favored by the word brokers of the Capitalocene, fewer eyeless shrimp, fewer unpolluted catfish, fewer humans whose lives are not compromised by warfare and its legacies, fewer banana trees, less cedar, less eucalyptus, fewer pecan groves, fewer children whose lives are not diminished by dependence on ruthless resource extraction, fewer elephants, fewer sharks, fewer whales, fewer families with access to potable water. The loss is overwhelming sometimes. "Perhaps the World Ends Here," Joy Harjo muses in one poem. But she localizes the poem in a house—at a kitchen table. There, she also acknowledges, "The world begins." The poems in this collection help give us language through which we might come to comprehend what we are losing, what we have already lost—and possibly even learn what is necessary to fight against such loss.

I am drawn to the poems in *Ghost Fishing* because of their expansive display of language. English is not the only language you'll encounter here. I am drawn to their global and diverse sources, and their reach across time. For much of the twentieth century we understood the provenance of nature writing to be something very different than what we are beginning to understand now, thanks, in part, to books like the one you are holding in your hands. As recently as 2006, when I conducted the literature review required to convince University of Georgia Press of the necessity of an anthology of African American nature poetry, I found a shockingly low representation of writers of color in the existing journals and anthologies of environmental writing—just a handful of poets of color repeated in publication after publication, mostly men. A lot of this had to do with the way we had defined who it was who wrote about the natural world—and how.

John Muir, bless his trailblazing heart, rejected the agrarian life of his father, married a wealthy concert-level pianist who refrained from playing her instrument when Muir was home writing, employed a Chinese cook who made sure Muir had food if he chose not to live only on stale bread, and was able to speak directly to the ears (and the pocketbooks) of many of the captains of industry. When John Muir got lost in nature, he could find himself again and then wander home to an estate overlooking a magnificent orchard he was not responsible for tending. I don't want to pick on Muir. I love Muir and his orchard. I have some almonds I picked there some years ago on my desk in my study. I have a desk in a study in a home; I have a spouse who also works to make a quiet space for me to write in; and I have the funds to order Chinese food if I don't feel like cooking. In these ways my positions of privilege are not that different from Muir's. But in other ways—my gender, my race, the wars and water shortages and sixth extinction that have magnified since Muir's time and that I worry will ravage my daughter's future—our positions are entirely different.

Muir's experience, the kind of experience many of us have understood as fundamental to the development of the great American nature writer, is not an experience we have all shared, nor one to which it would be reasonable for us all to aspire. Shifting the focus of the poems collected here away from a sense of the natural world untouched by humans and toward a space "of deep cultural attachment to the land," *Ghost Fishing* draws on voices from Gaza to Guam, Guatemala to Georgia. These poems are as likely to be set in the oil fields of Nigeria as the pipelines of Oklahoma and Canada. Poems here, as in Everett Hoagland's "Invocation," remind us that "Everything is / already connected." These poems record the perspectives of Asian men and black women, newly published poets and cornerstone voices of the twentieth century, working-class Americans and women who work on their knees clearing landmines "In Jordan's Northernmost Province." In fact, the poets represented between these covers represent far more demographic classifications than I could possibly name. The house built in this anthology is one of many interconnecting rooms.

It is the task of eco-poetics and eco-justice poetry to write about history, economics, politics, social justice, and the environment all at once. All that and more. Environmental crises and social crises are mutually and equally devastating. The mind of poetry is catching up with itself. Or it might be more accurate to say poetry is turning back into its own past. As many of the translations in this anthology prove, some environmentally oriented poetry has always grappled with history, politics, economics, love, and loss. I am grateful to Melissa Tuckey for compiling this collection. Spanning time and space, voice and vision, the poems in *Ghost Fishing* deliver necessary definition to this most crucial conversation.

Camille T. Dungy
Colorado, 2016

GHOST FISHING

INTRODUCTION

||||||||||||||||||||||||||||||||||||||||||||||||||||||||||||||||||||||||||||||||||||||||||||||||||||||||||||||||||||||||||||||||||||

Eco-justice poetry is poetry born of deep cultural attachment to the land and poetry born of crisis. Aligned with environmental justice activism and thought, eco-justice poetry defines environment as "the place we work, live, play, and worship." This is a shift from romantic notions of nature as a pristine wilderness outside of ourselves, toward recognizing the environment as home: a source of life, health, and livelihood. It is poetry at the intersection of culture, social justice, and the environment.

Ghost Fishing: An Eco-Justice Poetry Anthology began as a quest to better understand how poetry could respond to environmental and social crisis. I was looking for poems that hold *both* the complexity of this ecological moment and social consciousness, awareness that environmental crisis is both a social and political crisis. I was also looking for culturally diverse poetry because it is people of color and of low income who live disproportionately in harm's way with regard to environmental crisis, and such voices have been historically underrepresented among nature and eco-poetry collections.

The conversation around this book began at the 2012 Split This Rock Poetry Festival celebrating poet June Jordan and her contributions to social justice poetry. Wanting to explore June's connection to environmentalism as well as larger questions posed by her environmental poetry, I convened a panel titled "*(We) Who Would Be Free:* June Jordan and Environmental Justice Poetry." June's work opened new ways for me as a reader to think about nature poetry. In fact, as a longtime reader of her work, I had never thought of her as an environmental poet, perhaps because I had categorized her as a social justice poet and a black feminist writer, and in my mind, as a result of years of literary and cultural indoctrination, these identities were separate from what was most commonly defined as "nature poet." And yet, as I read her collected work again in search of nature poetry, I found it everywhere. June saw everything as connected, and she loved nature and spoke out on its behalf. Each poet on the environmental justice poetry panel, Homero Aridjis, Allison Adelle Hedge Coke, and Sherwin Bitsui, brought perspective to how their work intersected with both social justice and environmental concerns, and I came to realize my own poetry also lived at this intersection, though I hadn't thought of it in this way before.

I come to this work from a background in the military toxics and environmental justice movement, as someone who has lived near one of the nation's stockpiles of chemical weapons and advocated for safe disposal of these weapons. I come as a poet seeking the company of poems that speak to the complexity I witnessed as an activist. I come also as a middle-class white woman with working-class origins, navigating questions of race and class and gender, which inform and complicate my own understanding of the environment. I come to this work, over time, with humility.

Eco-justice poetry is recognition that the fate of the land is connected to the fate of people. Recent linguistics studies show that the most biodiverse parts of the world are also the most culturally diverse.[1] In places where biodiversity is threatened, linguistic diversity and culture are also threatened. While the correlation is not fully understood, current thinking in conservation acknowledges the connection between culture and environment: culture is how we negotiate with and survive in our environments; language is how we know the world. If cultural diversity is a sign of ecological health, it follows that an ecologically healthy eco-poetry would be as culturally diverse as the landscapes we seek to protect.

Poetry has a lot to offer a world in crisis. For centuries poets have given voice to our collective trauma: they name injustices, reclaim stolen language, and offer us courage to imagine a more just world. In a world out of balance, poetry is an act of cultural resilience.

Collecting poems for the anthology, I've come to a greater appreciation of the role of culture in connecting us to the environment, as well as of the historic way that colonization, war, white supremacy, and other forms of dispossession have robbed generations of their connection to the land. I've come to see how poetry and other arts have served throughout as a form of resistance, as an act of resurgence, and as cultural memory, just they have at times been used to justify a colonizing national identity. I've come to recognize as well that no experience of nature is monolithic, that all our relations to the natural world are grounded in cultural experience.

MAKING CONNECTIONS: ENVIRONMENTAL JUSTICE ACTIVISM

The environmental justice movement has been at the forefront of rethinking our human relationship to the natural world for more than forty years. In the United States, it has its origins in the civil rights movement, indigenous rights movements, and farmworker, labor, and feminist movements. It is, among other things, recognition that people of color and of low income are disproportionately burdened with exposure to toxic waste and recognition that environmental health and access to nature are human rights.

Rachel Carson's *Silent Spring* is a seminal work of environmental justice thought. A female scientist writing in the early 1960s, Carson described the impact of pesticides on birdlife and the eco-system, offering an early shift in Western scientific thinking toward recognition that the earth is a living system, one in which human shortsightedness has consequences. This text informed many environmental activists, who organized the first Earth Day actions and instigated establishment of the Environmental Protection Agency. It also informed early environmental justice activists, who began to make a connection between chemical contamination and public health in communities along the fencelines of hazardous waste disposal and production sites.

The first study to show a link between race, class, and pollution in the United States came in the form of a 1983 report from the General Accounting Office, which found that three-fourths of hazardous waste disposal sites in eight southeastern states were in low-income and African American communities.[2] This was followed by a United Church of Christ study in 1987, which showed that race, more than income, was a factor in where polluting industries and waste sites were located.[3] These studies galvanized the movement for environmental justice, as did the community experience of living and dying near toxic facilities.

The environmental justice movement is an international movement. At a historic gathering in 1991, more than 300 activists at the First International People of Color Environmental Leadership Summit developed a shared set of principles to guide their work, recognizing the "sacredness of mother earth, ecological unity, the interdependence of all species, and the right to be free from ecological destruction" as well as the "fundamental right to political, economic, cultural, self-determination of all peoples."[4]

Military accountability is also an environmental justice issue. According to the Center for Health, Environment, and Justice, the U.S. Department of

Defense is the country's largest polluter, with more than twenty-nine thousand sites in need of cleanup on more than eleven thousand properties in the United States alone. The majority of these sites are in low-income communities and communities of color. Abroad, the use of depleted uranium, white phosphorous, cluster bombs, and mines has created wastelands and public health catastrophes. The refugee crisis, likewise, is a product of war. A recent United Nations report estimates that "one in every 122 humans is now either a refugee, internally displaced, or seeking asylum."[5] Each of these displacements puts individuals, culture, and the environment at risk.

The environmental movement itself is not free of social division. As environmental scientist and cultural critic Carolyn Finney points out in her book *Black Faces, White Spaces*, the environmental movement continues to be divided by race. The big-ten mainstream environmental organizations are staffed mainly by white people, and many people of color feel marginalized and distrustful of these movements.

Though the environmental justice movement has done much to raise awareness and many communities are engaged in positive multiracial work, much work remains. As environmental sociologist Dr. Dorecetta E. Taylor writes in "American Environmentalism,"

> The environmental movement is a powerful social movement; however, the movement faces enormous challenges in the future. Among the most urgent, is the need to develop a more inclusive, culturally sensitive, broad-based environmental agenda that will appeal to many people and unite many sectors of the movement. To do this, the movement has to re-evaluate its relationship with industry and the government, re-appraise its role and mission, and develop strategies to understand and improve race, class, and gender relations.[6]

Carolyn Finney argues that those strategies must ultimately extend beyond the environmental justice framework, as any framework has the potential of limiting those categorized within it. She reminds readers that

> there is no monolithic African American experience. While there is arguably a collective experience of living in a country where racism is part of the nation's fabric, the personal experience for each African American (as it would be for anyone) is shaped by economic, generational, and gender differences, the place

where you live, your social and educational background, and ultimately the choices you make.[7]

Finney's words are especially useful in framing a discussion about environmental justice and eco-justice poetry: in reading multiculturally, in reading, as she defines it, "wildly," we must take care not to read any one particular human voice as speaking for an entire culture or category of people. At the same time, by reading widely and wildly, we have the opportunity to think beyond the limits of our own perspective and cultures, to enter human conversation from a deeper and more sustaining place. The right to form deep and sustaining bonds with the natural world, the right to enjoy nature and access health air, water, and food are human rights central to eco-justice literature.

POETRY AS MEMORY, IMAGINATION, AND RESISTANCE

Postcolonial literary critic Rob Nixon writes about pollution as a kind of unseen "slow violence" made all the more invisible because its victims are disproportionately poor and people of color; they also include future generations. According to Nixon, environmental justice literature can help make the unseen seen.[8] Eco-justice poetry brings poets of color, indigenous poets, women, and other marginalized voices (the unseen) to the center of eco-poetry.

Poetry's nonlinear approach to its subject matter allows us to imagine the link between past, present, and future and provides an opportunity to envision the "slow violence" Rob Nixon describes. It is not enough to understand that we have an impact on future generations—we must imaginatively *reshape* the way we think about the link between our actions and the future. Poetry offers this experience.

In this collection, for example, Lucille Clifton's poem, "generations," gives us a view of time from the perspective of grasshoppers, helping us to consider the intergenerational impact of "this business of war / these war kind of things." Similarly, Eleanor Wilner's "Trained on the Hill" gives us a telescopic and patient view of the erosion that follows the clear-cutting of trees on a distant hill. Such poems give us the opportunity to consider our own small space in time, whether we are living with history or looking ahead to the future.

The complexity of language is present in poetry's continual refreshing of it, through metaphors that connect seemingly disparate ideas to bring new understanding. Indeed, while "language is a cemetery," as Natalie Diaz writes in her harrowing intergenerational poem "Cloud Watching," language also rebirths itself in complex remakings that ask us to stay awake, the same way clouds are constantly remade. There is value in the way a poem can unmoor us from the familiar, reframing the way we see the world. Other times, we are asked to radically engage by listening to someone's story.

The participatory nature of poetry puts it at odds with monolithic thinking and political dichotomies, even within politically engaged poetry, as the poet looks inward to their/our complicity, such as in Pamela Alexander's poem "Makers," which addresses future generations: "we knew you were coming / but we couldn't stop." Poets in this collection ask us to rethink maps, topography, history, news, language, metaphor, economics, social relations, and culture. They ask also that we rethink the way we communicate with one another, even within activist movements, as Adrienne Rich does in her poem, "Trying to Talk with a Man," about disarmament activism:

> Your dry heat feels like power
>
> . . .
>
> when you get up and pace the floor
>
> talking of the danger
> as if it were not ourselves
> as if we were testing anything else.

Poetry is an act of inquiry and exchange, and the poems in this collection contain the kind of questions that reframe thinking. In "Focus in Real Time," June Jordan asks us, "Who grew these grains / Who owned the land / Who harvested the crop." In "Lunch in Nablus City Park," Naomi Shihab Nye asks, "Where do the souls of hills hide / when there is shooting in the valleys? / What makes a man with a gun seem bigger / than a man with almonds?" Whereas Wendell Berry, in "2008, XI," closes his poem about climate change with the profoundness of a riddle "to which the answer is a life / that none of us has lived."

When we are dulled by the disaster and deaths in our daily news feeds, poetry revitalizes our human connection to one another, as in Tarfia Faizullah's poem "Register of Eliminated Villages." Faizullah simultaneously invites critical thought about how the news is reported and offers a humanizing view, writing,

the scholar on tonight's
Frontline only counted each
town destroyed: three
hundred ninety-seven of them.

Who counts dolls, hand-
stitched, facedown in dirt?

A feeling of being overwhelmed by crisis sets in for those who are concerned about the fate of our communities, our oceans, our forests, and our planet. Only through imagination can we access the full extent of our grief, empathy, love, anger, and passion. Without it we are paralyzed. Poetry gives us access to difficult emotional landscapes and to the ferocity of hope. For example, Danez Smith's "summer, somewhere" asks us to imagine that somewhere (not heaven) black boys are safe: "please don't call / us dead, call us someplace better." This act of imagination makes it possible both to fully engage emotionally with social crisis and to imagine a world beyond it. Paradoxically, it is the presence of this imaginary unbroken world that allows us full access to our grief.

Like the romantics before them, eco-justice poets find resistance and resilience in the natural world. But nature in these inherently political poems is not free of civilization. In Brenda Hillman's "The Seeds Talk Back to Monsanto," the "Eco-terrorist seeds won't sprout." In Lorna Dee Cervantes's "Freeway 280," the seed again is a sign of resilience, the speaker of the poem scrambles "over the wire fence / that would have kept me out. // . . . that part of me / mown under / like a corpse / or a loose seed." In Cervantes's poem, the highway cuts like a scar through canning camps, through the "wild abrazos of climbing roses."

CONFRONTING PASTORAL AND ROMANTIC TRADITIONS

The romantic tradition of Eurocentric nature poetry, as commonly understood, was both a critique and an extension of Enlightenment thinking. It reflects the shift in Western thinking about nature, from nature as integral to human life to a nature that was available as a resource to be exploited. Romantic poets viewed nature as a place free of human corruption in opposition to industrialization and the industrialized view of nature. However, like the newly minted industrialists and capitalists, they valued individualism and saw nature as a resource in support of new ideals. And while this was an expansion of human freedom for a privileged minority, for others it was the beginning of enclosure, colonization, slave trade, and cultural and economic domination.

This way of thinking about nature as separate from civilization begins with the neopastoral, continues through romanticism, and persists in contemporary literature and thought. Unlike the early Greek pastoral, which showed the connection between labor and rural life and contained many tensions between the ideal and the realities of life, the neopastoral of the Renaissance, according to Raymond Williams, loses these crucial tensions, until selected images are "not in a living but enamelled world."[9] This polishing and mythologizing of rural life represents an erasure of cultural, political, and historical realities.

Romantic poetry offered both resistance to colonization and mythology to support it. The empty wilderness, with its romanticized natives, presented a vision to those with utopian dreams as well as an excuse for expansionist exploitation. And yet, this romantic vision was also a source of resistance to social injustice. For poets with a social conscience, the natural world offered a dream of a higher law. For William Blake, nature became part of his vision of a new world in which justice would prevail. For Henry David Thoreau, nature was a spiritual force with a higher law that compelled him to civil disobedience in response to the Mexican-American War and slavery. Walt Whitman's vision of an earth-based, culturally diverse, and democratic nation was an alternative to the broken physical world of civil war—and an inspiration for many poets since.

As idealistic and influential as these romantic poets were, their voices were not universal; they wrote from within their own limited cultural framework, as Langston Hughes reminds us in "I, Too, Sing America," his response to Whitman. Indeed, even before the American Civil War, African American poets such as James M. Whitfield were writing about their relationship to the natural world—and land culture traditions—as well as about their experience with slavery. As early as the 1700s, American Indians were writing poems in English, describing genocide and encroachment on their land and culture, arguing for self-determination.[10] Chicano poets were also writing nature-based poems. Women, too, had a story to tell beyond the domestic. Many of these poets were inspired by romantic tradition, but they wrote from outside American privilege, and they brought their own traditions, languages, and cultural understandings of the natural world to their work.

If we are to radically shift how we view our relationship to the natural world, we must be open to other viewpoints. When we acknowledge other cultural perspectives, we have an opportunity to examine our own cultural biases, and myths, many of which have served as a framework for ecological destruction.

Widening the parameters of nature poetry to include people of color and other marginalized people, we find a rich and diverse terrain reaching back hundreds of years in all directions. The forerunners of eco-justice poetry include not only environmental activist poets but also poets from American Indian poetry movements and traditions, the Harlem Renaissance, the Black Arts Movement, Chicano and Latino and Mestizo literary movements, Asian American traditions, traditions of activist and socially engaged poetry, feminist traditions, Appalachian culture, LGBTQ literary movements, and, of course, the many diverse cultures of storytelling and oral tradition that feed these traditions. These culturally diverse North American poetries have roots in international poetry reaching past the Eurocentric traditions to Africa, the Middle East, Asia, Latin America, and beyond.

What constitutes nature poetry and who counts as a purveyor of it have widened over the last forty years with the emergence of spoken word poetry and the greater accessibility of MFA writing programs, as well as the existence of culturally diverse literary organizations mentoring poets to produce a diverse and energized poetics among people of color, LGBTQ poets, low-income poets, women poets, and others. This wealth of cultural diversity brings with it innovation and stylistic diversity, as well as access to complex ways of thinking about the intersection of culture, the environment, and social justice. At the very moment in which biodiversity is threatened and languages and cultures are being lost, poets are staging an intervention, reclaiming culture and language, and resisting oppressive narratives, both in the United States and abroad.

NORTH AMERICAN ECO-JUSTICE POETRY . . . AND BEYOND
In constructing this anthology, I looked for thematic intersections of social justice, environment, and culture. The resulting sections reflect those intersections. I've arranged the book thematically to reflect the connection between the poems in the book and our individual and collective response to world events with the intention of focusing the conversation around key environmental concerns, such as borders and migration; war; food production and

distribution; animal-human relations; resource ownership and exploitation; environmental disaster; and cultural resistance. I've also included a Beyond North America section as an opportunity to connect concerns. Each of these thematic sections represents a key intersection of eco-justice concerns and an opportunity to widen conversations across disciplines.

At each of these intersections, I've sought poems that offer witness, fresh perspective, unique ways of looking/thinking, emotional catharsis, and imagination, as well as complexity of language and stylistic diversity. I've sought poems that both grapple with crisis and celebrate connections to the natural world. The majority of poems in this book are contemporary, written in the last twenty years. I have chosen to focus on these poems to explore the innovative ways that poets are responding to contemporary environmental and social crisis. I've included a few forebears going back to 1930 to ground some of the sections historically. One could go back further, of course, as environmental justice and eco-justice concerns are not new concerns in poetry. I wanted, however, to create a book of mostly living poets, a community of working writers who are engaged in naming this particular moment, with the knowledge that this conversation will continue to expand and grow beyond the confines of this anthology.

I've chosen to focus on North American eco-justice poetry because too little attention has been given to this mode of poetry in North America. However, environmental and social crisis are global, and the impact of U.S. foreign policy and North American consumer choices is felt globally. Moreover, the bonds between activists and citizens who care about the environment cross international borders. Therefore, any conversation about eco-justice poetry would be incomplete without acknowledging international perspectives. The "Beyond America" section provides an opportunity for readers to look beyond a North American perspective, with an emphasis on the Global South.

Many of the poets represented in this book have strong ties with other cultures and countries, and many of the indigenous poets in North America come from sovereign nations within U.S. borders. For the sake of simplicity, I define poets living in the United States as "North American" poets, and those beyond as "beyond North America," including those who have asked to identify as poets "beyond North America" because they live in multiple places.

Insisting that "Poetry is not a luxury," Audre Lorde writes, "Poetry is not only dream or vision, it is the skeleton architecture of our lives,"[11] In setting out to collect these poems, I'd hoped to find some poems to offset the despair these topics provoke. I imagined poems about alternative energy and farmer's markets and cooperatives, protests and community gardens, and although I did find some of these poems, in the end I was reminded that what poetry offers is something more fundamental than technology or political directives. It offers a way of seeing and connecting, an opportunity to widen our consciousness. Language creates neural pathways that allow us to imagine the future differently. The act of creating shared meaning is an act of community building at the deepest level. It is a journey in which we are changed.

Melissa Tuckey
Ithaca, New York

NOTES

1. L. J. Gorenflo, Suzanne Romaine, Russell A. Mittermeier, and Kristen Walker-Painemillad, "Co-occurrence of Linguistic and Biological Diversity in Biodiversity Hotspots and High Biodiversity Wilderness Areas," *Proceedings of the National Academy of Sciences of the United States of America*, 2012, http://www.ncbi.nlm.nih.gov/pmc/articles/PMC3361428/.

2. U.S. Government Accounting Office, "Siting Hazardous Waste Landfills and Their Correlation with Racial and Economic Status of Surrounding Communities," June 1, 1983, http://www.gao.gov/products/RCED-83-168.

3. Commission for Racial Justice, "Toxic Waste and Race in the United States," United Church of Christ, 1987, http://d3n8a8pro7vhmx.cloudfront.net/unitedchurch ofchrist/legacy_url/13567/toxwrace87.pdf?1418439935.

4. "Principles of Environmental Justice" (April 6, 1996), http://www.ejnet.org/ej/principles.html.

5. United Nations News Centre, "UN Warns of 'Record High' 60 Million Displaced amid Expanding Global Conflicts," June 18, 2015, http://www.un.org/apps/news/story .asp?NewsID=51185#.VcoK1_2Fv8E.

6. Dorceta E. Taylor, "American Environmentalism: The Role of Race, Class, and Gender in Shaping Activism: 1820–1995," *Race, Gender, and Class* 5, no. 1 (1997): 16–62, quote on p. 41.

7. Carolyn Finney, *Black Faces, White Spaces* (Chapel Hill, N.C.: The University of North Carolina Press, 2014), 98.

8. Rob Nixon, *Slow Violence and the Environmentalism of the Poor* (Cambridge, Mass.: Harvard University Press, 2011).

9. Raymond Williams, *The Country and the City* (New York: Oxford University Press, 1973), 18.

10. Robert Parker, *Changing Is Not Vanishing: A Collection of American Indian Poetry to 1930* (Philadelphia: University of Pennsylvania Press, 2011).

11. Audre Lorde, *Sister Outsider: Essays and Speeches* (Berkeley, Calif.: Crossing Press, 1985), 11.

SECTION I

||||||||||||||||||||||||||||||||||||||||||||||||||||||||||||||||||||||||||||||||||||||||||||||||||||||||||||||||||||||||||||||

La Frontera / Sin Fronteras
↦ Land, Culture, Possession, and Dispossession

At the heart of this section are questions of belonging and sovereignty. These are poems of survival, witness, and mourning; poems that question borders and citizenship; poems that celebrate complex identities. Within the poems, nature is a source of identity, sustenance, memory, resistance, and imagination.

Poems such as Jennifer Elise Foerster's "Leaving Tulsa" illuminate the speaker's struggle to remain connected to culture, history, and memory in a world of treaty violations, eminent domain, highways, pipelines, and vanishing land. In "Leaving Tulsa's" case, the culture is that of the Creek, and the land holds tradition and history; it is what keeps the speaker of the poem from becoming just another lost American.

In contrast, W. S. Merwin's poem "Native Trees" contemplates separation from the natural world from a migrant perspective:

> Neither my father nor my mother knew
> the names of the trees
> where I was born.

The child speaker attempts to understand how they could lack such vital knowledge, asking, "Were there trees / where they were children"?

Nature is a source of identity in many of the poems. In Aimee Nezhukumatathil's "What Are You/ Where Are You From?" the natural world is a source of resistance and beauty. Nezhukumatathil writes,

> I come from a place where scientists try to trick
> indigo buntings into following a false star
> in a darkened room.

Similarly, the speaker in Brenda Cárdenas's poem "Zacuanpapalotls" expresses Chicana/o identity in images of a natural world that celebrates complexity:

> We are between—
> the flicker of a chameleon's tail
> that turns his desert-blue backbone
> to jade or pink sand,
> the snake-skinned fraternal twins
> of solstice and equinox.

Poets in this section confront the violence of racism and mourn the intergenerational nature of displacement. In Margaret Walker's lyric 1942 poem "Sorrow Home," the African American speaker mourns the northern migration in response to post-Reconstruction racism and violence: "O Southland, sorrow home, melody beating in my bone and blood! How long will the Klan of hate, the hounds and the chain gangs keep me from my own?" Imagination opens a space for deep mourning in Danez Smith's poem "summer, somewhere," conjuring a world in which brown boys are safe, where murdered boys like Trayvon Martin and Sean Bell are returned to the earth unharmed. In the voice of the murdered boys, Smith writes, "please, don't call / us dead, call us alive someplace better" and asks "do you know what it's like to live / someplace that loves you back?"

Above all, these are poems of survival. Emmy Pérez's "Staying in the flood" shows the resilience of culture and nature in the midst of rising floodwaters, wondering,

> . . . why the busted-
> Up nopal like a bullet
> Target or a Just-
> Married sign
> In April
> Strung with
> Tecate cans
> Hitched to an
> El Camino
> Why is it still
> Blooming
> Yellow roses?

Sorrow Home
MARGARET WALKER

My roots are deep in southern life; deeper than John Brown or Nat Turner or
Robert Lee. I was sired and weaned in a tropic world. The palm tree and
banana leaf, mango and coconut, breadfruit and rubber trees know me.

Warm skies and gulf blue streams are in my blood. I belong with the smell of
fresh pine, the trail of coon, and the spring growth of wild onion.

I am no hothouse bulb to be reared in steam-heated flats with the music of
El and subway in my ears, walled in by steel and wood and brick far from
the sky.

I want the cotton fields, tobacco and the cane. I want to walk along the sacks
of seed to drop in fallow ground. Restless music is in my heart and I am
eager to be gone.

O Southland, sorrow home, melody beating in my bone and blood! How
long will the Klan of hate, the hounds and the chain gangs keep me from
my own?

Late Shift

TIM SEIBLES

Places—
maybe dreams

from which I cannot   return: the velvet

touch of Her lips, first light
fingering a cup: sacred dislocations

of mind—the way the right sound
becomes visible.

Where I am now
it's later—the clocks have been amended

to include all the strange hours—

and Someone cracked my name
as if all my life I'd been locked inside.

I know the shelves stay stocked, big cars lead the chase,
there's always more   and more to eat.

But was that ever   my country?

I was. Born there.
And I'd go back   if I could—

just to feel less lonely—
but what I took

to be a certain distance

was actually a late   shift in myself,

a different kind of listening:
the voice, a thread of honey—

the jar tipped   just enough to one side:

Listen.

We belong to no nation.

One day we will hold the earth
again   as if She were a love

nearly lost, Her rainy hair tangled in our hands.

The soul is what we are.
every life   a word the wind turns to say.

And though trouble grows back like a beard,
an unchained blood governs my tongue.

I have seen the door   that is not there

still open

☙☙☙

What Are You? / Where Are You From?

AIMEE NEZHUKUMATATHIL

I come from a place where scientists try to trick
indigo buntings into following a false star
in a darkened room. There is no other blue like these birds—
no other feather more electric. Not even a bright gumball
in a glass cage could match it. The weather I was born into
was a sort of drizzle on a singular day of sunshine, the kind
that unsettles you if you look out the window to search
for a funnel cloud. Somewhere, a wooden fence fell. Animals

did not know what to do with their fresh freedom, so they
huddled together at the edge of the property line until dark,
then slowly scattered away. On my first day of school, no one
could pronounce my name, and when they tried, it sounded like
bread sputtering as it bakes. My first love was a dandelion
gathered tenderly in the apron of my dress. I never
even noticed how quiet he was—a temporary silence—
as if he was only trying to figure out what to say.

⊕ ⊕ ⊕

Deleuze & Guattari: *Making love is not just becoming as one, or even two, but becoming as a hundred thousand.*
GREGORY PARDLO

Raise your eyes along the spires of Green-Wood Cemetery
or stand on the ball fields of Brooklyn College in Hopperesque
light. Quaker Parrots will appear to you like the visions
of St. Francis, lift the snatches of sound woven to make their
voices and call to you from their nests, a nation of cheer
trumpets and conch shells, a frenzied population of twitching,
toes. They seduce us not simply with their tropical verve. Listen
into the feathered shrubbery of their heat: they're chattering
lines from Emma Lazarus; they're trading fours on "Salt Peanuts";
they're mourning their cousin, the Carolina Parrot, reduced to
a flourish on ladies' headgear. Who flushed them from their ancestral
skies of Argentina? What love sustained the awareness of their bodies—
whether as chattel or deportees—such distance, and who speaks
for this Diaspora heedless of empire's mundane cartography?
If we ask why Brooklyn, we hear only our own reply:
If not here, where? then tease a final query from our minds like
thread from a lawn chair, parroting Hillel: *And if not now, when?*

֍ ֍ ֍

Leaving Tulsa

JENNIFER ELISE FOERSTER

for Cosetta

Once there were coyotes, cardinals
in the cedar. You could cure amnesia
with the trees of our back-forty. Once
I drowned in a monsoon of frogs—
Grandma said it was a good thing, a promise
for a good crop. Grandma's perfect tomatoes.
Squash. She taught us to shuck corn, laughing,
never spoke about her childhood
or the faces in gingerbread tins
stacked in the closet.

She was covered in a quilt, the Creek way.
But I don't know this kind of burial:
vanishing toads, thinning pecan groves,
peach trees choked by palms.
New neighbors tossing clipped grass
over our fence line, griping to the city
of our overgrown fields.

Grandma fell in love with a truck driver,
grew watermelons by the pond
on our Indian allotment,
took us fishing for dragonflies.
When the bulldozers came
with their documents from the city
and a truckload of pipelines,
her shotgun was already loaded.

Under the bent chestnut, the well
where Cosetta's husband
hid his whiskey—buried beneath roots
her bundle of beads. *They tell
the story of our family.* Cosetta's land
flattened to a parking lot.

Grandma potted a cedar sapling
I could take on the road for luck.
She used the bark for heart lesions
doctors couldn't explain.
To her they were maps, traces of home,
the Milky Way, where she's going, she said.

After the funeral
I stowed her jewelry in the ground,
promised to return when the rivers rose.

On the grassy plain behind the house
one buffalo remains.

Along the highway's gravel pits
sunflowers stand in dense rows.
Telephone poles crook into the layered sky.
A crow's beak broken by a windmill's blade.
It is then I understand my grandmother:
*When they see open land
they only know to take it.*

I understand how to walk among hay bales
looking for turtle shells.
How to sing over the groan of the county road
widening to four lanes.
I understand how to keep from looking up:
small planes trail overhead
as I kneel in the Johnson grass
combing away footprints.

Up here, parallel to the median
with a vista of mesas' weavings,
the sky a belt of blue and white beadwork,
I see our hundred and sixty acres
stamped on God's forsaken country,
a roof blown off a shed,
beams bent like matchsticks,
a drove of white cows
making their home
in a derailed train car.

↢↢↢

Zacuanpapalotls

BRENDA CÁRDENAS

in memory of José Antonio Burciaga, 1947–1996

> We are chameleons. We become chameleon.
> —José Antonio Burciaga

We are space between—
the black-orange blur
of a million Monarchs
on their two-generation migration
south to fir-crowned Michoacán
where tree trunks will sprout feathers,
a forest of paper-thin wings.

Our Mexica cocooned
in the membranes de la Madre Tierra
say we are reborn zacuanpapalotls,
mariposas negras y anaranjadas
in whose sweep the dead whisper.

We are between—
the flicker of a chameleon's tail
that turns his desert-blue backbone
to jade or pink sand,
the snake-skinned fraternal twins
of solstice and equinox.

The ashen dawn, silvering dusk,
la oración as it leaves the lips,
the tug from sleep,
the glide into dreams
that husk out mestizo memory.

We are—
one life passing through the prism
of all others, gathering color and song,
cempazuchil and drum
to leave a rhythm scattered on the wind,
dust tinting the tips of fingers
as we slip into our new light.

Anchorage

JOY HARJO

for Audre Lorde

This city is made of stone, of blood, and fish.
There are Chugatch Mountains to the east
and whale and seal to the west.
It hasn't always been this way, because glaciers
who are ice ghosts create oceans, carve earth
and shape this city here, by the sound.
They swim backwards in time.

Once a storm of boiling earth cracked open
the streets, threw open the town.
It's quiet now, but underneath the concrete
is the cooking earth,
        and above that, air
which is another ocean, where spirits we can't see
are dancing   joking   getting full
on roasted caribou, and the praying
goes on, extends out.

Nora and I go walking down 4th Avenue
and know it is all happening.
On a park bench we see someone's Athabascan
grandmother, folded up, smelling like 200 years
of blood and piss, her eyes closed against some
unimagined darkness, where she is buried
in an ache in which nothing makes sense.

We keep on breathing, walking, but softer now,
the clouds whirling in the air above us.
What can we say that would make us understand
better than we do already?
Except to speak of her home and claim her
as our own history, and know that our dreams
don't end here, two blocks away from the ocean
where our hearts still batter away at the muddy shore.

And I think of the 6th Avenue jail, of mostly native
and black men, where Henry told about being shot at
eight times outside a liquor store in L.A., but when
the car sped away he was surprised he was alive,
no bullet holes, man, and eight cartridges strewn
on the sidewalk all around him.

Everyone laughed at the impossibility of it,
but also the truth. Because who would believe
the fantastic and terrible story of all of our survival
those who were never meant
                                        to survive?

❧ ❧ ❧

Saguaros

JAVIER ZAMORA

It was dusk for kilometers and bats in the lavender sky
   like spiders when a fly is caught, began to appear.
And there, not the promised land, but barbwire and barbwire

   with nothing growing under it. I tried to fly that dusk
after a bat said *la sangre del saguaro nos seduce*. Sometimes
   I wake and my throat is dry, so I drive to botanical gardens

to search for red fruits at the top of saguaros, the ones
   at dusk I threw rocks at for the sake of hunger.

But I never find them here. These bats say *speak English only*.
   Sometimes in my car, that viscous red syrup
clings to my throat and I have to pull over—

   I also scraped needles first, then carved
those tall torsos for water, then spotlights drove me
   and thirty others dashing into palos verdes,

green-striped trucks surrounded us and our empty bottles
   rattled. When the trucks left, a cold cell swallowed us.

↭ ↭ ↭

Staying in the flood

EMMY PÉREZ

Why the tom
Spraying the screen
Window, why
Floodwater
Left over from
Hurricane Alex
A spring after last summer
Weed seeds sprouting
Downriver

Why the woodpecker's
Off and on wing
Pause causing
Vertigo, why
Confuse herons with
Egrets. Aztlán:
Land of white herons.

Why the sap stains
Like accidents
Why the border patrol
Woman in a blue truck
With camper big
Enough to haul
Livestock. Why
The anacahuita
Flowers, why one
Giant swallowtail butterfly

Why the debris
Of retama flowers
Gathering on asphalt
Edges like
The path of hair
Under your belly button
Or a path of marigold
Petals welcoming
The dead home

And why the busted-
Up nopal like a bullet
Target or a Just-
Married sign
In April
Strung with
Tecate cans
Hitched to an
El Camino—
Why is it still
Blooming
Yellow roses?

❧ ❧ ❧

summer, somewhere (excerpt)

DANEZ SMITH

somewhere, a sun. below, boys brown
as rye play the dozens & ball, jump

in the air & stay there. boys become new
moons, gum-dark on all sides, beg bruise

-blue water to fly, at least tide, at least
spit back a father or two. I won't get started.

history is what it is. it knows what it did.
bad dog. bad blood. bad day to be a boy

color of a July well spent. but here, not earth
not heaven, boys can't recall their white shirt

turned a ruby gown. here there is no language
for *officer* or *law*, no color to call *white*

if snow fell, it'd fall black. please, don't call
us dead, call us alive someplace better.

we say our own names when we pray.
we go out for sweets & come back.

———

this is how we are born: come morning
after we cypher/feast/hoop, we dig

a new boy up from the ground, take
him out his treebox, shake worms

from his braids. sometimes they'll sing
a trapgod hymn (what a first breath!)

sometimes it's they eyes who lead
scanning for bonefleshed men in blue.

we say *congrats, you're a boy again!*
we give him a durag, a bowl, a second chance.

we send him off to wander for a day
or ever, let him pick his new name.

that boy was Trayvon, now called *RainKing*.
that man Sean named himself *I do, I do.*

O, the imagination of a new reborn boy
but most of us settle on *alive.*

———

sometimes a boy is born
right out the sky, dropped from

a bridge between starshine & clay.
one boy showed up pulled behind

a truck, a parade for himself
& his wet red gown. years ago

we plucked brothers from branches
unpeeled their naps from bark.

sometimes a boy walks into his room
then walks out into his new world

still clutching wicked metals. some boys
waded here through their own blood.

does it matter how he got here if we're all here
to dance? grab a boy, spin him around.

if he asks for a kiss, kiss him.
if he asks where he is, say *gone*.

———

no need for geography
now that we're safe everywhere.

point to whatever you please
& call it church, home, or sweet love.

paradise is a world where everything
is a sanctuary & nothing is a gun.

here, if it grows it knows its place
in history. yesterday, a poplar

told me of old forest
heavy with fruits I'd call uncle

bursting red pulp & set afire,
harvest of dark wind chimes.

after I fell from its limb
it kissed sap into my wound.

do you know what it's like to live
someplace that loves you back?

———

here, everybody wanna be black & is.
look—the forest is a flock of boys

who never got to grow up, blooming
into forever, afros like maple crowns

reaching sap-slow toward sky. watch
Forest run in the rain, branches

melting into paper-soft curls, duck
under the mountain for shelter. watch

the mountain reveal itself a boy.
watch Mountain & Forest playing

in the rain, watch the rain melt everything
into a boy with brown eyes & wet naps—

the lake turns into a boy in the rain
the swamp—a boy in the rain

the fields of lavender—brothers
dancing between the storm.

———

if you press your ear to the dirt
you can hear it hum, not like it's filled

with beetles & other low gods
but like a mouth rot with gospel

& other glories. listen to the dirt
crescendo a boy back.

come. celebrate. this
is everyday. every day

holy. everyday high
holiday. everyday new

year. every year, days get longer.
time clogged with boys. the boys

O the boys. they still come
in droves. the old world

keeps choking them. our new one
can't stop spitting them out.

———

ask the mountain-boy to put you on
his shoulders if you want to see

the old world, ask him for some lean
-in & you'll be home. step off him

& walk around your block.
grow wings & fly above your city.

all the guns fire toward heaven.
warning shots mince your feathers.

fall back to the metal-less side
of the mountain, cry if you need to.

that world of laws rendered us into dark
matter. we asked for nothing but our names

in a mouth we've known
for decades. some were blessed

to know the mouth.
our decades betrayed us.

----

there, I drowned, back before, once.
there, I knew how to swim but couldn't.

there, men stood by shore & watched me blue.
there, I was a dead fish, the river's prince.

there, I had a face & then I didn't.
there, my mother cried over me

but I wasn't there. I was here, by my own
water, singing a song I learned somewhere

south of somewhere worse. that was when
direction mattered. now, everywhere

I am is the center of everything.
I must be the lord of something.

what was I before? a boy? a son?
a warning? a myth? I whistled

now I'm the God of whistling.
I built my Olympia downstream.

----

you are not welcome here. trust
the trip will kill you. go home.

we earned this paradise
by a death we didn't deserve.

I am sure there are other heres.
a somewhere for every kind

of somebody, a heaven of brown
girls braiding on golden stoops

but here—
            how could I ever explain to you —

            someone prayed we'd rest in peace
            & here we are

in peace   whole   all summer

ᘒᘒᘒ

We Who Weave

LECONTÉ DILL

On Tyrone Geter's "The Basket Maker #2"

Weave me closer
to you
with hands dyed indigo
that rake oyster beds
awake
Smell you long
before
I see you
Vanilla sweet
Sweetgrass weaving
wares that keep Yankees coming
on ferries, no bridge
Waters been troubled
Makes you wonder
who put the root on whom first
with doors dyed indigo
Pray the evil spirits away
at the praise house
Make John Hop to stave off John Deere
We migrants
fighting to stay put
Even nomads come home
for a Low Country Boil
a feast for hungry
prodigal sons
and daughters
with hearts dyed indigo
Dying for you to
weave us closer

❧ ❧ ❧

Bones—A City Poem

CHERYL SAVAGEAU

forget the great blue heron flying low
    over the marsh, its footprints
    still fresh in the sand

forget the taste of wild mushrooms
    and where to find them

forget lichen-covered pines
    and iceland moss

forget the one-legged duck
    and the eggs of the snapping turtle
    laid in the bank

forget the frog found in the belly of a bass

forget the cove testing its breath
    against the autumn morning

forget the down-filled nest
    and the snake swimming at midday

forget the bullhead lilies
    and the whiskers
    of the pout

forget walking on black ice
    beneath the sky hunter's bow

forget the living waters
    of Quinsigamond

forget how to find the Pole star and why

forget the eyes of the red fox
   the hornets that made their home
   in the skull of a cow

forget waking to hear the call of the loon

forget that raccoons are younger brothers
   to the bear

forget that you are walking
   on the bones of your grandmothers

Uptown

ALAN KING

after Tony Hoagland

A bee that sounds like an electric razor says something
to a bee that sounds like a punctured muffler.

The sun interrogates the grass that sambas when the wind
pulls its imaginary strings. Inside an apartment,

a cockatiel throws its song like an alley-oop

through an open window to a bird with a cry
like a dot matrix printer. Around here, flowers

are musk merchants enticing with their scents.
Trees hover like street ballers posing

for *Sports Illustrated*. No. They're emcees
kicking chlorophyll rhymes

while b-boy weeds uprock concrete around a strip mall
of liquor stores and carry-outs.

In all of this, pixie stix-powder colors the sunset tongues
of young mothers, wheeling their strollers

down the avenue. Their bodies tense as bluebell buds
to the ultraviolet stares of brothas.

Somewhere, sirens wail like horn-mouth babies,
like Miles at the Five Spot. Crushed
berries mark the street like chalk-outs.

In all of this, bodies fall like branches
blown away by hollow-tip winds while dead leaves

and petals litter cracked sidewalks
like shell casings.

Native Trees

W. S. MERWIN

Neither my father nor my mother knew
the names of the trees
where I was born
what is that
I asked and my
father and mother did not
hear they did not look where I pointed
surfaces of furniture held
the attention of their fingers
and across the room they could watch
walls they had forgotten
where there were no questions
no voices and no shade

Were there trees
where they were children
where I had not been
I asked
were there trees in those places
where my father and my mother were born
and in that time did
my father and my mother see them
and when they said yes it meant
they did not remember
What were they I asked what were they
but both my father and my mother
said they never knew

⊲⊳ ⊲⊳ ⊲⊳

Ghosts

FRANCINE RUBIN

The distant skyline backlit in cerulean, the city shimmered
with jewel-windows in skyscrapers, palatial bridges crowning
the Hudson—and whispered of great-grandparents who had lived
in rat-run hovels, who mixed hot water with catsup to make soup,
who feared pogroms burning them alive in their sleep.

From our perch on a suburban hill, we feared the city's darkened
corners filled with wraiths—the starving and wretched
who could traverse the distance in a second, who could sense
we were their descendants, and who could reverse time and space
to return us to our true birthright.

Crossing
BRIAN KOMEI DEMPSTER

No turning back. Deep in the Utah desert now, having left one home
    to return to the temple of my grandfather. I press the pedal
        hard. Long behind me, civilization's last sign—a bent post
           and a wooden board: *No food or gas for 200 miles.* The tank

    needling below half-full, I smoke Camels to soothe
my worry. Is this where it happened? What's left out there of Topaz
in the simmering heat? On quartzed asphalt I rush

    past salt beds, squint at the horizon for the desert's edge: a lone
        tower, a flattened barrack, some sign of Topaz—the camp
           where my mother, her family, were imprisoned. As I speed
                by shrub cactus, the thought of it feels too near,

        too close. The engine steams. The radiator
      hisses. Gusts gather, wind pushes my Civic side
to side, and I grip the steering wheel, strain to see

through a windshield smeared with yellow jacket wings, blood
    of mosquitoes. If I can find it, how much can
        I really know? Were sandstorms soft as dreams or stinging
           like nettles? Who held my mother when the wind whipped

        beige handfuls at her baby cheeks? Was the sand tinged
          with beige or orange from oxidized mesas? *I don't remember*
        my mother's answer to everything. High on coffee

and nicotine, I half-dream in waves of heat: summon ghosts
    from the canyon beyond thin lines of barbed wire. Our name
      Ishida. Ishi means stone, *da* the field. We were gemstones
        strewn in the wasteland. Only three days

and one thousand miles to go before I reach
San Francisco, the church where my mother was born
and torn away. Maybe Topaz in the desert was long

gone, but it lingered in letters, photos, fragments
of stories. My mother's room now mine, the bed pulled blank
with ironed sheets, a desk set with pen and paper. Here
I would come to understand.

❧ ❧ ❧

Cleaning
CAMILLE T. DUNGY

I learned regret at Mother's sink,
jarred tomatoes, river-mud brown,
a generation old, lumping
down the drain. Hating wasted space,
I had discarded what I could
not understand. I hadn't known
a woman to fight drought or frost
for the promise of winter meals,
hadn't known my great-grandmother,
or what it was to have then lose
the company of that woman
who, upon seeing her namesake,
child of her child, grown and gliding
into marriage, gifted the fruit
of her garden, a hard-won strike
against want. Opening the jar,
I knew nothing of the rotting
effect, the twisting grip of years
spent packing, of years spent moving,
further each time, from known comforts:
a grandmother's garden, her rows
always neat, the harvest: bright wealth
mother hoarded. I understood
only the danger of a date
so old. Understanding clearly
what is fatal to the body,
I only understand too late
what can be fatal to the heart.

‹›‹›‹›

Unpeopled Eden (excerpt)

RIGOBERTO GONZÁLEZ

> We died in your hills, we died in your deserts,
> We died in your valleys and died on your plains.
> We died 'neath your trees and we died in your bushes,
> Both sides of the river, we died just the same.
> "Plane Wreck at Los Gatos (Deportees)," Woody Guthrie

I

AFTER THE IMMIGRATION RAID

Beneath one apple tree the fruit
lies flung like the beads from
a rosary with a broken string.
Another tree stands amused
over the strangeness of a shoe
that pretends to be an apple
in its redness, though it'll never be
an apple with that lace stem
and a pit where a core should be.

The tree at the end of the row
will weep over the pillage
all week. Around its trunk, debris:
straw hats, handkerchief, a basket
going hungry for what's out
of reach. Somewhere in the orchard
a screech goes weaker by the hour.
A radio without paws, it cannot claw
its chords to end its suffering.

But silence comes, eventually,
and the apple trees will rest,
gathering the shadows to their roots
as the flame inside each apple
falls asleep. All the while, finches
perch among the branches—patient
vultures waiting for the fruit to rot.
For a wasp, intoxicated by the sugars,
this is the perfect place to nest.

The colony will thrive inside
decay: the apples softening until
their wrinkled skins begin to sink,
the seeds poking through like teeth.
The trees will sway without the wind
because the ground will boil
with larvae. A bird will feast
until it chokes and ants will march
into the belly through the beak.

. . .

V

AFTER THE CLEAN-UP ALONG LOS GATOS CANYON

What strange flowers grow
in the shadow. Without petals
and with crooked twigs for stems.
The butterflies that pollinated them
were bits of carbon glowing
at the edge. The solitary lone wolf
spider doesn't dare to bite
the scorched caul on the canyon.
It packs its fangs for brighter lands.

The footprints drawn in black
do not match the footprints
in the orchard though they also
bear the weight of the unwanted.
The chain gang called upon to gather
the debris sang the Prison Blues
all afternoon: Inmate, deportee,
in your last attempt to flee
every bone splits into three.

VI

AFTER THE COMMUNAL BURIAL

Twenty-eight equals one
deportation bus equals one
cell in the detention center, one
plane-load of deportees, one
plunge into the canyon, one
body in the coffin although one
was a woman—sister not alone
anymore among the chaperone
of angels with wings of stone.

Manuel Merino, Julio Barrón,
Severo, Elías, Manuel Calderón,
Francisco, Santiago, Jaime, Martín,
Lupe, Guadalupe, Tomás, Juan Ruiz,
Alberto, Ramón, Apolonio, Ramón,
Luis, Román, Luis, Salvador,
Ignacio Navarro, Jesús, Bernabé,
Rosalío Portillo, María, y José.
Y un Deportado No Identificado.

No papers necessary to cross
the cemetery. The sun floods
the paths between tombs
and everything pushes out
into light. No shame to be
a cherub without a nose.
The wreath will not hide
its decay. Cement displays
its injuries with no regrets.

This is the place to forget
about labor and hardship and pain.
No house left to build, no kitchen
to clean, no chair on a porch, no
children to feed. No longing left
except a wish that will never come
true: Paint us back into the blank
sky's blue. Don't forget us
like we've forgotten all of you.

How to Disappear the Stars
LAUREN CAMP

If you let them build a book of houses, the edges of a small world
will shave to sawdust; the moon will blue and fade.

Solitude will redraw as red lines that tear
your golden land to tiny parcels.

Ground will shift south into a suburb of metal streets and silent birds,
a breathless spine of two-by-fours talking to limbless trees.

Each small mound of affected dirt will sprout into a web of structure,
a coagulating noise of walls and floors tumbling all at once in your ears.

Each feverish city will extinguish the horizon
and erase the blueprint
of your open sky.

⤙⤙⤙

SECTION II

Instead of Flowers
↬ War

War is the largest contributor to environmental destruction, both in the use of toxic weapons and the massive displacement of local populations. Poets in this section consider the environmental consequences of war and the relationship between language, war, nature, and poetry. These poems explore the many ways war disrupts the human relationship to the environment.

Several poems in this section look directly at the toxic impact of war: Denise Levertov's "Overheard in S.E. Asia" and Yusef Komunyakaa's "You and I Are Disappearing" consider the damage of white phosphorous in Vietnam, what Levertov calls "mechanical snow." Shara Lessley writes about the women who clean up abandoned mines "In Jordan's Northernmost Province," a landscape where sheep graze on "restricted fields" and everyday life and survival are disrupted by war's legacy:

> Women go down on their knees hovering above a map-work of metalwork,
> brushing dust from cluster bombs like ash from flatbread.

Several poets examine the shared fate of animals in war. At times, humans find it easier to feel sympathy for animals than humans, as we are reminded in the poem "The Dogs of Ashdod," by Zein El-Amine. Sara Goudarzi's "Another Day" presents a nine-year-old child's view of war: "It is the birds I worry about . . . Because it's their song / that awakens me to another day."

Poets like Phil Metres examine the economic underpinnings of war. In "Mappemonde," Metres considers "the names of nations beneath the names of oil companies." Within the poem, in places like Mosul, history is layered between massacres and oil:

> The silt of rivers cradling the dead
> animal and vegetable on the bed
> of ancient seas, ancient continents, lust
> engulfed in the upheaving of earth's crust.

Elise Paschen looks at the connection between oil, trickery, and murder in "Wi'-gi-e," a poem about Anna Kyle Brown, an Osage Indian who was murdered in 1921 in Fairfax, Oklahoma, along with several members of her family in a plot by a wealthy white landowner to steal the family's oil rights.[1] Within this poem, nature is a witness and keeper of memory.

American poets question their distance from the war. In "Why I Don't Mention Flowers When Conversations with My Brother Reach Uncomfortable Silences," by Natalie Diaz, the speaker of the poem reports on a conversation with her brother, who has recently returned from war in Afghanistan. Her innocent question, "Were there flowers there?" yields horrific images of war.

Within these poems, nature serves as a source of opposition and contrast to war as well. Jennifer Atkinson's "Landscape with Translucent Moon" gives witness to the two-thousand-year-old tree planted by the historical Buddha from a slip of the tree in which Buddha sought enlightenment, and asks "how many wars / has that peace survived?"

We are reminded that war does not serve the natural world. Chickasaw poet Linda Hogan tells the story of the bamboo in her poem of the same name, associating with the first woman, who was "made of slender bones / like these that stand upright together." In an act of empathic imagination, the speaker reminds us that bamboo was not made for war:

> It did not give permission to soldiers.
> It is imprisoned in its own skin.
> The stalks are restless about this.
> They have lived too long in the world of men.
> They are hollow inside.

NOTE

1. "The Osage Murders: Oil Wealth, Betrayal and the FBI's First Big Case," *National Museum of the American Indian*, March 1, 2011, http://blog.nmai.si.edu/main/2011/03/the-osage-murders-oil-wealth-betrayal-and-the-fbis-first-big-case.html.

Dulce et Decorum Est

WILFRED OWEN

Bent double, like old beggars under sacks,
Knock-kneed, coughing like hags, we cursed through sludge,
Till on the haunting flares we turned our backs,
And towards our distant rest began to trudge.
Men marched asleep. Many had lost their boots,
But limped on, blood-shod. All went lame; all blind;
Drunk with fatigue; deaf even to the hoots
Of gas-shells dropping softly behind.

Gas! GAS! Quick, boys!—An ecstasy of fumbling
Fitting the clumsy helmets just in time,
But someone still was yelling out and stumbling
And flound'ring like a man in fire or lime.—
Dim through the misty panes and thick green light,
As under a green sea, I saw him drowning.

In all my dreams before my helpless sight,
He plunges at me, guttering, choking, drowning.

If in some smothering dreams, you too could pace
Behind the wagon that we flung him in,
And watch the white eyes writhing in his face,
His hanging face, like a devil's sick of sin;
If you could hear, at every jolt, the blood
Come gargling from the froth-corrupted lungs,
Obscene as cancer, bitter as the cud
Of vile, incurable sores on innocent tongues,—
My friend, you would not tell with such high zest
To children ardent for some desperate glory,
The old Lie: *Dulce et decorum est*
Pro patria mori.

Overheard in S.E. Asia

DENISE LEVERTOV

'White phosphorous, white phosphorous,
mechanical snow,
where are you falling?'

'I am falling impartially on roads and roofs,
on bamboo thickets, on people.
My name recalls rich seas on rainy nights,
each drop that hits the surface eliciting
luminous response from a million algae.
My name is a whisper of sequins. Ha!
Each of them is a disk of fire,
I am snow that burns.
              I fall
wherever men send me to fall—
but I prefer flesh, so smooth, so dense:
I decorate it in black, and seek
the bone.'

❧❧❧

For the Record

ADRIENNE RICH

The clouds and stars didn't wage this war
the brooks gave no information
if the mountain spewed stones of fire into the river
it was not taking sides
the raindrop faintly swaying under the leaf
had no political opinions

and if here or there a house
filled with backed-up raw sewage
or poisoned those who lived there
with slow fumes, over years
the houses were not at war
nor did the tinned-up buildings

intend to refuse shelter
to homeless old women and roaming children
they had no policy to keep them roaming
or dying, no, the cities were not the problem
the bridges were non-partisan,
the freeways burned, but not with hatred

Even the miles of barbed-wire
stretched around crouching temporary huts
designed to keep the unwanted
at a safe distance, out of sight
even the boards that had to absorb
year upon year, so many human sounds

so many depths of vomit, tears
slow-soaking blood
had not offered themselves for this
The trees didn't volunteer to be cut into boards
nor the thorns for tearing flesh
Look around at all of it

and ask whose signature
is stamped on those orders, traced
in the corner of the building plans
Ask where the illiterate, big-bellied
women were, the drunks and crazies,
the ones you fear most of all: ask where you were.

Cloud Watching

NATALIE DIAZ

Betsy Ross needled hot stars to Mr. Washington's bedspread—
    they weren't hers to give. So, when the calvary came,
        we ate their horses. Then, unfortunately, our bellies were filled
            with bullet holes.

Pack the suitcases with white cans of corned beef—
    when we leave, our hunger will go with us,
        following behind, a dog with ribs like a harp.

Blue gourds glow and rattle like a two-man band:
    Hotchkiss on backup vocals and Gatling on drums.
        The rhythm is set by our boys dancing the warpath—
            the meth 3-step. Grandmothers dance their legs off—
                who now will teach us to stand?

We carry dimming lamps like god cages—
    they help us to see that it is dark. In the dark our hands
        pretend to pray but really make love.
            Soon we'll give birth to fists— they'll open up
                black eyes and split grins— we'll all cry out.

History has chapped lips, unkissable lips—
    he gave me a coral necklace that shines bright as a chokehold.
        He gives and gives—census names given to Mojaves:
            George and Martha Washington, Abraham Lincoln,
                Robin Hood, Rip Van Winkle.

Loot bag ghosts float fatly in dark museum corners—
    I see my grandfather's flutes and rabbit sticks in their guts.
        About the beautiful dresses emptied of breasts . . .
            they were nothing compared to the emptied bodies.

Splintering cradleboards sing bone lullabies—
　　they hush the mention of half-breed babies buried or left on riverbanks.
　　　　When you ask about officers who chased our screaming women
　　　　　　into the arrowweeds, they only hum.

A tongue will wrestle its mouth to death and lose—
　　language is a cemetery.
　　　　Tribal dentists light lab-coat pyres in memoriam of lost molars—
　　　　　　our cavities are larger than HUD houses.
　　　　　　　　Some Indians' wisdom teeth never stop growing back in—
　　　　　　　　　　we were made to bite back—
　　　　　　　　　　　　until we learn to bite first.

❧ ❧ ❧

Wi'-gi-e

ELISE PASCHEN

Anna Kyle Brown. Osage.
1896–1921. Fairfax, Oklahoma.

Because she died where the ravine falls into water.

Because they dragged her down to the creek.

In death, she wore her blue broadcloth skirt.

Though frost blanketed the grass she cooled her feet in the spring.

Because I turned the log with my foot.

Her slippers floated downstream into the dam.

Because, after the thaw, the hunters discovered her body.

Because she lived without our mother.

Because she had inherited head rights for oil beneath the land.

She was carrying his offspring.

The sheriff disguised her death as whiskey poisoning.

Because, when he carved her body up, he saw the bullet hole in her skull.

Because, when she was murdered, the *leg clutchers* bloomed.

But then froze under the weight of frost.

During *Xtha-cka Zhi-ga Tse-the, the Killer of the Flowers Moon.*

I will wade across the river of the blackfish, the otter, the beaver.

I will climb the bank where the willow never dies.

❧ ❧ ❧

In California during the Gulf War

DENISE LEVERTOV

Among the blight-killed eucalyptus, among
trees and bushes rusted by Christmas frosts,
the yards and hillsides exhausted by five years of drought,

certain airy white blossoms punctually
reappeared, and dense clusters of pale pink, dark pink—
a delicate abundance. They seemed

like guests arriving joyfully on the accustomed
festival day, unaware of the year's events, not perceiving
the sackcloth others were wearing.

To some of us, the dejected landscape consorted well
with our shame and bitterness. Skies ever-blue,
daily sunshine, disgusted us like smile-buttons.

Yet the blossoms, clinging to thin branches
more lightly than birds alert for flight,
lifted the sunken heart

even against its will.
                                  But not
as symbols of hope: they were flimsy
as our resistance to the crimes committed

—again, again—in our name; and yes, they return,
year after year, and yes, they briefly shone with serene joy
over against the dark glare

of evil days. They *are*, and their presence
is quietness ineffable—and the bombings *are*, were,
no doubt will be; that quiet, that huge cacophony

simultaneous. No promise was being accorded, the blossoms were not doves, there was no rainbow. And when it was claimed the war had ended, it had not ended.

Landscape with Translucent Moon
JENNIFER H. ATKINSON

Palm trees, like old pilings, tip
in the sand toward the Maldive Islands still.
The moon,
                a slice of green coconut, floats
in a sky streaky with cloud.

Ten winters after the tsunami hit,
                         offshore
the coral reef is reinventing itself
by fits and starts, by hook and foot
and reef-wasn't-built-in-a-day
                             steady calm.
Patience comes easy to gastropods.

The after-war
news is of atrocity, in this like
                    before-, during, after-
war news everywhere: rape, torture, mass graves,
the usual list, human power
reasserting itself
                on the bodies of others.

Deep in the once
                jungled, once war-riven
Tamil north, a Buddha carved in living stone
still falls smiling into death,
                    serene these last thousand years.
How many wars
has that peace survived?

It's said that just before he died,
the historical Buddha
                    sent south to Sri Lanka
a slip from the original
enlightenment tree at Bodh Gaya.

That tree planted between the sites of tsunami and war
is now the oldest tree on earth, a living
                            emblem of compassion
for these last two thousand years.
It's guarded night and day at gunpoint.

❧ ❧ ❧

Awe is the entrance
CHRISTI KRAMER

It was a mistake they said, of the map,
                    when one country accidently invaded another,
                                        set up camp.

            Anasheed he sings: *it is the same sea*

Or this is euphemism for   refugees fled.

Number is not   new name not   what each person walking away   sings

        a ccapella: the ocean in a single beat

Or the soldier breathes out   Or the child in the hedge by the door
                                                          breathes in

No barrier between the cry of the oppressed and God, something to fear

Said, suitcase or coffin, as in sole options   departure:
(I've carried both but not quite)

Farmer, bus driver, student don't know when they will be hit
by what drops from drone that buzzes above and hovers and whirs and
                                        does not leave

          when, because of the way we've built this temple, it is given

the roof caves in

this dome meant to receive silence, or if not, the vocation of longing;
                              moist whispered prayer

when sanctuary is riddled   rats pull flesh from rubble
(I didn't want this image here but it's true).

teacher filled tea cup to overflowing, point: must be empty to receive

farmer's hoe and till imagine   carrot, labour, wheat

          if two stories: one of empire one of creation
                              in which is the digging done

          suitcase is empty, all there was time to pack before run

run   not a figure   of speech,
          it is the body reaching, unaware of tendon or root,
                              broken glass, pocked asphalt

          Where do you go when the door has been blown from the hinges?

There is a roof that looks like sky

☙ ☙ ☙

Mappemonde

PHILIP METRES

for Vahan Cardashian

―――

The foreman's shout, the donkey's squeal,
now caught in the oil's glue. Lashed
peons roused, the rush for ropes to extricate it.
In that minute, animal vanished.

―――

"I charge two of the President's Cabinet
bartered the Armenia case at Lausanne . . .
the expulsion of nearly one million
from ancestral homes for a share in Mosul oil . . ."

―――

The silt of rivers cradling the dead
animal and vegetable on the bed
of ancient seas, ancient continents, lust
engulfed in the upheaving of earth's crust.

Like the maps of the Middle East:
the names of nations beneath the names of oil companies.

֎֎֎

Lunch in Nablus City Park

NAOMI SHIHAB NYE

When you lunch in a town, which has recently known war
under a calm slate sky mirroring none of it,
certain words feel impossible in the mouth.
Casualty: too casual, it must be changed.
A short man stacks mounds of pita bread
on each end of the table, muttering
something about more to come.
Plump birds landing on park benches
surely had their eyes closed recently,
must have seen nothing of weapons or blockades.
When the woman across from you whispers
I don't think we can take it anymore
and you say there are people praying for her
in the mountains of Himalaya and she says
Lady, it is not enough, then what?

A plate of *hummus*, dish of tomato,
friends dipping bread—
I will not marry till there is true love, says one,
throwing back her cascade of perfumed hair.
He says the University of Texas seems remote to him
as Mars, and last month he stayed in his house
for 26 days. He will not leave, he refuses to leave.
In the market they are selling
men's shoes with air vents, a beggar displays
the giant scab of leg he must drag from alley to alley,
and students argue about the best way to protest.

In summers, this cafe is full.
Today only our table sends its laughter into the trees.
What cannot be answered checkers the tablecloth
between the squares of white and red.
Where do the souls of hills hide
when there is shooting in the valleys?
What makes a man with a gun seem bigger
than a man with almonds? How can there be war
and the next day eating, a man stacking plates
on the curl of his arm, a table of people
toasting one another in languages of grace:
For you who came so far;
For you who held out, wearing a black scarf
to signify grief;
For you who believe true love can find you
amidst this atlas of tears linking one town
to its own memory of mortar,
when it was still a dream to be built
and people moved here, believing,
and someone with sky and birds in his heart
said this would be a good place for a park.

The Dogs of Ashdod

ZEIN EL-AMINE

The dogs of Ashdod are nervous
because of the sirens. Their plight
is catalogued in the *Jerusalem Post*.
Uri inquires, is this for The Onion?
The reporter replies, this is a serious
problem for the southern pet owner.
A 3-year-old in Gaza crawls under
his bed, makes a lullaby of the rebar
hum in the concrete. He assures
his aunt that his parents can beat back
the bombs, but if that fails, he tells her,
he has a cache of candy he can offer
the enemy. 15-year-old Mohammad
is on Skype, his face, fading in
and out of the computer light.
He tells me, it sounds like a monster
DJ playing disco outside. His voice
is drowned by the deadly beat
and by the dogs of Ashdod barking.

⊕ ⊕ ⊕

If It Were

JAVIER ZAMORA

for Monseñor Romero

Bless today, leaves crawling back on trees, ashes
washed from sidewalks, and the collecting of names

at the "appeared" parade. No more war: woodpeckers
prove deadwood, students shout their own names—

the roses of roses growing in mouths. Bless
the drought of bullets, cured cholera, and the comfort

of earthquakes. No more marriages between safety pins
and craters. Bless all things we didn't know we loved:

exiles, silent skies, buses, midnight walks, radios,
firecrackers. Bless tin rooftops, cane burning,

and palms singing: here, we only thought of loss. Bless
the surrendered M-16s propped next to rusting

artillery. There's nothing left to reminds us of
the marching of boots, as if it were rain.

୧ଦ୧

For the Missing in Action

JOHN BALABAN

Hazed with heat and harvest dust
the air swam with flying husks
as men whacked rice sheaves into bins
and all across the sun-struck fields
red flags hung from bamboo poles.
Beyond the last tree line on the horizon
beyond the coconut palms and eucalyptus
out in the moon-zone puckered by bombs
the dead earth where no one ventures,
the boys found it, foolish boys
riding buffaloes in craterlands
where at night bombs thump and ghosts howl.
A green patch on the raw earth.
And now they've led the farmers here,
the kerchiefed women in baggy pants,
the men with sickles and flails, children
herding ducks with switches—all
staring from a crater berm; silent:
In that dead place the weeds had formed a man
where someone died and fertilized the earth, with flesh
and blood, with tears, with longing for loved ones.
No scrap remained; not even a buckle
survived the monsoons, just a green creature,
a viney man, supine, with posies for eyes,
butterflies for buttons, a lily for a tongue.
Now when huddled asleep together
the farmers hear a rustly footfall
as the leaf-man rises and stumbles to them.

֍ ֍ ֍

You and I Are Disappearing

YUSEF KOMUNYAKAA

—*Björn Håkansson*

The cry I bring down from the hills
belongs to a girl still burning
inside my head. At daybreak
  she burns like a piece of paper.
She burns like foxfire
in a thigh-shaped valley.
A skirt of flames
dances around her
at dusk.
  We stand with our hands
hanging at our sides,
while she burns
  like a sack of dry ice.
She burns like oil on water.
She burns like a cattail torch
dipped in gasoline.
She glows like the fat tip
of a banker's cigar,
  silent as quicksilver.
A tiger under a rainbow
  at nightfall.
She burns like a shot glass of vodka.
She burns like a field of poppies
at the edge of a rain forest.
She rises like dragonsmoke
  to my nostrils.
She burns like a burning bush
driven by a godawful wind.

☙☙☙

Supreme

FRANCES PAYNE ADLER

*Dedicated to Atta Jaber, a Palestinian grape grower whose land borders Kiryat
Arba, a Jewish settlement just outside Hebron, in the West Bank*

> A petition was filed to the Israeli Supreme Court to let Palestinians
> harvest their grapes, and the High Court told the Army that they must
> let them harvest. They can check them before they let them come in, but
> people have rights to this land and there's no law that takes these rights
> away.
> —Avital Sharon, an Israeli lawyer with Rabbis for Human Rights

My client, Atta, wants to go harvest his grapes
and he can't go because what used
to be his vineyard, the settlement took
as their shabam, their security zone,
and he can't go because he doesn't
have a permit and he doesn't have
a permit because they won't give him
one and this is the problem, so I
called the Army and they said he can't
get a permit because he has to prove
this is his land and he has to get an
expert to show that this is his land
and I said that he did that, he came
to your office and showed you the map,
and he said I don't have it, and I said,
could you look again because he even
remembers the date he was there and
Palestinians don't usually remember
the date and he called me back and
said, yes, I have his date, but I don't
have his map. But a map costs a lot
of money, I said, could I send it to you
on the computer and he said, no, I don't

like that and here's what we could do,
I could come to his land and you and I
and him, we could walk and he could
show me. So we agree on a date and
Atta and I are there and this guy doesn't
show for the meeting, and here we are,
this has been going on for three years.
Last year, they let him come in to harvest
his grapes, just for a day or two, and you
should've heard his voice on the phone,
calling from his vineyards, picking his grapes,
the joy. And now he wants to go in again, and
they're saying ever letting him in was a mistake

Confiteor: A Country Song

PATRICIA MONAGHAN

Evening. Red sky. Standing at the door
I sense a shadow presence here:
the one who loved this land before.

These harmless hills bear scars of war.
Someone stood here, full of fear.
This is not a metaphor.

Above me, turkey vultures soar;
below the garden, seven deer.
Someone loved this land before,

loved it as I do, maybe more.
She did not simply disappear
and she is not a metaphor:

This was some woman's home before
pale soldiers came to clear
a land that someone loved before.

What to do with facts like this? Ignore
them? Hope they disappear?
Someone loved this land before.
None of this is metaphor.

❖ ❖ ❖

Descent

GABRIELLA M. BELFIGLIO

"Get Inside
Before I Fucking Knock You Out,"
my middle-aged neighbor
screams at her granddaughter.
The little girl
is wearing a purple dress that falls
just past her knees;
yellow polka dots
on the collar
frame her neck.

A shrill wail escapes
as she shifts away.
She crouches behind
the decaying Chevy.
"Don't Start That Shit Now—
You're Gonna Get It
Even Worse If You Don't Shut Up."

Later the girl
grinds her crimson sandals
into the pavement
again and again
steadily killing
a colony of ants
who are making hills
between cracks
in broken concrete.

⊕ ⊕ ⊕

Daisy Cutter

CAMILLE T. DUNGY

Pause here at the flower stand—mums
and gladiolas, purple carnations

dark as my heart. We are engaged
in a war, and I want to drag home

any distraction I can carry. Tonight
children will wake to bouquets of fire

that will take their breath away. Still,
I think of my life. The way you hold me,

sometimes, you could choke me.
There is no way to protect myself,

except by some brilliant defense. I want
the black iris with their sabered blooms.

I want the flamethrowers: the peonies,
the sunflowers. I will cut down the beautiful ones

and let their nectared sweetness bleed
into the careless air. This is not the world

I'd hoped it could be. It is horrible,
the way we carry on. Last night, you catalogued

our arsenal. You taught me devastation
is a goal we announce in a celebration

of shrapnel. Our bombs shower
in anticipation of their marks. You said this

is to assure damage will be widely distributed.
What gruesome genius invents our brutal hearts?

When you touch me I am a stalk of green panic
and desire. Wait here while I decide which

of these sprigs of blossoming heartbreak I can afford
to bring into my home. Tonight dreams will erupt

in chaotic buds of flame. This is the world we have
arranged. It is horrible, this way we carry on.

Why I Don't Mention Flowers When Conversations with My Brother Reach Uncomfortable Silence

NATALIE DIAZ

> Forgive me, distant wars, for bringing flowers home.
> —Wislawa Szymborska

In the Kashmir mountains,
my brother shot many men,
blew skulls from brown skins,
dyed white desert sand crimson.

What is there to say to a man
who has traversed such a world,
whose hands and eyes have
betrayed him?

Were there flowers there? I asked.

This is what he told me:

In a village, many men
wrapped a woman in a sheet.
She didn't struggle.
Her bare feet dragged in the dirt.

They laid her in the road
and stoned her.

The first man was her father.
He threw two stones in a row.
Her brother had filled his pockets
with stones on the way there.

The crowd was a hive
of disturbed bees. The volley
of stones against her body
drowned out her moans.

Blood burst through the sheet
like a patch of violets,
a hundred roses in bloom.

Cousins

BRIAN BRODEUR

for David Brodeur (1976–2011)

1.

Last night, after the Air Force official
told your folks what happened to you in Kabul,

your brother called. I almost didn't answer.
The bullet to the face, which you survived,

pierced one cheek, he said, then the other,
but you rose from the floor and staggered after

the man who'd shot you, grabbing for his hand
as a second bullet severed your spinal cord.

I was going to say it was too much to hear
but I didn't have the right—you weren't *my* brother.

He called you a hero, asked if I had any questions.
"Questions?" I said, and he hung up the phone.

2.

It was rare to get the three of us together.
When you flew into DC, we drove to Skyline Drive

in separate cars, and hiked the Whiteoak Trail
to see if the falls were running. They were dry.

On the gravel path, fresh piles of horse dung
swarmed with monarchs and swallowtails

who feasted on something they'd found there.
For a long time we watched their wings

opening and closing in the hot wind,
their bodies pulsing with what resembled

pleasure, their legs and forked tails trembling,
their abdomens thick as pinky fingers.

3.

I don't know why I'm telling this to you.
You were there. You saw the butterflies, the view

of the Shenandoah Valley from the falls.
Draining my water bottle, I coughed and wheezed—

I promised to join the gym and quit smoking.
Your brother walked ahead. You stayed behind.

We parted at the lot—I can't remember
if we shook hands before we found our cars.

In my rear-view, the sun blazed off your hood,
slices of light flashing as you entered.

Your windshield glinted as if lit from within.
It hurt to look at you is what I mean.

֍ ֍ ֍

In Jordan's Northernmost Province

SHARA LESSLEY

for the Middle East's first all-female de-mining team

Women go down on their knees
hovering above a map-work of metalwork, brushing
dust from cluster bombs like ash from flatbread.
Delicate metal-filled bomblets glisten, scaring off
the crows. In fields where men once braided their hair,
a wife trades her niqab for goggles
and armor, sifting the topmost soil
from behind her rake. She knows the mines
never sleep. She knows better to fear
the snakes, scorpions, heat,
her brother's pasture where running
water dislocates the dragon's teeth, toy-like
mines disguising themselves as butterflies
and yams. Shepherds herd their sheep
in restricted fields, their daughters more afraid
of sniffing dogs than the cross-shaped pressure
plates lying in wait. Today begins
where yesterday ends: brushes, detectors,
mallets and stakes prodding twenty square meters
grain by grain, searching for wires
attached at the pull switch. And the ragged
finch perched on the fencepost,
does it prophesy something
among the fruit trees—a thimble-
sized device, perhaps, its firing pin needling
a young boy's eyes? Who knows what
the ordinary arbor holds. Hundreds of
underground cages ready to unloose the clay-
more birds in air, their blackened gullets canting
for the boy's mother, now downed

among the silent grasses, as if unclasping a barb
from her stocking, or bending to sweep back
the wild herbs clutched at her jilbab's hem.

Bamboo

LINDA HOGAN

First woman was made of slender bones
like these that stand upright together
in the rich, green world of daylight.

At night, they are a darkened forest
of sisters who grow quickly
in moving water
and talk in the clattering breeze
as if each is an open throat, rising
to speak.

I tell a man about this beautiful,
creaking world, how it flowers all
at once. He has been to war. He says
with bamboo they do terrible things
to men and women.

I look at this bamboo.
It did not give permission to soldiers.
It is imprisoned in its own skin.
The stalks are restless about this.
They have lived too long in the world of men.
They are hollow inside.

Lord, are you listening to this?
Plants are climbing to heaven
to talk to you.

҉ ҉ ҉

Little Fires (excerpt)
CHRISTINA LOVIN

There are witnesses. There were plans:
Bats would be eased into cold sleep
deep in the bellies of bombers,
strapped with incendiary explosives
the size and shape of their young,
so as not to alarm, but rather, when warmed
and wakened, encourage their swift flights
to safety beneath the eaves of paper houses,
balsa wood shops, and flammable factories.
So, when their time was up, the bombs
would set off a holocaust of small blazes
across Japan. That was the plan,
and in the trials a million little fires
burst, flamed, then cooled to carbon.
But Praise the Lord and Pass the Ammunition:
the A-bomb came along to "save more lives."

Birthday Poem, March 31, 1999

SARAH BROWNING

—Kosovo

Today, the blue moon,
my son's first birthday,
the freakish warm March
blue moon, happy birthday

Today, we tolerate the war
the radio announcer tells us,
saying the air war is *immaculate*
the moon blue, my son one

Boys pulled from their homes
Women walking days alone with babies
Men driven to stadiums, again

The blue moon, the second blue moon
this year, this first year my hands hold him

I am a mother who holds her son
this warm day in March, who asks for hugs
and gets them, whose war
is *immaculate*

I raked the lawn
I listened as the professors
were shot, as my son
waved to me
and said *Hi*

as my son grinned, as the bombs fell
as I tried—and failed—to imagine
being some other mother
I heard birds, I heard cars on the highway

My yard was practically *immaculate*
the ground drying out, the bulbs shooting
I tried on that other mother, her son,
her extraordinary son, what kind of stadium

could hold him, I ask you that, what answer
what twiggy earth, what cacophony of birds

❧ ❧ ❧

Another Day

SARA GOUDARZI

It is the birds I worry about
when the streets become shadows
and planes litter the sky
when my father wraps my hand in his
and we're headed down to the basement again
where it's safest.
It is the birds I worry about
when the anti-aircraft tracers are brighter than the stars
and I'm watching through a small window
praying to a god I won't believe in when the sky clears.
It is the birds I worry about
when the bomb of the night finally drops
and a family is dust.
It is the birds
the birds
that I, the nine-year-old,
worry about.
Because it's their song
that wakes me to another day.

↫↫↫

Pomegranate Means Grenade

JAMAAL MAY

> The heart trembles like a herd of horses.
> —Jontae McCrory, age 11

Hold a pomegranate in your palm,
imagine ways to split it. Think of the breaking
skin as shrapnel. Remember granada
means pomegranate and granada
means grenade because grenade
takes its name from the fruit;
identify war by what it takes away
from fecund orchards. Jontae,
these are the arms they will fear from you.
There will always be at least one like you:
a child who gets the picked-over box
with mostly black crayons. One who wonders
what beautiful has to do with beauty as he darkens
a sun in the corner of every page,
constructs a house from ashen lines,
sketches stick figures lying face down—
I know how often red is the only color
left to reach for. I fear for you.
My heart trembles like a herd of horses.
You are writing a stampede into my chest.
This is the same thumping anxiety that shudders
me when I push past marines in high school
hallways, moments after their video footage
of young men dropping from helicopters
in night vision goggles. I want you to see
in the dark without covering your face,
carry verse as countermeasure to recruitment videos,
and remember the cranes buried inside poems
that hung in Tiananmen Square—

remember because Huang Xiang was exiled
for these, exiled for this, the calligraphy of revolt.
You stand nameless in front of a tank against
those who would rather see you pull a pin
from a grenade than pull a pen
from your backpack. Jontae,
they are afraid.

Register of Eliminated Villages

TARFIA FAIZULLAH

> I have a register which lists 397 eliminated villages, Kurdish villages in
> Northern Iraq . . . it's a very decorative, pretty thing . . .
> —Kanan Makiya, *Frontline*, 2002

Somewhere in this insomniac night
   my life is beginning
without me. In Northern Iraq,
   it is high noon, the sun there

perched over fields shriven
   with lilies, the petals of orange
poppies red with a light
   that a gauze of gray sparrows

glides through over sheaves
   of bone too stubborn to burn,
all that is left of those razed
   towns. Mother turns to Father

in the cold room they share,
   offers her hands to his spine.
I curl inside her, a silver
   bangle illuminated by candle's

flame. I curl beside you, lay
   my head close to the vellum
of your smooth back, try
   again to sleep. *Count to 1,000,*

you suggest. Count to two.
    Three. As someone must count
hacked date trees, hollowed
    hills paved into gardens, though

the scholar on tonight's
    Frontline only counted each
town destroyed: three
    hundred ninety-seven of them.

Who counts dolls, hand-
    stitched, facedown in dirt?
Count to five. Six. Count
    cadaver, stone, belongings: pots,

spun from red clay. Who
    will count the amputated
hands of thieves? Mother
    presses a hand to me. Inside

her, I thrash, a stalk of wheat
    blistered by storm. Sleep comes,
brief as it is bright. I startle
    awake, turn to you. The register,

I know, is real and beautiful,
    filled with the names of the dead,
elegant strokes of sharp pencil
    etched into thick pages. Father

presses an ear to Mother's
    belly. I am wide awake. Count
to seven. Eight. Nine. You
    murmur, turn to me. Someone

must be counting hours
    spent weaving lace the color
of moonlight for a young girl's
    dowry. But I don't have

the right to count hours,
    girls, dowries—only the skin-
thin pages of the *Qur'an*
    I once cut a hollow into, condoms

I stored there, cigarettes.
    Count each minute I waited
for my parents to fall
    asleep. Count nights I sat alone

on the curb, held smoke
    inside my mouth, released
whorls of it into the air.
    Father leaves Mother asleep

on her side, the crocus
    of my fetus nestled inside her.
I draw the thin sheet
    over us. Father reaches

for the *Qur'an*, thumbs through
    page after illuminated page,
runs a fingertip beneath
    each line of verse, looks everywhere

for the promise of my name.

๑ ๑ ๑

Moving Still (excerpt)

MARTHA COLLINS

July 2007

5

Honor the sun that sheds the light
that falls upon us, honor the clouds
that gather and make the rain
that falls upon us, honor the earth
that holds and keeps us, honor
That Which made us, gave us
honor, the sun, the hurting earth.

6

Earth: mantled mother big
blue marble pale blue dot not

blue until we got out there we
thought talked green forgot

the water now we let green
go cut it burn it turn it into

stuff, junk, shall her bones live?

7

Live from our own
dawn air, featuring song
sparrow, cardinal, mourning

dove, alive and well
in our bed my love, his slow
sleeping breathing, low continuo

entered into this summer score

8

Score one for sea, one for sky, blue
meets blue, line, tie,
                    one for sand,
now exposed, turning tide,
leaving sand,
                    birds for all, least
terns hover, dart, piping
plovers scurry,
                    can we all agree
with these on earth sea air

9

Sky items: Yesterday I disturbed
the nesting terns, they charged
like planes,
                    in May the osprey flew
away from the camera raised
to count eggs,
                    today NATO planes
killed 105 in a village, today
clouds, then rain, then—

10

Then he said *love* and by
that summer we were settled

months before the Wall fell and we
said *peace*, years before the Towers
fell and we said *war* Iraq Iraq Iraq

Afghanistan Darfur how to save
what's been lost oh little world

❧ ❧ ❧

SECTION III

||||||||||||||||||||||||||||||||||||||||||||||||||||||||||||||||||||||||||||||||||||||||||||||||||||||||||||||||||||||||||||||||||||||||||||

Little Farm, Big Farm

↵ Food, Culture, and Capital

Food connects us to one another, to our culture, and to the larger ecosystem. It is a source of health and sustenance and also a source of profound injustice in our current economic system. These poems look at the relationship between food, culture, survival, and economics.

As Joy Harjo's "Perhaps the World Ends Here" reminds us, the kitchen table is where the world begins; it is a place for family and community ritual central to our existence: "no matter what, we must eat to live."

Poets in this section explore the connection between culture and subsistence. Food in these poems is a connection to the natural world, to what Lucille Clifton calls "the bond of live things everywhere" in her poem, "cutting greens."

We learn from our elders how to take care of our gardens and feed our families. The oldest of these traditions are based in sustainability and care for the land: "Bury the fish and let the birds be, / she said. There will enough," Cheryl Savageau writes in "The Sweet and Vinegary Taste."

Poets examine the link between culture and food. Martín Espada's "Coca-Cola and Coco Frío," looks at the cultural and environmental impact of colonization on the food system. In this poem, an American child visiting Puerto Rico marvels, after his first sip of coco frío, that his relatives in Puerto Rico are all drinking Coca-Cola instead,

> while so many coconuts in the trees
> sagged heavy with milk, swollen
> and unsuckled.

Culture, economics, and agriculture also come together in Dan Vera's poem "Abcedarian Yellow," which offers a lesson in monoculture agriculture, American intervention, Panama disease, and banana republics.

Poets in this section question the means of production and the basic injustice central to our global food system, as June Jordan does in "Focus in Real Time":

> Who grew these grains
> Who owned the land
> Who harvested the crop
> Who converted these soft particles to money
> Who kept the cash

These poems also hold abundance—of backyard and urban fruit trees, of olive trees and gardens. This section teems with gleaners, givers, and sharers of food. Poems offer gratitude for sustenance, awareness of the complicated interaction between hunger and survival, as Linda Hogan reminds us in "Milk,"

> Something must hold me this way,
> and you,
> and the thin blue tail of the galaxy,
> to keep us from leaving
> as life unfolds behind us.

Harvest Song
JEAN TOOMER

I am a reaper whose muscles set at sundown. All my oats are cradled.
But I am too chilled, and too fatigued to bind them. And I hunger.

I crack a grain between my teeth. I do not taste it.
I have been in the fields all day. My throat is dry. I hunger.

My eyes are caked with dust of oatfields at harvest-time.
I am a blind man who stares across the hills, seeking stack'd fields of other
  harvesters.

It would be good to see them .. crook'd, split, and iron-ring'd handles of the
  scythes. It would be good to see them, dust-caked and blind. I hunger.

(Dusk is a strange fear'd sheath their blades are dull'd in.)
My throat is dry. And should I call, a cracked grain like the oats . . . eoho—

I fear to call. What should they hear me, and offer me their grain, oats, or
  wheat, or corn? I have been in the fields all day. I fear I could not taste it. I
  fear knowledge of my hunger.

My ears are caked with dust of oatfields at harvest-time.
I am a deaf man who strains to hear the calls of other harvesters whose throats
  are also dry.

It would be good to hear their songs .. reapers of the sweet-stalk'd cane,
  cutters of the corn .. even though their throats cracked and the strangeness
  of their voices deafened me.

I hunger. My throat is dry. Now that the sun has set and I am chilled, I fear to
  call. (Eoho, my brothers!)

I am a reaper. (Eoho!) All my oats are cradled. But I am too fatigued to bind them. And I hunger. I crack a grain. It has no taste to it. My throat is dry. . .

O my brothers, I beat my palms, still soft, against the stubble of my harvesting. (You beat your soft palms, too.) My pain is sweet. Sweeter than the oats or wheat or corn. It will not bring me knowledge of my hunger.

❧❧❧

Focus in Real Time
JUNE JORDAN

A bowl of rice
  as food
  as politics
  or metaphor
  as something valuable and good
  or something common to consume/exploit/ignore

Who grew these grains
Who owned the land
Who harvested the crop
Who converted these soft particles to money
Who kept the cash
Who shipped the consequences of the cash
Who else was going to eat the rice
Who else was going to convert the rice to cash

Who would design the flowers for the outside of the bowl
Who would hold the bowl between her hands
Who would give the bowl away
Who could share the rice
Who could fill that bowl with rice how many times a day
   how many times a week
Who would adore the hands that held the bowl that held the rice
Who would adore the look the smell the steam of boiled rice
    in a bowl

Who will analyze the cash the rice becomes
Who will sit beside the bowl or fight for rice
Who will write about the hands that hold the bowl
Who will want to own the land
        A bowl of rice

❧ ❧ ❧

From the Field

LENARD D. MOORE

Certainly they are the same weathered trees
we carved our names on,
played on as children, making
an insistent sound. Two elms rub together
and bend. Out here, no one listens.
They go on pulling tobacco plants
from the damp black earth.
Some load plants on flatbeds
on the puddled side roads.
Only a young girl stands
at the end of a row
not working.
Twenty years ago,
we pulled plants
at any age. Children
won't do field work anymore.
Who is content on bent knees,
except when praying? I would kneel
to uproot plants
in warm daylight.
But I stand dreaming
about my people's labored hands.
The thick clouds do not move.
The day goes on this way
until sun leaves
like yesterday
into the deepest stillness
of tobacco country.

Rich soil linked us
like blessings that speak to us
without a sound.

❧ ❧ ❧

Umpaowastewin

MARGARET NOODIN

Ode'iminibaashkiminasiganke
She makes strawberry jam

ginagawinad wiishko'aanimad, waaseyaagami
mixing sweet wind and shining water

miinawaa gipagaa nibwaakaa,
with thick wisdom

bigishkada'ad, dibaabiiginad
pounding, measuring

gakina gaa zhawenimangidwa
everything we've cared for

gakina gaa waniangidwa
everything we've lost

nagamowinan waa nagamoyaang
the songs we have not yet sung

miigwanag waa wawezhi'angidwa
the feathers yet to decorate

ezhi-zhoomiingweyaangoba
and all the ways we've smiled

mooshkine moodayaabikoong
into jars filled to the brim

ji-baakaakonid pii bakadeyaang
to be opened when we are thin

boozangwamyaang biboong besho
sleeping deeply in winter near

gaa oginiig endazhi-ginibigiwag
where the tomatoes once grew.

❧❧❧

While they sing they have no names

LEE SHARKEY

They sang as they gleaned   not to waste any of the abundance
the common grape of the second harvest   potatoes souring in the sun
To the rhythm of snapping shears   their song rose clear water above
them bent at the pelvis all day   mosquitoes were biting
come night   old aches darkened the brew
mouth harp formed from the dark   they were centuries risen
the sum of the sum of labor   turned joy in the lamenting
As for the master   of sheep and white cattle
who keeps them   from his figs and apples
theirs by right   following the harvest
let his own weight topple him

☙ ☙ ☙

Suddenly in Grace

HONORÉE FANONNE JEFFERS

How in the bowl the collards steamed,
hiding gifts of meat and tomatoes.
How the chicken was cloaked
in its brown robe of singing fat.
How the cornbread could have been supper alone,
had been to others in starved times.

Again, look at the table.
How my mother plucked the greens
from her modest garden out back
and through the summer she chased
away creatures from the tomatoes,
righteously planting marigolds.
How she could have grown corn
so tall, she said, if only she had the land.
How her hands did not wring this chicken's
neck but her mother's did another.

Again.
How she baptized the greens in gallons
of water, scrubbed the stiff, unforgiving leaves.
How her back was turned to me
where she stood at the sink.
How she kept from speaking to my anger, lips tucked,
a bland face, head bowed suddenly in grace.
How she was determined to feed me.

Again.
How she plunged the greens over and over,
watched the water run free of dirt
and tried to teach me this way back,
though I had no interest then.
How she finally taught me, insistent.
How a last meal must be clean.

How We Live

VALERIE NIEMAN

Bay leaf and pepper, mushrooms,
garlic, sometimes juniper berries,
vinegar and onion: I have my own
familiarity with the doe
you shot in our third field;
my hands trim
the yellow rinds of fat, wake
the spark lying quiet
in this dense red grove.
Sometimes,
despite your scrupulousness,
I find a fine brown hair,
zoned with the colors
of concealment like fur from the cat's back
or the way my hair turns white.

Some people cannot abide wild
meat, the resinous aroma,
the color
like knife-openings
in the palms of their hands,
blood loamy as old
wine and thick, unmingled with water.
To eat and live:
like breathing in and out,
and acknowledged or not
there is always
some spiral toward coldness.

Still, those of us who eat
have a duty to know—hunker down
and smell fresh droppings gleaming
like berries on the path,
hear the snort
of the lead doe warning
into white flight
a band of yearlings,
in uncut fields
to walk our way into the beds of deer,
rounded as the stopping-place
of boulders, where a moraine
knuckles under inexorable glacier.

Now I Pray

KATHY ENGEL

Ashen face, wool hat bobbing,
the young boy's eyes dart to me,
then up at the man pulling a roll-y
suitcase, whose hand he holds,
then back at me. His legs move
as if without gravity. The man asks:
Do you know a church on this street
that serves free food? I want to say
I know. That the names of churches
on an Avenue called Americas roll
out of me. I want to tell you
it is temporary, their condition:
suitcase, darting eyes, seeking free
food at 9 pm in a big city on a school night.
I want to tell you I don't for a moment
wonder if that is really the boy's father
or uncle or legitimate caretaker—
something in the handholding and
eyes, having watched too many
episodes of *Law and Order*. I want
to tell you I take them to a restaurant
and pay for a warm meal or empty
my wallet not worrying how
offensive that might be because
in the end hunger is hunger.
I want to tell you I call someone
who loves them—that there is someone—
and say your guys are lost, can
you come? I want to tell you I sit
down on the sidewalk at the corner
of Waverly, and pray—that all
passing by, anonymous shoes

marking the pavement, join
in a chorus of prayer humming
like cicadas in the Delta. I want to
tell you the boy and the man eat food
encircled by the warmth of bodies.
I want to turn the cold night into a feast.
I will tell you I am praying.

Wealth
ALLISON ADELLE HEDGE COKE

When it was over

everything dust   blown
chickens, ducks, horses, plows
Model A, Mark III

   Dad still keeps the key
mounted to this tin shed wall.

Dust, then,
      everything blown.

Dust, dust, dust.

Still they came around
asking for whatever he held
       to feed,
eleven of them he carried
and the others,   dozens.

Grandpa the generous
gave his last rhyme
in riddle rhythms
without capital consensus.

"I thought you were rich."
They said.

As Granddad and his family
walked away from this
repossessed dugout,
chunk of ground,
earthen home,

flushed and empty,
chin up, Cherokee . . .

"Am, my family's alive."
He affirmed, shaking his head loose
from assumption
he had anything left to give.

As if he'd ever been fund wealthy
longer than a week.

Still Granny fed them
before they walked on.

He insisted. She couldn't imagine
                    any other way.
It was their manner. Their spark.

Once, his land had put out,
he gave away 'cause others called,
split between closer relatives
who camped all alongside throughout.

Until it was done.
Back to corn, squash, beans, tomatoes.
Back to working for railroads,
farmers, farriers, friends, foes.

Back to the shoulder plow,
another hold, far from rooted homes,
rotted worlds behind them,
then the dust,

        dust,   dust,   dust.

Still, in this world,
down generations now.
Others come wanting
      something
           they're sure we have.

We pull out our checkbooks, cards,
overdraw ourselves.

Feed them.

❧ ❧ ❧

Almonds

ELIZABETH JACOBSON

Of course you would think *tree*

a farm, water

the California sun.

Each nut a seed in the center of a sage green—

nappy like the outside of a peach—

testicle-shaped—

protector. Spongy, yet

fibrous underneath the fuzz.

We found some at a gourmet food shop,

   whole like this

opened them with a scissors,

the meat surprisingly white,

   tasteless

   a short drink of water.

Of course you would think *protein.*

Hopefully organic, vitamin E, phenols.

You would think, *heart friendly and antioxidant*

  you would feel *content.*

The almond, the center of a fruit,

the shape of the eyes of our ancestors

  a whole food

not a global concern.

Of course you wouldn't think

bee death

or *drought, or gill rot,*

the way everything this good becomes Big Money.

Of course you wouldn't ask

  this almond, or the lives of many salmon?

  This almond, or my daily dose of water?

❧ ❧ ❧

harvest
QURAYSH ALI LANSANA

yellow-gold overgrowth

wheat like children raising
arms high to be picked. everywhere
is shaft scraping cloud, every
where is nowhere, what's behind
looks like what's ahead.

a boy no more than twelve
commanding earth, tiny monarch
in green glass, a southwestern
pope-mobile sweating progress.

the smooth hand of machine.

after harvest
QURAYSH ALI LANSANA

from mullet to buzz cut

used-up breadbasket for a world
that barely cares, tips cereal
box. braided rows half unkempt, tossed
by god's breathing. jagged stubble
in blistering sun, the almost

bald head endless flat. mane cropped
by fortress that blocks traffic in both
directions. vaulted cockpit a telephone
booth with hips, helix of blade a sinister grin

idle, only sky to fill time.

๏ ๏ ๏

Federico's Ghost

MARTÍN ESPADA

The story is
that whole families of fruitpickers
still crept between the furrows
of the field at dusk,
when for reasons of whiskey or whatever
the cropduster plane sprayed anyway,
floating a pesticide drizzle
over the pickers
who thrashed like dark birds
in a glistening white net,
except for Federico,
a skinny boy who stood apart
in his own green row,
and, knowing the pilot
would not understand in Spanish
that he was the son of a whore,
instead jerked his arm
and thrust an obscene finger.

The pilot understood.
He circled the plane and sprayed again,
watching a fine gauze of poison
drift over the brown bodies
that cowered and scurried on the ground,
and aiming for Federico,
leaving the skin beneath his shirt
wet and blistered,
but still pumping his finger at the sky.

After Federico died,
rumors at the labor camp
told of tomatoes picked and smashed at night,
growers muttering of vandal children
or communists in camp,
first threatening to call Immigration,
then promising every Sunday off
if only the smashing of tomatoes would stop.

Still tomatoes were picked and squashed
in the dark,
and the old women in camp
said it was Federico,
laboring after sundown
to cool the burns on his arms,
flinging tomatoes
at the cropduster
that hummed like a mosquito
lost in his ear,
and kept his soul awake.

❧ ❧ ❧

Sweetgum Country

ANN FISHER-WIRTH

Billy shows us his arm, burned by the sun
where pesticides sensitized his skin
those years of his childhood, playing
in Delta cotton fields. A charred,
hand-sized lozenge marks the tender crease
inside his elbow. Alex holds up her chart
that shows the sickness and death
in her mother's family, from cancer
in Cancer Alley. She has made red circles
for "fought," green crosses for "died,"
she has put stars around her name,
my pretty dark-haired student.
They come to class, my sixteen freshmen,
and no matter what their topics,
they all say, "I never *knew* this . . ."

Fords and Chevies that will barely crank
one more time are parked in the reeds
and slick red mud. Early evening sun
pours down on the cypresses and sweetgum,
the Tallahtachie swamp at the edge
of Marshall County. Turtles poke their heads up.
Cottonmouths zipper through black water
or stretch out long and bask on the abandoned
railroad bridge. Men and women of all ages
beguile the hours after work,
the idle hours, with soft talk or silence,
with bamboo poles and battered coolers.

They could use the food.
They fish for buffalo, catfish, bass,
despite the fish advisories, the waters laced with mercury.

❧ ❧ ❧

Monsanto, Drunk in the Garden
MELISSA TUCKEY

She whispers to plant life: come up
come up, my sleeping herds of thistle,
my stinging and resolute theocracies,
my unbound glory, my sunning stars,
my stranglehold of monopoly.
Come up. Come up and waddle
through the dirt with me, drink deep
this chlorinated song, sprung
lonely from a nozzle of pure joy where
I find myself most mornings weeping.

Be brave my little florets. Make haste
to catch the light before it's gone.
Open your petals to science.
Surface the hidden world.
Break blues and purples and reds
in a riot of contradiction. My parrots,
my garden of lambs, my pig parts,
my onions. Come stir on a light breeze
as bees fall to sleep in the crimson afterlife.
We will be wealthy and famous forever.

෯෯෯

Abecedarian Yellow

DAN VERA

A is for apple.

B is for banana—treasure fruit of the tropics,

which replaced the apple on the breakfast table of Victorian America.

C is for Carmen Miranda smiling

from the label of the bunch of bananas.

D is for drugs to disrupt nature's cycle,

for longevity to cut and ship and freight by steamship

a green banana to the market and your table.

E is for ethylene gas, which is what the drugs suppress in fruit,

for longevity to cut and ship and freight by steamship

a green banana to the market and your table.

F is for fruit, obviously.

G is for Guatemala.

H is for Honduras,

or H could be for O. Henry, who gave them a name:

"banana republics"—governments ruled by giant fruit companies

like Dole and United Fruit through American intervention.

Yes, I is for intervention. Are you still with me?

J is for junta, with an h-like *j* from the Spanish,

as in "military junta" set up by intervention to sustain control

and ensure cheap labor in countries like Honduras and Guatemala

so that bananas can get to your table cheaper

than an apple which grows in your yard.

K is for kitchen—your kitchen,

where history and blood commingle each morning

in the green curve of an L-shaped fruit

from countries with Monoculture agriculture,

which is nuts.

N is for nuts, because we've been through this before,

over and over again.

P is for "Panama disease," which wiped out

the last variety of shippable banana in the 1950s

and may soon wipe out our current one.

¿Que? ¿Que?

R is for ripe.

S is for surprise!

T is for trouble—

Undeniable trouble.

V is for Victoria—Queen Victoria, who died in 1901—

we've been at this that long with bananas.

W is for wrapping up.

X is for eXtinction of a species of yellow fruit

or berry, depending on your view.

Y is for yellow and

Z is for zed,

which signifies end.

❧ ❧ ❧

Coca-Cola and Coco Frío
MARTÍN ESPADA

On his first visit to Puerto Rico,
island of family folklore,
the fat boy wandered
from table to table
with his mouth open.
At every table, some great-aunt
would steer him with cool spotted hands
to a glass of Coca-Cola.
One even sang to him, in all the English
she could remember, a Coca-Cola jingle
from the forties. He drank obediently, though
he was bored with this potion, familiar
from soda fountains in Brooklyn.

Then, at a roadside stand off the beach, the fat boy
opened his mouth to coco frío, a coconut
chilled, then scalped by a machete
so that a straw could inhale the clear milk.
The boy tilted the green shell overhead
and drooled coconut milk down his chin;
suddenly, Puerto Rico was not Coca-Cola
or Brooklyn, and neither was he.

For years afterward, the boy marveled at an island
where the people drank Coca-Cola
and sang jingles from World War II
in a language they could not speak,
while so many coconuts in the trees
sagged heavy with milk, swollen
and unsuckled.

⊖ ⊖ ⊖

Urban Warming

TRUTH THOMAS

Stoned by no Rosetta,
merchants allowed through the fence
learn to misspeak "black speak,"

in Edgar's harbor village,
at Hip Hop Fish & Chicken
on Route number 4 x 10.

"Baby Girl" becomes XX.
"My Man" assumes all XY.

For salt & pepper curls,
& baby stroller crowds,
their broadcast is the same:

"Baby Girl, your diabetes
is ready." "My Man, your
stroke order is up."

They know their audience:
french fried lives, french fried
luck, french fried us.

They know corner markets
of cornered markets, seldom
scale the wall. Their shit

is always hot. Their shit is
always cheap. Their shit is

always landmark of poison
in pens, along with: windows
wearing boards, hubcaps

leaning curbs, the sound of
"bitch," the sound of "mother-
fucker," the sound of "niggah"

sounding off, projectile vomiting
from children's lips—our hush
puppy young, made beasts

behind these bars. Some days
you will see them, dirt bike
knights, riding Edmondson

Avenue, armor-less. They are
wheelies, jousting against traffic,
wheelies, jousting against stop-

lights, gas tanks bleeding out
on stretchers, as sirens serenade,
metal flies hover. There are

skeletons of chickens scattered on
the ground. There are meeting bones
of children fractured in the street,

cordoned off.

This is urban warming. This is
underwear in exhibition, pants
saddened to sag, hanging off ass

cracks, like wet clothes on a line.
This is the ecology of locks, since
our country is locks, since our

color is locks, since this block is
locked. When your order is up,
you will eat anything tossed inside

the cage.

♦ ♦ ♦

The Sweet and Vinegary Taste

CHERYL SAVAGEAU

for my grandmother, Rose LeBlanc Meunier

Summer overflowed the kitchen
where Memere made pepper relish
and piccalilli,
cooked up tons of beans,
and served us cucumbers and tomatoes
three times a day.

Every morning I followed her
down the cellar stairs
and out the back door
a load of laundry in her arms,
a bag of clothespins in mine.

A big girl now,
I grabbed the pole
and lowered the clothesline.
I hung the little things,
socks, underwear,
while Memere hung the sheets.

The line heavy with clothes,
Memere helped me push the pole
until the sheets swung
above my head,
closer to the wind, Memere said,
and safe from dogs.

But laundry was just an excuse.
The garden was what pulled us out,
and after clothes were hung
we walked our usual path
in and out among the beans and squash,
pulling a weed here, flicking a caterpillar
from the tender vines.
We buried fish
to make the plants grow.
We tied pie plates to strings
to keep the birds away, and
Memere wasn't bothered if
it didn't work. Birds flew
above and walked through the corn.
When I raised my arms and ran
to chase them Memere's voice would come,
Bury the fish, she said, and let the birds be.

Her knobby hands
working in the dark brown
New England soil
never seemed to doubt
there'd be enough.
This piece of earth
we called garden
was home, she knew,
to many, and not ours alone.

Bury the fish and let the birds be,
she said. There will be enough.

And there was enough.
Enough for everybody,
for birds, and rabbits,
and caterpillars, enough
and more than enough
to overflow the kitchen,
to fill the winter shelves
with the sweet and vinegary taste
of life, the mystery
flowing from the earth
through her hands
to our open mouths.

cutting greens
LUCILLE CLIFTON

curling them around
i hold their bodies in obscene embrace
thinking of everything but kinship.
collards and kale
strain against each strange other
away from my kissmaking hand and
the iron bedpot.
the pot is black,
the cutting board is black,
my hand,
and just for a minute
the greens roll black under the knife,
and the kitchen twists dark on its spine
and i taste in my natural appetite
the bond of live things everywhere.

Her Fruit

CELESTE GUZMÁN MENDOZA

She's given me twenty grapefruits from her family's stash
out back in the bed of the broken down pickup truck—a Ford.
She picked these grapefruits in the fields with her husband,
his sack full of sunburst. How could she not love him? Years

of working side by side, down the same row of grapefruit
trees, cotton, watermelon, spinach, strawberries; crops
that took them from Mission to Denver to patches of Michigan
and back. I find it hard to take her fruit home while she struggles

to find aluminum foil to insulate the one bedroom trailer for her
seven kids, husband, and two dogs. But she's double-bagged the fruit
in plastic. Grapefruit I've promised to eat and share with my husband

because, *Los maridos son nuestra razón, dios también.* God
and husband the two reasons why she works in 103° heat
wearing long sleeves to keep the sun   from burning.

↔ ↔ ↔

To the Fig Tree on 9th and Christian

ROSS GAY

Tumbling through the
city in my
mind without once
looking up
the racket in
the lugwork probably
rehearsing some
stupid thing I
said or did
some crime or
other the city they
say is a lonely
place until yes
the sound of sweeping
and a woman
yes with a
broom beneath
which you are now
too the canopy
of a fig its
arms pulling the
September sun to it
and she
has a hose too
and so works hard
rinsing and scrubbing
the walk
lest some poor sod
slip on the
silk of a fig
and break his hip
and not probably

reach over to gobble up
the perpetrator
the light catches
the veins in her hands
when I ask about
the tree they
flutter in the air and
she says *take*
as much as
you can
help me
so I load my
pockets and mouth
and she points
to the step-ladder against
the wall to
mean more but
I was without a
sack so my meager
plunder would have to
suffice and an old woman
whom gravity
was pulling into
the earth loosed one
from a low slung
branch and its eye
wept like hers
which she dabbed
with a kerchief as she
cleaved the fig with
what remained of her
teeth and soon there were
eight or nine
people gathered beneath
the tree looking into
it like a

constellation pointing
do you see it
and I am tall and so
good for these things
and a bald man even
told me so
when I grabbed three
or four for
him reaching into the
giddy throngs of
yellow-jackets sugar
stoned which he only
pointed to smiling and
rubbing his stomach
I mean he was really rubbing his stomach
like there was a baby
in there
it was hot his
head shone while he
offered recipes to the
group using words which
I couldn't understand and besides
I was a little
tipsy on the dance
of the velvety heart rolling
in my mouth
pulling me down and
down into the
oldest countries of my
body where I ate my first fig
from the hand of a man who escaped his country
by swimming through the night
and maybe
never said more than
five words to me
at once but gave me

figs and a man on his way
to work hops twice
to reach at last his
fig which he smiles at and calls
baby, *c'mere baby*,
he says and blows a kiss
to the tree which everyone knows
cannot grow this far north
being Mediterranean
and favoring the rocky, sun-baked soils
of Jordan and Sicily
but no one told the fig tree
or the immigrants
there is a way
the fig tree grows
in groves it wants,
it seems, to hold us,
yes I am anthropomorphizing
goddammit I have twice
in the last thirty seconds
rubbed my sweaty
forearm into someone else's
sweaty shoulder
gleeful eating out of each other's hands
on Christian St.
in Philadelphia a city like most
which has murdered its own
people
this is true
we are feeding each other
from a tree
at the corner of Christian and 9th
strangers maybe
never again.

֍ ֍ ֍

ورق

PHILIP METRES

———

consider the olive: it gnarls as it grows
into itself / a veritable thicket / it throws

———

up obstacles to the light to reach
the light / a crooked path in the air

———

while beneath our sight it wrestles the rock
wrests water from whatever trickles

———

beneath / it doesn't worry it looks like hell
refuses to straighten for anyone

———

each spring offers itself meat to be eaten
first brambles / then olives

❧❧❧

Detroit

ALISON SWAN

Scrub and brush
reassert grow

after so much assembly
so much undone

I learned asphalt isn't forever
He was twelve

And I was dragging
decades of concrete

behind me without even realizing—
Drop them then

Tear them up and plant
vegetables in a parking lot

goats and chickens behind
the last house standing

Totally illegal
but no one complains

He was probably forty-something
What's there to complain about

And Eastern Market fills up with flowers
and a hundred thousand people

↬ ↬ ↬

Milk

LINDA HOGAN

At night
inside the steamed windows
of the milk barn,
the milking machines are at work,
steel amidst the animal warmth
of cattle, nipples just washed,
brought in from the field.

I remember the smell of my mother's milk,
the taste of beginnings
when she was food for another child.
I am a body
grown from nipple,
from when we were
sharers of the same body,
one lost
in the waters of the other.

Milk is the beginning of a journey
that opens into other journeys,
cattle brought in the dark
holds of ships
from other bodies of land,
across waters.
They were hungry,
with angled bones
poking through the darkness
where they stood,
ate, weakened,
coupled and gave birth afraid
their kind would not go on,
and the milk sellers

hoisting up the dying
thirsty cow
too weak to stand
in leather straps and milking death,
drinking its watery milk,
eating land,
they were hungry.

At the river one day
the women were washing cloth
blue as the flowing light of milk.
It could have been stolen by water,
carried away, except for the hands that held it.
Something must hold me this way,
and you,
and the thin blue tail of the galaxy,
to keep us from leaving
as life unfolds behind us
over long roads and intricate, human waters.

❧ ❧ ❧

Perhaps the World Ends Here

JOY HARJO

The world begins at a kitchen table. No matter what, we must eat to live.

The gifts of earth are brought and prepared, set on the table. So it has been since creation, and it will go on.

We chase chickens or dogs away from it. Babies teethe at the corners. They scrape their knees under it.

It is here that children are given instructions on what it means to be human. We make men at it, we make women.

At this table we gossip, recall enemies and the ghosts of lovers.

Our dreams drink coffee with us as they put their arms around our children. They laugh with us at our poor falling-down selves and as we put ourselves back together once again at the table.

This table has been a house in the rain, an umbrella in the sun.

Wars have begun and ended at this table. It is a place to hide in the shadow of terror. A place to celebrate the terrible victory.

We have given birth on this table, and have prepared our parents for burial here.

At this table we sing with joy, with sorrow. We pray of suffering and remorse. We give thanks.

Perhaps the world will end at the kitchen table, while we are laughing and crying, eating of the last sweet bite.

ᘯ ᘯ ᘯ

||||||||||||||||||||||||||||||||||||||||||||||||||||||||||||||||||||||||||||||||||||||||||||||||||||||||||||||||||||||||||||||||||||||||||||||||||||||||||||||||||||||||||||

Tell the Birds

↪ Human-Animal Relations

These poems examine divergent cultural perspectives on human-animal relations, ranging from the hierarchical thinking found in Western science, religion, and philosophy to an animist view that all living beings are interrelated.

Some of the poems in this section stand clearly in the human position, looking out at the animal world. Others step into the animal position to offer empathy and recognition of shared fate. Still other poems look at ways in which our own survival is linked to the survival of animals with recognition that colonization, war, and economic exploitation affect the animal world as well as human worlds.

Clare Rossini's "The Great Chain of Being" opens the section with an inquiry into the hierarchical way of cataloging that continues to dominate Western thought, asking, "What extremity roosts / In the small hard hut of a snail?"

Kathy Engel offers a vision of interconnectedness and healing in her poem "Return"—a vision in which humans and animals are inseparable:

> the animals camp out in the farm
> of my body, a field of muscle, fat
> and bone, sea of nerves; they mend.

Poets mourn the loss of species and habitat with a sense of their own loss. Ojibwe poet Louise Erdrich, in "I Was Sleeping Where the Black Oaks Move," mourns the herons, who lost their habitat when the water on the reservation rose and washed their nests away. The loss is one of profound kinship and identity, as Grandpa says in the poem, *"These are the ghosts of the tree people / moving among us unable to take their rest."*

Morton Marcus, in "There Are Days Now," describes the extinction of elephants and whales, a loss the speaker feels in his own body:

> I am resigned to this,
> but with each of these premonitions
> there is a crumbling
> along the banks of my blood stream.

Poets bring awareness that our political and economic disturbances affect the animal world as well as humans. The otherness so present in Western thinking with regards to the animal and nonhuman world is a shared sorrow in Chickasaw poet Linda Hogan's "Mountain Lion," in which the speaker and a mountain lion pass each other on the road and see each other "inside mortal dusk" where nothing is hidden "in the land of the terrible other." Hogan writes,

> Red spirits of hunters
> walked between us
> from the place where blood
> goes back to its wound
> before fire
> before weapons.

Craig Santos Perez further explores colonization in his poem "*ginen* the micronesian kingfisher [*i sihek*]," a poem that traces the extinction of the wild Micronesian kingfisher and mourns its fate in zoo cages, offering empathy from the indigenous perspective of living in a postcolonial and colonized world. He writes,

> invasion is
> a continuous chain of
> immeasurably destructive
> events in time—

generations
LUCILLE CLIFTON

people who are going to be
in a few years
bottoms of trees
bear a responsibility to something
besides people
        if it was only
you and me
sharing the consequences
it would be different
it would be just
generations of men
        but
this business of war
these war kind of things
are erasing those natural
obedient generations
who ignored pride
        stood on no hind legs
        begged no water
        stole no bread
did their own things

and the generations of rice
of coal
of grasshoppers

by their invisibility
denounce us

֍ ֍ ֍

The Great Chain of Being

CLARE ROSSINI

The rain cowing ferns   the feral twittering of stars—
    What extremity roosts

In the small hard hut of a snail?
    Furiously, creation exudes   particulars

We put them in order   one fine medieval day
    God at the top, angels next   and beneath

The dimpled *putto*   wingless man
      Canceling forests   grinding down

The extravagant mountains   the bees in fluorescent hives
    Sweatshopping honey

Yes, we dreamed ourselves   on high, nailed every frog
    And sparrow in place   below us—

A kind of comfort, I suppose   when the wind begins to blow
    And the sea, rising   comes looking

❧ ❧ ❧

Return

KATHY ENGEL

The animals camp out in the farm
of my body, a field of muscle, fat
and bone, sea of nerves; they mend
my vessels, sew back my arteries, sing
my stutter, gallop my missteps—first a
horse, then the others claim their places,
even snakes and insects swivel and swarm.
I thought the rupture within was all
a human thing—the mother, the father,
the lost girl—now I understand, the earth
itself is calling and the animals, buried,
scattered, those who rise, snort, bellow,
murmur, hiss; their hooves, wings, fins,
and tentacles seed the soil,
repair the soul.

Spider's Orb
KATY RICHEY

The cocoons are set and protected
for months before the wind sets them loose.

These are the last days of waiting.

Now tiny drops of dust cling like catchweed.
The web will float if disturbed.

This is the last doting.

Nothing moves in winter. Its silence
is an idle breath, sunlight reticent.

Soon this world will break.

Spring comes,
the exodus is like precipitation.

Nothing is left behind, no tendrils
or sweet balm. Only whispers, prophecy—

❦ ❦ ❦

Crossing a City Highway
YUSEF KOMUNYAKAA

The city at 3 a.m. is an ungodly mask
the approaching day hides behind
& from, the coyote nosing forth,
the muscles of something ahead,

& a fiery blaze of eighteen-wheelers
zoom out of the curved night trees,
along the rim of absolute chance.
A question hangs in the oily air.

She knows he will follow her scent
left in the poisoned grass & buzz
of chainsaws, if he can unweave
a circle of traps around the subdivision.

For a breathy moment, she stops
on the world's edge, & then quick as that
masters the stars & again slips the noose
& darts straight between sedans & SUVs.

Don't try to hide from her kind of blues
or the dead nomads who walked trails
now paved by wanderlust, an epoch
somewhere between tamed & wild.

If it were Monday instead of Sunday
the outcome may be different,
but she's now in Central Park
searching for a Seneca village

among painted stones & shrubs,
where she's never been, & lucky
she hasn't forgotten how to jig
& kill her way home.

Blackbody Curve
SAMIYA BASHIR

Stairs: a rushed flight down thirty-eight; French doors unlocked always.

Always: a lie; an argument.

Argument: two buck hunters circle a meadow's edge.

Edge: one of us outside bleeding.

Bleeding: shards of glass; doors locked.

Locked: carpet awash with blood.

Blood: lift and drop; a sudden breeze.

Breeze: its whistle through bone.

Bone: the other was looking at —

Bone: cradled to catch drips.

Drips: quiet as a meadow fawn.

Fawn: faces down each hunter each gun.

Gun: again.

Again: somebody call someone.

Someone: almost always prefers forgetting.

Forgetting: an argument; a lie.

Lie: a meadow; a casement; a stair.

❧ ❧ ❧

Mountain Lion

LINDA HOGAN

She lives on the dangerous side
of the clearing
in the yellow-eyed shadow of a darker fear.
We have seen each other
inside mortal dusk,
and what passed between us
was the road
ghosts travel
when they cannot rest
in the land of the terrible other.
Red spirits of hunters
walked between us
from the place where blood
goes back to its wound
before fire
before weapons.
Nothing was hidden
in our eyes.
I was the wild thing
she had learned to fear.
Her power lived
in a dream of my leaving.
It was the same way
I have looked so many times at others
in clear light
before lowering my eyes
and turning away
from what lives inside those
who have found

two worlds cannot live
inside a single vision.

Whole Notes

PAMELA USCHUK

God is the tongue of the female timber wolf
slathering my face, rough as a snowshovel
scraping back the pages of Red Riding Hood,
                        revising my ears. Listen,
says this wolf tongue speaking its severed
language of love and sorrow, its history
of stick games, its guileless pups,
history of rifleshot from airplanes,
forelegs snapped in steel-toothed traps, trailing
blood through snow.
Listen.

      Have you ever heard eighty wild throats howling their ghosts at noon,
eighty fanged angels buzzed by yellow jackets and the belch
of oil tankers downshifting just
                       over the ridge? Have you heard
their long-boned whole notes of goodbye?

Wolfwood Wolf Refuge
Ignacio, Colorado

❧ ❧ ❧

Whale Song

ELISE PASCHEN

> Pilot whales have a close-knit social structure that can cause them to
> follow sick or lost members of their pod and then resist leaving those
> animals.
>
> —*Los Angeles Times*

At counters in grocery stores
friends purchase turkeys large enough
to feed twelve siblings, thirty cousins,

while our family table grows
smaller. Across the continent
the pilot whales click, call and keen

as one, then another, dry-docks.
Hovering nearby in shallow waters,
the pod can't be lured to the deep.

On linens we station pale candles,
marshal chrysanthemums in vases,
balance wedding glasses for five,

while in the graveyards the headstones
wait to be carved. Around the table:
ghost of song, empty chairs.

✺ ✺ ✺

There Are Days Now

MORTON MARCUS

There are days now
when I can see the souls of elephants
being towed to heaven.
Soon the trees
will be loosed from their moorings
and sail off like a chorus of Greek women
rigid with grief.
And the whales—soon the whales
will be hulks full of sand.

I am resigned to this,
but with each of these premonitions
there is a crumbling
along the banks of my blood stream.
So if I touch you now,
my friend,
how can it be with my whole hand,
the fat resting firm beneath the palm,
and not with clutching fingers,
as though I had grabbed you in passing
and were holding on?

❧ ❧ ❧

I Was Sleeping Where the Black Oaks Move

LOUISE ERDRICH

We watched from the house
as the river grew, helpless
and terrible in its unfamiliar body.
Wrestling everything into it,
the water wrapped around trees
until their life-hold was broken.
They went down, one by one,
and the river dragged off their covering.

Nests of the herons, roots washed to bones,
snags of soaked bark on the shoreline:
a whole forest pulled through the teeth
of the spillway. Trees surfacing
singly, where the river poured off
into arteries for fields below the reservation.

When at last it was over, the long removal,
they had all become the same dry wood.
We walked among them, the branches
whitening in the raw sun.
Above us drifted herons,
alone, hoarse-voiced, broken,
settling their beaks among the hollows.
Grandpa said, *These are the ghosts of the tree people*
moving among us, unable to take their rest.

Sometimes now, we dream our way back to the heron dance.
Their long wings are bending the air
into circles through which they fall.
They rise again in shifting wheels.
How long must we live in the broken figures
their necks make, narrowing the sky.

ginen the micronesian kingfisher [*i sihek*]
CRAIG SANTOS PEREZ

~

[our] nightmare : no
birdsong—
the jungle was riven emptied
of [*i sihek*] bright blue green turquoise red gold
feathers—everywhere : brown
tree snakes avian
silence—

the snakes entered
without words when [we] saw them it was too late—
they were at [our] doors sliding along
the passages of [*i sihek*]
empire—then

the zookeepers came—
called it *species survival plan*—captured [*i sihek*] and transferred the last
twenty-nine micronesian kingfishers
to zoos for captive breeding [1988]—they repeated [*i sihek*]
and repeated :

"if it weren't for us
your birds [i sihek]
would be gone
forever"

what does not change /

last wild seen—

~

exterior features : quarter inch plywood
screened mesh cage front [*i sihek*] with bumpers
and burlap shield—

~

"a rare micronesian kingfisher chick, weighing five grams, hatched at the
national zoo's conservation and research center [2004] [*i sihek*]

~

interior ceiling : foam rubber or burlap stuffed
with straw—external minimum size :
nine inch by nine inch—internal height :
minimum ten inch clearance between floor and
ceiling padding—perching : [*i sihek*] half inch diameter—

~

"our newest pair of micronesian kingfishers at the san diego zoo is currently
raising a chick [2007] [*i sihek*]

~

the minimum enclosure
size for breeding pairs : ten feet by eight feet
with a height of ten feet containment—
this cage [*i sihek*]
can be either solid material wire mesh
or glass—
on these displays [*i sihek*]—

what does not change / is

is born and fed and grows and dies—

~

for wire enclosures
mesh size should not exceed one inch—
kingfishers have attacked

their images reflected
in glass cage fronts—these
are not legends—
the birds are
birds—inside
snake belly [*i sihek*]—no
longer averting pests or
spreading
seeds—

"two of guam's endangered micronesian kingfishers were released from quarantine at the department of agriculture. the female birds arrived on guam about a month ago from the philadelphia zoo (both were hatched at the st. louis zoo), courtesy of continental airlines petsafe program [2008] [*i sihek*]

nest logs
should be a minimum
of two feet in length with a diameter of no
less than fifteen inches—
it may be difficult to place nest logs
at this height in
captivity—[*i sihek*] the core of
the log should be exposed
so the birds have access to the soft
center [*i sihek*]
without excavating
the hard outer
bark—the national

zoo has had success using a pulley
system to lower and raise
the nest
log to check for
eggs—

~

"the saint louis zoo has hatched 41 chicks since 1985. recent modifications
to bird house habitats have now made it possible to house [*i sihek*] a pair of
these rare birds for visitors

~

what does not change / is the will

to see

~

"a mated pair of guam micronesian kingfishers . . . laid two fertile eggs this spring deep inside a hollowed-out palm log in a special breeding room of the lincoln park zoo bird house. keepers promptly stole one of the eggs . . . The parents incubated and hatched one egg in the hollow log . . . the other egg hatched [a few days later] inside an incubation machine in a lab, where the chick now lives, fed by keepers from tweezers protruding beneath the beak of an oversized kingfisher hand puppet [2010]

[*i sihek*]

~

invasion is
a continuous chain of
immeasurably destructive
events in time—

is the death of [*i sihek*]
origins—
is a stillborn [*i sihek*]
future—is the ending of
all nests this
choked thing [we] [*i sihek*]
rise
above cages
i sihek

☙ ☙ ☙

Midwestern Zoo

KAREN SKOLFIELD

We speak of the polar bear solitary
in his polar pen and watch his red ball
hopefully, the bear slumped by his shallow cave.

The crowd wills the bear to play or walk
his usual bear circuit, just the width
of two paws, a battered and tedious oval.

We are a species that admires paths:
the track worn in the carpeted stairs' center.
Treadmarks into the garage, then out again.

The boy says the bear's looking
thinner, the fur darkened.
For two years they've needed a new bear.

A pair that will wrestle like kittens,
fall into water oddly free of seals.
Even in our zoo animals we find the world wanting.

The boy says maybe three bears, imagine
three little bears, or six! and that's
what we wish for, a line of blindingly

white polar cubs that stay small and frolicsome.
Still, we are benevolent. When the bear raises
its weary head, we are polite enough to cheer.

This is the bear we've got.
Our applause goes on longer than it should.
You can hear it all the way to the tiger's cage.

❧ ❧ ❧

Hum

JOSHUA MCKINNEY

When I smelled green through the blur
where its wings were, felt
the whir of their arc, heard the red
of its ruby throat-scales, tasted the dart of its forked tongue
afloat in the foxglove—my only desire was
to tell you.

My weed-work stopped. Hands
in earth, I knelt by the garden wall,
and suddenly that world seemed remote.

I called to you, aloud, and the words I spoke
were rote, broken, each one an arbitrary token
of the tiny bird that came to kiss the flowers.

It was then I knew my exile's full extent.
The phenomenon of pungent sound is brighter—
sheer iridescent now there then—
than the hours of thought without flesh. Once, to be
at one meant to act, so I have tried to make this
matter.

ଚ-ଚ-ଚ

Raining in the Fields

DOUG ANDERSON

When a horse dies something ancient dies
that links to our beginnings after which
we'll be less than we were, less noble,
less connected to the old world
that may itself be going,
so grievously have we broken it.
The vet will come, the horse
will lie down one last time
and then the man with the backhoe
will dig a hole big enough.
You might expect to find bones beneath
the bones that will be—
something there waiting to receive
this old Pegasus. The silence here is huge,
and the grave a tunnel to another truth.

300 Goats
NAOMI SHIHAB NYE

In icy fields.

Is water flowing in the tank?

Will they huddle together, warm bodies pressing?

(Is it the year of the goat or the sheep?

Scholars debating Chinese zodiac,

follower or leader.)

O lead them to a warm corner,

little ones toward bulkier bodies.

Lead them to the brush, which cuts the icy wind.

Another frigid night swooping down—

Aren't you worried about them? I ask my friend,

who lives by herself on the ranch of goats,

far from here near the town of Ozona.

She shrugs, "Not really,

they know what to do. They're *goats*."

ཨ ཨ ཨ

The Bee People

AMY MILLER

sat quiet while the council droned
about the ugly new plaza
and knots of traffic
tying up North Main.
They sat in their sandals
and blue t-shirts painted
with the tiger backs of bees
and waited for the vote
about hives and lots and setbacks
and neighbor notification
and EpiPens and the relative
aggression of wasps and the range
of the average working bee
and colony collapse and fields
east of the rain shadow. Some
hummed. One trembled. I noticed
their hair, a golden sheen
on every head as if—
well, as if the bees
had somehow had a hand
in getting them here, had pushed them
down the walk with wings
that hovered magic and precise
like small hands
steering them by the sun
to where they had to go.

֍ ֍ ֍

The Barnacle and the Gray Whale
CECILIA LLOMPART

Said the Barnacle,

You enchant me, with your carnival
of force.

Yours is a system of slow.

There is you, the pulley
and there is you, the weight.

Your eyes wide on a hymn.

Your deep song like the turn
of that first,

that earliest of wheels.

Said the Whale,

I have seen you, little encruster,
in that business of fouling the ships.

Known, little drum machine, you
to tease out food from the drink.

Little thimble of chalk and hard water.

You could be a callus of whiter skin.

You could be a knucklebone. You
who hang on me,

like a conscience.

❧❧❧

Magnifying Glass

TIM SEIBLES

No one
would burn
your name
for not seeing
the ant's
careful antennae
testing the air
next to your
shoe, six legs
almost rowing
it along. Who

would be upset
if you brushed one
off-handedly off
your arm, undone
by the tiny
steps: *what do
they want,*
you ask—unaware
that they breathe
through their
sides. Do they
sleep? Do they
dream
anything? No
one should

mark your soul
short   if you
mash one: when
two ants meet
there's no tongue
for hello—it's a
bug, a nearly
less than
little thing: at most,
made to chisel
crumbs
under the fridge
with eyes that,
even in brightest
day, see not reds
or greens but gray
and gray again.
Who would

curse your life
if you bring out
the *Raid*?
How many
books have they
read?—that
brain   a virtual
speck. Is all
they carry
really work

or just some
dumb old daily
ado?—the heart
spending
what blood, what
prehistoric nudge
on that
handsome,
brittle head.

Strategy against Dying

MONICA SOK

We fashioned party cups
to catch bees, wasps,
sprayed the green hose
to drown them, then freeze them,
little blue flowers, milkweed
from the field, pulled grass
dead as hair.
We trapped the queen butterfly,
so free we suffocated her—
at the touch of water, her wings
went limp, they hinged shut
inside a yellow cave.
We froze her.
The ice pulled her apart,
opened her wings.
In the garage, we rested her
inside her own cup of sun
beside cut meats.
Dad found her in the freezer,
asked us *Why?*
as he held her grave
like a drink in his hand.

✧✧✧

Eviction Notice
BRIAN PATRICK HESTON

After it came, my mother went out and walked the trail
along the river in the high morning heat. This place used to be only
weeds and garbage. We called it hobo heaven because of the train
that ran here, and all the veiled spaces to hide a refrigerator box.
Now, everywhere, it was blooming and oblivious: juvenile poplars
bloated with leaves, peaceful joggers, lovers holding hands.

She sat at a bench overlooking the water, a brown froth
swirling with plastic debris. She hung her head, wondering
how she could tell us the news. "Whatado? Whatado?"
birds asked from the trees. "Screwed! Screwed!"
other birds replied. She looked back to the river, thinking.

That's when she saw the two mallard corpses floating
towards her on the river's surface, feathers black and filthy
as an engine block. As they passed by, falling into the distance
like dreams, she struggled to make out the thin white rope
of their necks hanging beneath the murk.

❧ ❧ ❧

Albatross

KEVIN SIMMONDS

after Chris Jordan's photograph series Midway: Message from the Gyre

opened like a purse
bellies of rotted
bird bodies

lay burst
with shiny things
parents thought
good
food

not
bottle cap
button
bottle's green
shard

the contents never shifted
during flight

never flew

☙ ☙ ☙

The Dreams of Antelope
DANE CERVINE

In Yosemite, they introduced wolves back into the mountains, which fed again on the antelope, which stopped over-eating the willow trees, so the birds returned to sing and beavers started making dams again from the fallen branches, resurrecting the marshes, and once more everything started turning green because a wild predator was allowed back into the dreams of antelope.

✦ ✦ ✦

The Parable of St. Matthew Island
DANE CERVINE

In the Bering Sea, the Coast Guard brought twenty-nine reindeer to the island as back-up food supply for the nineteen soldiers stationed there. After World War II, the base was closed. Thirteen years later, a thousand reindeer fed on the four-inch thick mat of lichen that covered the island, then six thousand a decade later. In just three more years, travelers found only a small herd, not much lichen, and fields of reindeer skeletons. Soon, it was only skeletons.

✦ ✦ ✦

Too Many

DAVID BAKER

my neighbors
say, when what they mean
       are deer—the foragers, the few at a time, fair

if little more
than rats, according to
                a farmer friend nearby, whose corn means plenty.

They nip the peaches,
and one bite ruins;
       hazard every road with their running-

into-headlights-
not-away; a
       menace; plague; something should be done.

   Or here in town,
where I've
       found a kind of afterlife—the townies hate

the damage to their varie-
gated hostas,
       shadeside ferns—what they do inside white bunkers of

the county's one good
course is "criminal,"
       deep scuffs through the sand—that's one thing—but

lush piles of polished-
olive-droppings, hoof-
       ruts in the chemically- and color-enriched greens . . .

Yet here's
one more, curled
    like a tan seashell not a foot from my blade, just-

come-to-the-
world fawn, speckled,
    wet as a trout, which I didn't see, hacking back

       brush beneath my tulip
poplar—it's not afraid,
        mews like a kitten, can't walk: there are so many, too

many of us,
the world keeps saying,
       and the world keeps making—this makes no sense—
  more.

❧ ❧ ❧

The Dogs and I Walked Our Woods
GRETCHEN PRIMACK

and there was a dog, precisely the colors of autumn,
asleep between two trunks by the trail.
But it was a coyote, paws pink
with a clean-through hole in the left,
and a deep hole in the back of the neck,
dragged and placed in the low crotch
of a tree. But it was two coyotes,
the other's hole in the side of the neck,
the other with a dried pool of blood below
the nose, a dried pool below the anus,
the other dragged and placed
in the adjoining low crook, the other's body
a precise mirror of the first. The eyes were closed,
the fur smooth and precisely the colors
of autumn, a little warm to my touch though the bodies
were not. The fur was cells telling themselves
to spin to keep her warm to stand
and hunt and keep. It was a red
autumn leaf on the forest floor, but
it was a blooded brown leaf, and another, because
they dragged the bodies to create a monument
to domination, to the enormous human,
and if I bore a child who suffered to see this,
or if I bore a child who gladdened to see this, or if
I bore a child who kept walking, I could not bear
it, so I will not bear one.

❧ ❧ ❧

Serengeti Afternoon
LISA RIZZO

To stand upright,
a wildebeest struggles,
wobbly, his legs broken.
In the thin arms
of a baobab tree
vultures,
ink splotches
across the deep blue sky.
They are waiting
for the wildebeest's
last fall
before they drop
down around him.
I watch stunned
as the first one, brazen,
tears a strip of flesh
from the still-shuddering flank.
Red means only one thing
in the Serengeti.
My silent vigil
is all I offer
the dying.
For the first time
in my life
I wish for a gun.

෴ ෴ ෴

SECTION V

Unquiet Air
↪ Resource Extraction

Poems in this section examine the impact of resource extraction and industrialization on local populations and local environments. Whether describing pollutants such as the "roaring flowers of the chimney-stacks," as Muriel Rukeyser does in her poem "Alloy," or the greed for light given by whale blubber—"a hill made of fat / and blood, a town built on it"—as Linda Hogan does in "Fat," poets in this section examine the environmental and human impact of extraction economies. They question the value of living resources traded for capital or stolen, whether those resources are human bodies, trees, or entire mountains.

The poets challenge cultural values. As Molly McGlennen reminds the reader in "Snake River IV," the indigenous perspective is to value our connectedness to the living river rather than to exploit the river:

> We could say parent
> or grandmother river.
>
> . . .
>
> But down from us, she surges between
> urbanity's survival kit:
> hydro-electric plants, Prairie Island
> radioactivity.

Landscapes of benzene, brown fields, chemical dumps, coal-burning plants, plastic factories, radioactivity, charred river banks and stunted trees, tailings ponds, tank farms, and fracking trucks exist side-by-side with human and animal communities.

The destruction does not come from nowhere; it is part of a living history. In "the killing of the trees," Lucille Clifton, with her "witness eye," sees the bulldozing of trees in her suburban neighborhood not just as the destruction of forest but as the destruction of indigenous people. The speaker of the describes the scene as "trees huddle in a camp weeping":

> he was a chief. he was a tree
> falling the way a chief falls,
> straight, eyes open, arms reaching
> for his mother ground.

Poems in this section tell of a scarred and dangerous landscape, but nonetheless a peopled one. In Elee Kraljii Gardiner's "Refinement," "Oil is an unctuous tongue" in a world where "What's good for business / is not good for you":

> . . . saturation
>
> in the center of discourse. You soften, remember
> your brother-in-law works the pipe line
> collapses on the couch at the end of his shift.

Similarly, Heather Lynn Davis reminds us in "29 Men" of lives lost mining coal:

> The lights in your home channel 29 men, their
> soot stained clothes, last breaths, crystalline sweat
> let loose on black rock.

Cultures collide and connect across borders of unequal power; "*hellofuckyou,*" the kids in Muynak yell at American visitors in a place "doomed / to die from the inside out" in Jaime Lee Jarvis's poem "Aral." It is a world increasingly connected by crisis and destruction. In Lisa Wujnovich's "To Haiti from Mountain Dell Farm," the narrator makes a connection between deforestation in Haiti, agricultural destruction, and resource exploitation in the United States:

> . . . we've been told:
> your disasters are all natural,
> our injuries unconnected,
> none of us related.

The section ends with lullaby and cradlesong in a land of tank farm and fracking waste trucks. "For now," Lilace Mellin Guignard's poem croons, "Daddy still has a job to lose," and "Spin-dizzy in the sweet threshold of this benzene lullaby," Vivian Faith Prescott writes: "Go to sleep, little children, go to sleep."

Alloy

MURIEL RUKEYSER

This is the most audacious landscape. The gangster's
stance with his gun smoking and out is not so
vicious as this commercial field, its hill of glass.

Sloping as gracefully as thighs, the foothills
narrow to this, clouds over every town
finally indicate the stored destruction.

Crystalline hill: a blinded field of white
murdering snow, seamed by convergent tracks;
the travelling cranes reach for the silica.

And down the track, the overhead conveyor
slides on its cable to the feet of chimneys.
Smoke rises, not white enough, not so barbaric.

Here the severe flame speaks from the brick throat,
electric furnaces produce this precious, this clean,
annealing the crystals, fusing at last alloys.

Hottest for silicon, blast furnaces raise flames,
spill fire, spill steel, quench the new shape to freeze,
tempering it to perfected metal.

Forced through this crucible, a million men.
Above this pasture, the highway passes those
who curse the air, breathing their fear again.

The roaring flowers of the chimney-stacks
less poison, at their lips in fire, than this
dust that is blown from off the field of glass;

blows and will blow, rising over the mills,
crystallized and beyond the fierce corrosion
disintegrated angel on these hills.

the killing of the trees
LUCILLE CLIFTON

the third went down
with a sound almost like flaking,
a soft swish as the left leaves
fluttered themselves and died.
three of them, four, then five
stiffening in the snow
as if this hill were Wounded Knee
as if the slim feathered branches
were bonnets of war
as if the pale man seated
high in the bulldozer nest
his blonde mustache ice-matted
was Pahuska come again but stronger now,
his long hair wilde and unrelenting.

remember the photograph,
the old warrior, his stiffened arm
raised as if in blessing,
his frozen eyes open,
his bark skin brown and not so much
wrinkled as circled with age,
and the snow everywhere still falling,
covering his one good leg.
remember his name was Spotted Trail
or Hump or Red Cloud or Geronimo
or none of these or all of these.
he was a chief. he was a tree
falling the way a chief falls,
straight, eyes open, arms reaching
for his mother ground.

so i have come to live
among the men who kill the trees,
a subdivision, new,
in southern Maryland.
I have brought my witness eye with me
and my two wild hands,
the left one sister to the fists
pushing the bulldozer against the old oak,
the angry right, brown and hard and spotted
as bark. we come in peace,
but this morning
ponies circle what is left of life
and whales and continents and children and ozone
and trees huddle in a camp weeping
outside my window and i can see it all
with that one good eye.

Eloquence of Earth (excerpt)

KIMBERLY BLAESER

Each season gavels strike new bargains with our oldest enemies
maji-manidoog, handsome fast-talking strangers disguised as prosperity.

Daily we watch patient warnings swim the Wolf River,
wash up on the shores of our great lakes,
migrate to absent wetlands, trumpet old calls.
How do we translate the flashing fins of poisoned fish?
What other alphabet do you know to spell *contaminated waters*?
Like banned books words still burn on my tongue—*reciprocity,*
sacred, preservation, earth, tradition, knowledge, protect.
Even the vellum of *justice* disdained, crumbled in quick greedy fists.
Meanwhile we gather here, descendants of *ajijaak* and *maang*
lift our ancient clan voices in longing, for a chant of restoration
in a Faustian world.

If I say *Gichigami*—Lake Superior—a turquoise plain, stretches
infinite, *gete-gaming.* If I say *Wiikonigoyaang,* she invites us to her feast,
how many will remember the eloquence of earth itself?
At dawn when *jiibay* mist backstrokes across the copper of northern prairies
eerie white hovering, damp and alive,
will you stretch out your hands in hope
cup the sacred like cedar smoke,
draw it toward you—a gesture
fervent and older than language?
Now I say *wiigwaasikaa,* everywhere we look
there are many white birch,
bark marked with sign, scrolls a history.
I say *ritual, continuum, cycle of belonging,*
I say *daga,* please; *ninandotaan,*

you must listen for it—*aki*.
Yes, our very earth speaks.
Who among us will translate?

֍֍֍

2008, XII
WENDELL BERRY

> My people are destroyed for lack of knowledge
> —Hosea 4:6

We forget the land we stand on
and live from. We set ourselves
free in an economy founded
on nothing, on greed verified
by fantasy, on which we entirely
depend. We depend on fire
that consumes the world without
lighting it. To this dark blaze
driving the inert metal
of our most high desire
we offer our land as fuel,
thus offering ourselves at last
to be burned. This is our riddle
to which the answer is a life
that none of us has lived.

❧ ❧ ❧

Fat

LINDA HOGAN

This is the land
where whales were mountains
pulled in by small boats,
where fat was rendered
out of darkness
by the light of itself,

where what fell through
the slaughtering decks
was taken in by land

until it became a hill made of fat
and blood, a town built on it.

The whale is the thick house of yesterday
in red waters.
It is the curve of another fortune,
a greasy smell and cloud
of dark smoke
that hides our faces.

At night
in this town
where hungers
are asleep,
we sleep
on a bed of secret fat.

A whale passes.
From dark strands of water,
it calls
its children by name,
Light, Smoke, Water, Land.

I hear it singing,
I sit up, awake.
It is a mountain rising,
lovely and immense.
I see myself
in the shine of it
and I want light.
I am full
with greed.
Give to me
light.

✧ ✧ ✧

Money

JANE MEAD

Someone had the idea of getting more water
released beneath the Don Pedro Dam
into the once-green Tuolumne,—

so the minnows could have some wiggle room,
so the salmon could lunge far enough up
to spawn, so that there would be more salmon

in the more water below the dam.
But it wasn't possible—by then the water
didn't belong to the salmon anymore, by then

the water didn't even belong to the river.
The water didn't belong to the water.

❧ ❧ ❧

Epithalamia

JOAN NAVIYUK KANE

Butane, propane
and lungful of diesel.
I did not stand a chance.

Always with poison
breath, bill, responsibility:
a man with rote hands.

Everything in exchange,
rain in a frozen season.
Our roof, roofs strung

with hot wire. Our love,
what was, an impression
of light, gaunt: there is

nothing to get.

֍ ֍ ֍

Benefit of the Doubt

J. D. SMITH

Someone may have wondered
How much does a mountain weigh?

There was no great balance to set it on,
no human scale, but the question
could be divided, layers taken and tallied
with rounding of inevitable error.

Perhaps the only way to pay for this answer
was to sell off the resulting heaps
of shorn stone and dust,

which some believed
would lighten, if not the earth,
our passage over it.

⊕ ⊕ ⊕

A Hakka Man Farms Rare Earth in South China

WANG PING

First of all, it's not rare nor earth, as they call it.
The metal lies under our feet, sparkling in the soil we farm,
Red, green, yellow, blue, purple, sky of grass
And buffalos, patches of rice, bamboos, sweet yams.
We came here as guests—Hakka—fleeing from angry
Lords. Year after year, we bent over the earth
Feet and hands in the neon soil, our sweat
Fertilized the fields, children, ancestors' graves
Our stove cooked the fragrance from the sun and moon.

Now we dig, deep in the mud, our boots
Rotting in the rainbow sludge . . . Dig, and we dig
Hoes, pickaxes, guns, explosives, acid wash
Ten yuan a sac, this red dirt speckled with
Blue and yellow. Home, we cry,
A small haven painted with green.
Now the mountains are lifted.
Deep crates in the fields, blood and pus
In streams and rivers . . . all because the world
Wants this earth—"Vitamins" for I-pods
Plasma TVs, wind turbines, guided missiles—
Things that make the world
Cleaner and more beautiful, as they say

And here we are, in the waist-deep sludge
A sac of mud—a tail of greed
Leaching in our stove.
Fire licks my wife's slender hands
Acid fumes in her lungs, liver, stomach
Till she can no longer sip porridge laced
With the thousand-year-old egg.
In our cooking woks, we exhume
Dysprosium, Neodymium, Promethium
All the names of Gods, they say.

If gods have eyes, would they see us
Slaves on this earth that no longer holds us?

In the distance, a mushroom of dust—
Boss and his Prius, powered by the sludge
That chokes my eyes, ears, nose . . . One *Rich Field*
twenty-five pounds of metal, ten-thousand sacs of earth
Ripped under our feet. We're slipping,
Our chests soaked in blood, backs broken
Digging, pulling, no food or water.
Our quota still short, the boss will be mad,
But no matter. I light a cigarette, each puff
Is the last. Tomorrow is gone, like our village.
Here and far away, where horses ran wild
Under the sky, where we, children of
Genghis Khan, return every night in our dream,
which is gone, too, they say. Mongolia
Our origin, now a rare earth pit for the world.

Oh, Hakka, Hakka, forever a guest
Wandering on this bare earth.

NOTES

Hakka: Nomads from Mongolia, scattered all over China and world. Most of them now live in Guandong, where the rare earth metals are mined and leached in stone-age methods. Inner Mongolia and Guangdong produce 95 percent of the rare earth supplies for the world.

Rich Field: The meaning of Toyota; the Chinese name is FengTian.

᧡᧡᧡

29 Men

HEATHER LYNN DAVIS

If any of you have been asked by your group president, supervisors,
engineers, or anyone else to do anything other than run coal, you need to
ignore them and run coal.

—Don Blankenship, CEO of Massey Energy, owner of the Upper Big Branch
Mine

The lights in your home channel 29 men, their
soot stained clothes, last breaths, crystalline sweat
let loose on black rock.

The lamps in your den cast 29 men
from West Virginia to your retinas, making night
like day, closing the circle.

Did the bulbs in their kitchens pop and spark, the floors
revolt when the methane blew, stopping the hearts
of family members for what seemed like hours?

When he left that morning he said, "Love you too, buddy.
     Now I'm gonna
          Cut me some coal."

Along with the brilliance in your bedroom you get 29 men
so cheaply it's like nothing, an easy find
at the second hand store, a keeper.

I heard about Don Blankenship, King of Coal, Massey CEO.
How he made it his crusade to crush the union
so the men could start working 12-hour shifts.

I heard about Don Blankenship, Pied Piper, 1,000 violations
studding his golden belt, how it wasn't enough, how he
wooed those boys to the precipice like hard used toys.

Your porch light out front floods the yard and sings
29 men, electric lives exuberant, giving everything. Don't
turn away. This is what we pay for.

⸙ ⸙ ⸙

Wampum

HONORÉE FANONNE JEFFERS

> In the early contact period New England Indian
> wampum consisted of small tubular-shaped
> shells drilled and strung as beads.
> —Alfred A. Cave

The breaking of clouds begins with seizure.

    A man grabs another, reasons ransom.

A murder averted in the thing's scheme.
    A cape's shell transformed, more than one supposed.

What stands behind this? Enemy or friend?
    (Yes, they can be both. Don't you think I know?)

List: Dutch. Indian. Pequot. Puritan.
    List: Then. War. Event. Now. History. List.

The shell buys glories of iron and pelt.
    Wampum is dismissed. Joke. Sneer. Currency

of the disappeared whose children live still.
    List: Blessing. Curse. Wife. Slave. Savior. Savage.

The shells make their noise. The robbed graves cradle.
    He who brings food to the starving gets cooked.

֍ ֍ ֍

New Jersey Poem

MARIA MAZZIOTTI GILLAN

In New Jersey, with one of the highest cancer
rates in the nation, with its brown fields and
chemical dumps, with its rivers that reek
of death and floating sewage, with its air tainted
by the coal-burning plants in Ohio, with its
towns where all the trees are dying, there are
moments still if I look beyond the surface
of all the ruin we have brought to the earth,
when I can drive the soft fold of hills through
Long Valley, climb the steep ledges of the roads
in Sussex, see the vistas from Newton's highest
hills, moments I can believe that some of the
world I remember, the daisies and black-eyed
susans that seeded the vacant lots of my
childhood, the sky crammed full of chunky
stars, the air so clean I breathe it in and sigh,
the snow that fell in thick flakes and that we ate
sprinkled with sugar and coffee after we
scooped it into cups off the ground. If the air
and the earth were already destroyed then, we
did not know it, licking this fresh fallen snow
off a spoon, not aware that the world we were
given was not the one we'd pass on.

∾∾∾

Snake River IV

MOLLY MCGLENNEN

Tucked away,
a zip lock baggie holds our river maps —
hidden signatures of this one tributary
we move upon
and its own traveling to the main stem.

We could say parent
or grandmother river.

She, too, is a body we know well.
Exposed not in lines and bar scales,
but seasonal stories of late ice,
foot paths, walleye nests.

But down from us, she surges between
urbanity's survival kit:
hydro-electric plants, plastic
factories, Prairie Island
radioactivity.

Endowments
of toxic carcinogens and
congenital disorders.

It appears no matter; this slow
and sinister winding.

Still
she bifurcates,
multiplies.

Offerings are made
amidst the reinforced-steel cans
and fuel pools. We acknowledge
her persistent current

and posterity. While, our feet press
the canoe's flanks
feeling river tempo; patterns reveal
tobacco gifts
and the sweet ache of long days
that a body fragilely stores.

❧ ❧ ❧

Refinement

ELEE KRALJII GARDINER

after Oil and Sugar #2, 2007 by Kader Altia

Sweaty gloss of oil insinuates
itself into crystals—
this sinuous discord is
brittle poison. What's good for business
is not good for you.
    Seepage, reports of accommodation
bleed into column inches.
Oil is an unctuous tongue, obliterates
the angles, rounds down
numbers where it suits. The dialogue is fluid
versus structure, saturation

in the center of discourse. You soften, remember
your brother-in-law works the pipeline,
collapses on the couch at the end of his shift.
Twin towers of economics and race
dissolve in a slow-motion tsunami over the plate
of middle-American techtonics.
You eat it up, the policy—the promises
    crash and glitter in waves. You salute
like a child at a parade. Your shelf-life is mined
with hazard. Slowly, you nourish a worry
    about containment
and the proximate distance of irreversibility.

⊷⊷⊷

In This Place
MATTHEW SHENODA

From the air, you understand
topography is a child's feet
dragging through sand.

The coral heads of the Red Sea
dotting a map from Africa
to the Levant.

In between, the sea and the rise of Sinai,
the Nile, and the streets of Cairo,
the air hangs heavy with trepidation
calling for the weaver to save the sky
with cotton yarn and indigo dye.

We promise ourselves that this world will sustain us
that the spring will not dry before our children's thirst.

We run our fingers on sandstone
speak stories in rivets and impressions.

We cup our hands for water
and pray the birds will learn to drink.

The architecture of the streets we rise from
is shaped from fragility and resilience.

The peddler's kufiyah woven with understanding
wind can kill or save in this desert.

Beneath the scarves which cover these furrows
lives colored by the farmer's plow.

We wonder why the children's eyes have grown so large—
igniting this charcoal landscape.

❧❧❧

Aral

JAIME LEE JARVIS

> The children of Muynak have made a playground out of the wrecks of
> ships
> —BBC News, March 16, 2000

Was it the rush of words in that language
we understood only when we cocked our heads,
speaking on the slant, slurring our way
through the grammar of another way of life?

Was it the whirr of metal shards the ragged
children hucked at our heads
the way they delivered their greeting

hellofuckyou

obscenity blunted by effervescence but
still bearing that cutting edge?

Was it the slow groan of the abandoned barges
that sheltered them, crumbling through
geologic time, salted and sharp-jointed
like the people living among them
—their desiccated hope?

Or the whoosh of power as we hurled
words back at them in their own language,
mouths stretching and puckering to make
the sounds they sang? Our speech waxed formal
and the children

armed to their rotten teeth with the remnants
of a fishing industry—brandishing scythes torn
from rotten hulls—laughed at the village accents
we'd worked so hard to own.

Maybe it was knowing
they were doomed
to die from the inside out,
that their empty sea was brimming with
what had already killed them.

Maybe it was the shimmer in the distance,
the heat shining like water, mocking us
with what we had come to see, mocking us
with what we would never learn to see.

  ⇛⇛⇛

Paddling the Nickel Tailings near Sudbury

AARON KREUTER

after Edward Burtynsky's Manufactured Landscapes photographs

We put in at the edge of the tailings pond,
our canoe loaded with gear and food
to take us on the four-day loop trip,
our nylon tent and stainless steel pots.
The river at first is like any other river
but not, a photo with the colours twisted,
stunning, rich orange fluorescence,
tailing off into the blackened valley bed.
The slurry so thick it takes a dozen strokes
before we learn how to move in it,
but by mid-aft we're paddling well,
elbowing with the river's curves,
the blades of our paddles sizzling
as we dig through the golden slur.
We pass charred river banks,
stunted trees subsumed in industrial after-thought,
the refinery puffing away on the horizon
busy piping out the iron chaff
that ends in the tailings impoundment
we're set on exploring
(*I think: iron, ironic, nickel*).
We enter a delta and pick our way
through; later, on the only portage
of the day—from Wet Tailings Outflow 3
to Wet Tailings Outflow 7—
the ground gives like fresh bread,
endless salt-and-pepper spongy loam.
The canoe on our shoulders
we sink knee-deep in the gummy effluent.
There are no animal tracks, no
beaver dams to break through

(I think: terrestrial habitat disturbance,
I think: various tailings disposal alternatives
at a conceptual design level,
think: slurry trench cut-off wall).
We put back in at Stony Waste Basin.
The sun, coalish through the haze,
is lowering. We're an hour or so
from the main tailings pond, can
smell the tangy iron-oxide (*I think: fact, faction,*
factor. I think: Factory).
Stew, my paddling companion, coughs, says:
"I didn't think I'd miss the insects
as much as the potable water,
the blue sky, green." We
haven't used the bathroom
since parking at the quarry.
It's started raining fire, pitch.
Our faces black, our hands glowing.
We need to set up camp.
We need to find someplace
to hang the food barrel.

✤ ✤ ✤

Ghost Fishing Louisiana

MELISSA TUCKEY

> These people are in prison and there's poison loose.
> —Rev. Willie T. Snead Sr., Mossville, Louisiana

That's not an ambulance
that's the sun
going down in your rearview mirror

It gets in your clothes it gets in
the way you talk

And the thunder late at night
railroad cars full of poison
bumping into one another

Gambling boats ghost fishing
on Lake Charles

Sugar is refined here for sweet tea
flour bleached white
men selling melons the size of heads

Her house held the cancer
like fish in a locked box

❧ ❧ ❧

To Haiti from Mountain Dell Farm

LISA WUJNOVICH

> Research carried out by UTIG scientists suggests that earthquakes in
> some parts of Texas may be induced by the pumping of fluids at oil and
> gas fields.
> —Institute for Geophysics, University of Texas at Austin.

I've seen the earth's need
rise up in a wet field,
plowed too early.
Sticky rolled mud
in a farmer's hand wept—
too much, too much,
you take too much.

I've seen rain roll off
in rivulets,
through cabbage jungles,
pooled at his knees.
I've seen him know
what not to do,
his mind break like a branch,
too heavy with fruit,
before the slow seed of renewal
grew one sprout at a time.

And we've been told: we need
our forests thinned,
quarries emptied,
farms and towns
drowned in reservoirs.

And we've been told: we need
gas drilling to pay
our bills: houses,
health insurance,
credit cards,
and food.

And we've been told:
your disasters are all natural,
our injuries unconnected,
none of us related.

Finding Water on Mars

GRANT CLAUSER

By October my skinny apple tree
that never bore fruit finally
looks dead enough to give
up on, the withered fist
of one dry apple balanced
in front of an orange moon.

Beneath these birdless skies
with the ground crackling
under frost, I think of my favorite hills,
fracked and draining into mud,
trucks gray and heavy in the breathy
dawn breaking up silence and years.

Yesterday a robot dragged itself
over Mars' red hollows
and sent us messages of rivers, rain,
glaciers that carved continents

while in Florida pilot whales kill
themselves by dozens, lungs
collapsing under their own weight
because they follow their injured
brothers onto sandbars, refusing
to let a loved one die alone.

❦ ❦ ❦

It's What They Do

JUDITH SORNBERGER

Last week two of the swarm of drillers
who claw through our hills'
mottled breasts for gas
got liquored up and brawled their way
through the donut shop's plate glass.

That's what happens, neighbors nod,
when folks are far from home,
work too many hours, have too few connections.

Who knows what the pines
lining the ridge above us—
or the earth they cling to—
tell each other, hope for.

Just outside our glass the hawk survives,
as does the dove it clutches,
talons digging, digging in.
It's what they do, my husband whispers
as his palms cup my shoulders.

I swear the dove
looks me in the eye—
not with a plea—or any hope—
only with pain, with dread,
and something like forbearance.

⊷⊷⊷

Looking Out over an Abyss in Boone County

BETH WELLINGTON

for Larry Gibson

Picture our fifty
acres, just one family's piece
of Kayford Mountain.

That metal farm gate
used to mark our line, the steep
farm road wound, benign,

though old growth hardwoods,
song birds in flight, both sides a
blessed continuum

of Almost Heaven
West Virginia. Our farm gate's
now The Gates of Hell.

The smell's not brimstone
but ANFO, ammonium
nitrate and fuel oil.

———

The same Devil's brew
at Oklahoma City
Belfast, Gaza Strip:

terrorists, they call
truck bombers, but Blankenship's
"a big employer."

Such liars, he hires
so few to drive the drag lines:
maggots chewing up

our hills to rubble,
burying headwater streams
that sang us to sleep.

We keep thinking we'll
wake and the knobs will be there.
We keep thinking no

family photos
need be bolted to our walls
to withstand the blasts.

Big Coal has its way
they will blow up Blair Mountain.
Permits are pending.

———

Eighty years ago
10,000 miners rose up
ten days at Spruce Run

while federal troops
fired: civil war to keep
us company slaves.

Blow up Blair Mountain?
Feature Vicksburg, Bull Run gone
for thirty year's coal.

Mountains should abide
but Massey plays God
scattering our peaks.

How can we be the
Mountain State without mountains,
our home, a war zone?

❧ ❧ ❧

Lullaby in Fracktown

LILACE MELLIN GUIGNARD

Child, when you're sad put on your blue shoes.
You know that Mama loves you lollipops
and Daddy still has a job to lose.

So put on a party hat. We'll play the kazoos
loud and louder from the mountaintop.
Child, when you're sad put on your blue shoes

and dance the polka with pink kangaroos,
dolphin choirs singing "flip-flop, flip-flop."
Hey, Daddy still has a job to lose—

don't be afraid. Close your eyes, snooze,
because today our suns have flared and dropped.
Tomorrow when you wake, put on your blue shoes.

Eat a good breakfast. Be good in school.
Good boys go to college goody gumdrops
so someday too you'll have a job to lose.

Waste trucks clatter by as the gray bird coos.
Flames pour forth when the faucet's unstopped.
Child, when you're sad put on your blue shoes.
For now, Daddy still has a job to lose.

ఢ ఢ ఢ

Living by a Tank Farm Cradle Song
VIVIAN FAITH PRESCOTT

The fuel man's yelling again, 3:00 a.m., a January night at 10 below, *Put out your goddamn woodstove, it's sparking the sky.* You'll blow up the town like the 4th of July. Our backyard: the black sludge dump where dead cats seep in soppy mud holes. And every night so far, I sing to the marrow of our tomorrows, to my drowsy children—Don't let your tiny red chambers weep into your colorless stem-celled dreams. Spin-dizzy in the sweet threshold of this benzene lullaby—Go to sleep, little children, go to sleep.

SECTION VI

To See the Earth
↤ Eco-Disaster

Poems in this section respond to eco-disaster in its many forms, among them: drought, climate change, collapse of civilizations, die-offs and species extinction, floods, nuclear disaster, collapse of bee colonies, loss of habitat, cancer, orange alerts, nuclear bomb tests, oil spills, hurricanes, and the Eastern Garbage Patch. Poets wrestle with their own consciences, the emotional weight and shock of these disasters, and the question of how to respond. They seek to put the ineffable into words: our fear, our fascination, our grief in response to ecological change. As Ed Roberson writes in "To See the Earth before the End of the World,"

> People are grabbing at the chance to see
> The earth before the end of the world
> The world's death piece by piece each longer than we.

Disaster overwhelms us. Jason Frye writes in response to the Buffalo Creek flood and mining disaster that killed 118 people in West Virginia: "What happened to us? / What happened? It was morning and time / for breakfast."

Poets explore our disconnect, participation, and denial. In an intimate second-person accounting, Camille T. Dungy writes in "A Massive Dying Off,"

> When the fish began their dying you didn't worry.
>
> You bought new shoes.
> They looked like crocodiles:
> snappy and rich,
> brown as delta mud.

There are confessions and accountings for wrongs as well: "We dried rivers or dammed them, made / music, treaties, money, promises," Pamela Alexander writes in "Makers." The address is an accounting to future generations:

> We knew you were coming
> but we couldn't stop. We leave you photos.
> We leave you orange skies.

In the midst of crisis, poets also give voice to our search for hope. As Jennifer Atkinson articulates in "At the Chernobyl Power Plant Eco-Reserve," we live in a series of if/then moments:

> If ravens perch on the ferris wheel
> outside of town, if owls
> nest in the silos and swallows circle
>
> ...
>
> ... if then, if then, if

Or as Dorianne Laux writes in "Evening," there is beauty despite the presence of disaster, and it is beauty perhaps that keeps our hearts from closing:

> We know we are doomed,
> done for, damned, and still
> the light reaches us, falls
> on our shoulders even now.

Other poets move toward action. June Jordan's "Who Would Be Free, Themselves Must Strike the Blow" borrows its title from abolitionist Frederick Douglass, bringing this historic activist and orator into a conversation with nuclear contamination. Brenda Hillman's "A Violet in the Crucible," evokes poet Percy Bysshe Shelley's edict that "the poet is the unacknowledged legislator," making an argument for why poets must be politically engaged:

> Shelley wants you to visit Congress when he writes
> *a violet in the crucible* & when he notes
> *imagination is enlarged by a sympathy*
>
> ...
>
> When Shelley says ‹ the poet is the legislator › he means as
> the duskytail darter from Tennessee, legislates or
> the Indiana bat, *myotis sodalist*, the dwarf wedgemussel
>
> ...
>
> he means send the report with your body—

The Corrosive Season
LYNN RIGGS

We will need even these stumps of cedar,
The harsh fruit of the land
Our thirst will have to be slaked, if at all, by this thin
Water on the sand.

If we have demanded this corrosive season
Of drought, if we have bent
Backward from the plow, asking
Even less than is sent,

Surely we may be no bitterer
Than the shrunk grape
Clinging to the wasted stem
It cannot escape.

⊰⊱⊰⊱⊰⊱

Trained on the Hill

ELEANOR WILNER

The telescope is trained on the hill where they had disappeared,
was it weeks ago, or years? The fogs roll in; it's hard to see
exactly where we are, or what's out there. Even with this high

magnification, we find it hard to focus movement on the hill—
the hill that we've been watching for so long, and with such
distant but persistent hope. When they were first lost to view,

we left, came back; we thought to watch for their return.
That was before the hill began to change its shape, almost
at first without our noticing—new hollows, dark fissures

like shadows crawling on the ground, as if to eat the hill.
The mists never entirely clear; we are forever wiping
the glass of the telescope lens; it's almost like weeping

the way drops form, keep sliding down the glass, a trail
of tears that smear the view. It isn't clear if it's the rain,
or mist, or our own grief, or some slight defect in the glass

that blurs our perfect sight, or some aversion to the slow
erosion of the hill. And now we're running out of coins
to focus the pay-to-view, though we came with bags and bags

of coins, not knowing how long it all might take, but somehow
didn't count on years. It's been so long that now we doubt
our memory of the ones who disappeared, last seen

through the upper branches of the trees, those trees long gone,
the hill bare, and with the cave-ins, the erosion, the silence
on the hill, really we can't be sure of what seemed once so dear,

long lost to view; we only know our coins are running out,
the clink-clink you hear—the last pair dropping in the slots.

❧ ❧ ❧

To See the Earth before the End of the World
ED ROBERSON

People are grabbing at the chance to see
the earth before the end of the world,
the world's death piece by piece each longer than we.

Some endings of the world overlap our lived
time, skidding for generations
to the crash scene of species extinction
the five minutes it takes for the plane to fall,
the mile ago it takes to stop the train,
the small bay   to coast the liner into the ground,

the line of title to a nation   until the land dies,
the continent uninhabitable.
That very subtlety of time between

large and small
Media note   *people chasing glaciers*
in retreat up their valleys   and *the speed. . . .*

watched ice was speed made invisible,
now—   it's days, and a few feet further away,
a subtle collapse of time between large

and our small human extinction.
If I have a table
at this event, mine bears an ice sculpture.

Of whatever loss it is   it lasts as long as ice
does until it disappears   into its polar white
and melts   and the ground beneath it, into vapor,

into air.   All that once chased us and we
chased to a balance chasing back, tooth for spear,
knife for claw,

         locks us in this grip
   we just now see

            our own lives taken by
taking them out.   Hunting the bear,
we hunt the glacier with the changes come
     of that choice.

❧ ❧ ❧

Makers

PAMELA ALEXANDER

We didn't waste them. We used the trees
to build, to burn. Jungles
got in our way, and animals,
especially the bears.

Sucked oil from the ground,
and coal, and gold, drank Coke
at 90 miles an hour, flicking
cigarette butts out the window
into unimportant air.
Talked, always, wired,
wireless, words glowing
on screens continents away.
Beamed messages to stars. Billions
of billions of messages, billions of us.

We dried rivers or dammed them, made
music, treaties, money, promises.
Made more and more of our kind,
which made the cars and the wars
necessary, the droughts and hurricanes.

Grains of soil flew in flocks, water hid
in clouds. A few of us raised wolves
that others shot. It didn't matter
in the end. We had to eat. We ate
wetlands and tops of mountains.
Drank water from roots of plants,
from beaks of birds. Redstarts
sent up flares we didn't see.
All the foxes went to ground.

Some said it was written in holy books,
others said we could change. But we couldn't
reassemble glaciers, button the molecules together;
couldn't fill dry riverbeds with the silver flash
of fish. Couldn't find the bears.

We knew you were coming
but couldn't stop. We leave you photos.
We leave you orange skies.

their dying you didn't worry.

>You bought new shoes.
>>They looked like crocodiles:
snappy and rich,
>brown as delta mud.

>>Even the box they shipped in was beautiful,
>>bejeweled.

>You tore through masses of swaddling paper,
>>these shoes!

>carefully cradled
in all that cardboard by what
>>you now understand
must have been someone's tiny, indifferent hands.

———

The five-fingered sea stars you heard about on NPR.

You must have been driving to Costco.
It must have been before all the visitors arrived.

You needed covers, pillows, disposable containers.
At Costco, everything comes cheap.

Sea stars, jellies, anemones, all the scuttlers and hoverers
and clingers along the ocean floor. *A massive dying off, further displacing
depleted oxygen,* cried the radio announcer.

You plugged in your iPod.
Enough talk. You'd found the song you had been searching for.

————

One cargo ship going out. One cargo ship coming in.

Crabs crawling up trawler lines.
Giant lobsters walking
right onto the shore.

You've been sitting in your car
watching the sunset over the Golden Gate.
NPR again.

One cargo ship going out. One cargo ship coming in.

Those who can are leaving.

The Marin Headlands crouch
toward the ocean,
fog so thick on their side of the bay
you can't tell crag from cloud from sea.

One cargo ship headed out, another coming in.

They're looking for a place
where they can breath.

You've been here less than an hour.
When the sun has finished setting
you'll go home.

————

In the dream, your father is the last refuse to wash ashore.
                          This wasn't what you wanted.
                                              Any of you.
                                                        The first sign

of trouble was the bottle with the message.
    That washed up years ago.
Then, so many bottles
            the stenographers couldn't answer all the messages anymore.

                    The women of the village wept when your father died.

Then they lined up to deliver tear-stained tissue to the secretary of the
        interior
    who translated their meaning
and had it writ out on a scroll.

These were the answers your people had been waiting for!

            That papyrus wound around your father like a bandage.
        The occasion announced,
                you prayed proper prayers, loaded him onto an outrigger,
set him off,
                        but here he is again. Stinking.
        Swelling.

You can't dispose of the rising dead and you're worried.
            What can you do?

☙ ☙ ☙

Inundated

HAYES DAVIS

after watching Hurricane Katrina coverage on CNN

What tides move in him? At what watermark
did survival instinct kick in? How much water
is too high for wading? At what pitch
of a baby's cry does the father think diapers,
food, instead of *too deep, too much wind?* On film

his trudge out of the French Quarter Walgreen's
will be labeled "LOOTING," his visage, gait
indistinguishable (to the casual viewer)
from people clutching stereos, sneakers, alcohol,
any item the newsroom seems to suggest
black people grab first. But look closely:

see Huggies under his right arm, gallon of milk
gripped in his left hand. Who can know his story?
Who wouldn't grab a twelve-pack, if the bad day
that sends you to Scotch on a Tuesday
were strung together for months, for lifetimes,
if what a teenager makes working a summer job
had to feed a family, if healthcare, a house
were fleeting dreams? So look again—

he carries milk with the Huggies and he's
black and he might not have made it home but you
wouldn't, probably, have heard if he didn't so call him
father, or husband, maybe Larry, or Junior, handsome,
thoughtful, drenched, scared, but not "Looter."

༅ ༅ ༅

Buffalo Creek

JASON FRYE

The river belches out its dead, and they flood
the banks with dragging feet asking *What happened to us?*
What happened? It was morning and time
for breakfast. They gather in puddles outside your window
and listen closely for the *hmm-click* of the burner
as you cook your morning eggs. They gather in the yard
behind the church and in the Foodland parking lot. They gather
in the fog and rockdust and orange pall of tipple lights.
They gather on the banks from Kistler to Chapmanville
to Salt Rock and the Ohio and ask *What happened?*
It was morning and time for breakfast.

At the Chernobyl Power Plant Eco-Reserve

JENNIFER H. ATKINSON

If ravens perch on the ferris wheel
outside of town, if owls
nest in the silos and swallows circle
the tipped watchtower, if catfish
bloat in the cooling pool and elk
graze on perennial beard grass,
if boars rake their tusks
among the roots, if black
storks claim the cloud-blighted
pines of Red Forest, if wire
succumbs to rust, if lichen,
if shingles unhinge in the snow,
if untrafficked lots cede land
to yarrow, if mirrors, if spoons
reflect the sky, if watches tick
in unopened drawers, if swollen,
if stiff-maned Przewalsi horses
foal, if wolves, if then, if then, if

❧ ❧ ❧

Dance, Dance, While the Hive Collapses

TIFFANY HIGGINS

Oh my, oh my, I lose myself
I study atlases and cirrus paths
in search of traces of it, of you

> of that thing, of that song
> I keep pressing my ear to the current
> of air to hear . . .

>> I hear it and it disappears
>> It was all I wanted to do in this
>> life
>> to sense that phantom tap

on my nerves, to allow myself
to be hit by it, attacked, aroused
until, as if someone else, I arise

> I dance my part in paradise
> ~~~~~~~~~~~~~~~~~~~~~~~

I read that bees who've drunk
imidacloprid

> can't waggle to indicate
> to others where the best
> nectar is located

(you and I also long to map
for each other the sweetest
suck of sap)

Workers carry far less food
back to the waiting hive.

                            They wander, wobble
                            can't bring their way
                            home alive

The imidacloprid-imbibed
can't bring it back
to the colony.
                Some hives collapse
                entirely.
                        I desire to say that I, I
                        would do it differently
                            I would be the bee, bloomed
                            with pesticide

that still would shake out a wiggle
like the finger's signature
on the iPad at checkout:

    not quite you, but still identity
    more like a wave than solid you
    yet enough to signify
                    There, there, in the far off field
                    spiked acanthus, trumpets of datura

                            in the abandoned lot
                            on the corner of International and
                          High

                            the mystic assignation
                            the golden throat of light:

Gorge, gorge, take
your fill, I would cry

before I too failed
and my bumbling body lain
down to die

I'd dance my last dance
to rescue the hive
Yes, I'd carry the amber whirrers
out alive   ~~~~~~~~~~~~~~~~~~~~~~~

        Or not. Perhaps I too would succumb

to the corn syrup, chemical
piped into our supply.

        (I, too, longing to find my
        way to you,
        would go off course.)

            Alas. There is still melody,
            rhythm, someone is streaking
            out in air, droning

                around the phonograph, which is the grooved
                heart valve of the black vinyl
                divine who is winding this universe.
                ~~~~~~~~~~~~~~~~~~~~~~~

Someone is dancing us.
Will it be you?   ~~~~~~~~~~~~~~~~~~~~~~

Dance, dance, as the hive collapses
Dance, dance, while the colony disassembles
Dance the occasion
Dance the gorgeous design

~~~~~~~~~~~~~~~~~~~~~~

inside the honey
of our lit up veins

~~~~~~~~~~~~~~~~~~~~~~~

between the stripes and streams
of these swift rays

↫ ↫ ↫

Requiem

MELISSA TUCKEY

Unable to sleep,
    the blankets wrapped in waves, waves
    as tall as dreams,
the dream world trying to make sense
    of the waking—

    Strange dream of flooded rivers,
entire cities underwater. Look how the dead float,
    hair blossoming on the surface,
    and the daily hustle into streets filled with water,
    going to get bread,
going to get gasoline, and the dogs
    tied to lampposts, and the elders,
in chest high water, waiting for rescue. And always
    the water rising, and we never know
who it will take next—except that some houses
    are more sturdy than others,
and some rescues come quicker, or do not come at all.

    Remember when our beds were filled
with oil—the sea was whispering from an open door
    as that viscous dark came spilling
up and out and into every crevice of our dreams
    how many days it gushed, all over our newspapers,
    into our laundry and hair, how it covered our hands
and it wouldn't wash out? We couldn't sleep at night.
    And the President ate shrimp and said none of this,
though tragic, should interrupt our dinner.

We who crawled once to these shores, having risen
    single celled from the ocean floor,
        now standing in the midst of an invented world.
Each morning, we step into our clothes,
    light the stove for breakfast, and those of us
with privilege, we gas up and go.
    We who once had no claws, no hands,
no way of grasping what we desired.
    And the waters keep seeping back in.

Look how carefully zookeepers pack up
    those dolphins, airlifting them to safety
giving them massages to ease the stress.
    After the flooding
the houses so weak they are crumbling,
    and before the flooding also.
Elsewhere drought brings flame.
    Fires consuming the west coast
        of our country. Easy breathing only when
the wind is blowing the other direction,
    firefighters fighting to protect
        the houses as animals come screaming
from the flames. Give them water,
    foresters beg, let them recover.

Give me a dog who isn't drowning,
    a tree not in flames,
a flag that is not betrayal.
    Teach me how to help build an ark big enough
for everyone who needs rescue.

֎ ֎ ֎

Who Would Be Free, Themselves Must Strike the Blow

JUNE JORDAN

—Frederick Douglass

The cow could not stand up. The deadly river
washed the feet of children. Where the cows
grazed the ground concealed invisible
charged particles that did not glow or make
a tiny sound.

It was pretty quiet.

The cow could not stand up. The deadly clouds
bemused the lovers lying on the deadly ground
to watch the widening nuclear light
commingle with the wind their bodies set
to motion.

It was pretty quiet.

The cow could not stand up.
The milk should not be sold.
The baby would not be born right.
The mother could not do anything about the baby
or the cow.

It was pretty quiet.

✤ ✤ ✤

The Orange Alert

DOUGLAS KEARNEY

Picture the upturned millipede, dead,
    and see the streets of Altadena:
palm tree rows against the concrete, stiff
    to the horizon.
There have been no birds big enough,
    we are comforted, to pluck
the chitins from before our yards
    and vanish
into the sun like dog-fighting MiGs.
    War bears litters of similes.

Altadena, smog hugs the foothills like mustard gas
    where our rich peer through their blinds
into ravines, Santa Anas sway the mustard plants, yuccas
    bob, some man—his cigarette,
a full gas-can, an itch. We've known
    the orange alert, fires reaching for helicopters
like cartoon cats clawing at panicked birds.

Yesterday, fire engines and HAZMAT trucks
　　jostled at Alameda and El Molino
like beetles eating a four-legged spider.
　　That morning, radios warned of orange.
Neighborhood kids watched officers climb in
　　and out an open manhole,
consulting the entrails of the great dead millipede.
　　We watched the ground;
the sun hotter than all year.
　　The mountains hid Santa Anas,
the smog went orange with dusk, the growing shadows
　　of lingering birds.

A Violet in the Crucible

BRENDA HILLMAN

Shelley wants you to visit Congress when he writes
       a violet in the crucible & when he notes
              imagination is enlarged by a sympathy
    that you may intuit environments
as endangered creatures do when 7 million pounds
       of nitrogen flow into the Chesapeake—;
as you push open the cherry wood door
       & the intern looks up from her
map of wheels beside the philodendron with streaked
anemic arrows & a jar
          of pens from pharmaceutical firms,
Shelley knows you are endangered
       as the eyeless shrimp *Stygobromus hayi* living
          among rocks upstream in Virginia feeding on dying
      leaves is, or the Congressman you came to visit
         is endangered, feeding
in the Rayburn cafeteria with the lobbyist from Bechtel, having left his
aide endangered in a faux-maple carrel
    to work on the war funding bill
        where seedlings of the law have finished sprouting.
    You look at things to make them speak.
    You have threadlike legs found only in your species.
The cogs are selling credits to the dams
    for phosphorous to go into the sea.
When Shelley says ‹ the poet is the legislator › he means as
    the duskytail darter from Tennessee legislates or
the Indiana bat, *myotis sodalist*, the dwarf wedgemussel
        half buried in Maryland with your bivalve
        in silt of your wetland habitat, as you, the vanishing
northeastern bulrush from Massachusetts
    legislate by shrinking; he doesn't mean you will live,
he means you could live on listen. As the sturgeon

in a million pounds of phosphorous or

the snowy plover from Cascadia might.

The aide is living on listen too,

he takes your words, there's a little you

in his left eye which tries to focus on your nervous

speech, a stubby tassel

swinging on his shoe; he's got a friend in the Marines

who likes it over there instead of working

in the tire shop after high school. The punctuation

falling from your eyes its eyes their eyes his eyes

is merging with uh·· uh·· uh·· uh·· uh·· uh·· as he explains

the Pentagon budget uh·· uh·· uh·· uh·· his sentences forming

a five-star alkaline: *We cannot leave them*

there without weapons uh-uh-uh-uhuhuh.

He cannot see the stars camped in your heart,

the bunchy bunched-up stars, though he also

has stars in his heart & his friend the Marine has stars.

When Shelley notes ‹ the poet is meant to cheer › he means

your name is on the list right here, he means

if you don't survive this way there are others,

he means send the report with your body—

᭜᭜᭜

Did It Ever Occur to You That Maybe You're Falling in Love?

AILISH HOPPER

We buried the problem.

We planted a tree over the problem.

We regretted our actions toward the problem.

We declined to comment on the problem.

We carved a memorial to the problem, dedicated it. Forgot our handkerchief.

We removed all "unnatural" ingredients, handcrafted a locally-grown
    tincture for the problem. But nobody bought it.

We freshly-laundered, bleached, deodorized the problem.

We built a wall around the problem, tagged it with pictures of children, birds
    in trees.

We renamed the problem, and denounced those who used the old name.

We wrote a law for the problem, but it died in committee.

We drove the problem out with loud noises from homemade instruments.

We marched, leafleted, sang hymns, linked arms with the problem, got
    dragged to jail, got spat on by the problem and let out.

We elected an official who Finally Gets the problem.

We raised an army to corral and question the problem. They went door to
    door but could never ID.

We made www.problem.com so You Can Find Out About the problem, and
    www.problem.org so You Can Help.

We created 1-800-Problem, so you could Report On the problem, and
    1-900-Problem so you could Be the Only Daddy That Really Turns That
    problem On.

We drove the wheels offa that problem.

We rocked the shit out of that problem.

We amplified the problem, turned it on up, and blew it out.

We drank to forget the problem.

We inhaled the problem, exhaled the problem, crushed its ember under our
    shoe.

We put a title on the problem, took out all the articles, conjunctions, and
    verbs. Called it "Exprmntl Prblm."

We shot the problem, and put it out of its misery.

We swallowed daily pills for the problem, followed a problem fast, drank
    problem tea.
We read daily problem horoscopes. Had our problem palms read by a seer.
We prayed.
Burned problem incense.
Formed a problem task force. Got a problem degree. Got on the problem
    tenure track. Got a problem retirement plan.
We gutted and renovated the problem. We joined the Neighborhood
    Problem Development Corp.
We listened and communicated with the problem, only to find out that it had
    gone for the day.
We mutually empowered the problem.
We kissed and stroked the problem, we fucked the problem all night. Woke
    up to an empty bed.
We watched carefully for the problem, but our flashlight died.
We had dreams of the problem. In which we could no longer recognize
    ourselves.
We reformed. We transformed. Turned over a new leaf. Turned a corner,
    found ourselves near a scent that somehow reminded us of the problem,
In ways we could never
Put into words. That
Little I-can't-explain-it
That makes it hard to think. That
Rings like a siren inside.

Trying to Talk with a Man
ADRIENNE RICH

Out in this desert we are testing bombs,

that's why we came here.

Sometimes I feel an underground river
forcing its way between deformed cliffs
an acute angle of understanding
moving itself like a locus of the sun
into this condemned scenery.

What we've had to give up to get here—
whole LP collections, films we starred in
playing in the neighborhoods, bakery windows
full of dry, chocolate-filled Jewish cookies,
the language of love-letters, of suicide notes,
afternoons on the riverbank
pretending to be children

Coming out to this desert
we meant to change the face of
driving among dull green succulents
walking at noon in the ghost town
surrounded by a silence

that sounds like the silence of the place
except that it came with us
and is familiar
and everything we were saying until now
was an effort to blot it out—
Coming out here we are up against it

...t here I feel more helpless
with you than without you
You mention the danger
and list the equipment
we talk of people caring for each other
in emergencies—laceration, thirst—
but you look at me like an emergency

Your dry heat feels like power
your eyes are stars of a different magnitude
they reflect lights that spell out: EXIT
when you get up and pace the floor

talking of the danger
as if it were not ourselves
as if we were testing anything else.

✤ ✤ ✤

As If Hearing Heavy Furniture Moved on the Floor above Us

JANE HIRSHFIELD

As things grow rarer, they enter the ranges of counting.
Remain this many Siberian tigers,
that many African elephants. Three hundred red egrets.
We scrape from the world its tilt and meander of wonder
as if eating the last burned onions and carrots from a cast iron pan.
Closing eyes to taste better the char of ordinary sweetness.

Transients

VIVIAN FAITH PRESCOTT

At the window in the bar overlooking the bay, stretch your neck back to
Bligh Reef where you worked spring of '89. See killer whales: sleek black
canoes, cruising through water. A dozen or more rounded the point and
last in line, a towering dorsal fin like a huge sail on a boat. Now, walk along
petroglyph beach, see only shadows. In grooved rock, trace a killer whale fin
with your finger. Remember, his fin collapsing, lesions on his skin. Pack for
the next job: your hazmat certificate, your rubber boots. Carry his story to
the Gulf.

Malebolge: Prince William Sound

SAM HAMILL

"This world knows them as a blind people,
greedy, invidious, and arrogant;
cleanse yourself of their foul ways."

—Ser Brunetto Latini to Dante,
in the bowels of Hell's seventh circle,
and he named them:
gent' è avara, invidiosa e superba.

And Brunetto said, "Know that I keep company
with clerics and with the literati
and with those who know grand fame,
and for each, the sin against earth is the same."

And going deeper, Virgil used Dante's belt
to summon Geryon from the depths,
to carry them on his back to the edge of Malebolge
where flatterers are immersed in excrement.

Teals. Terns. Eagle and raven. Sea otter, clam, and salmon.
The world's tallest mountains
are all under water. Porcupine, beaver, muskrat.
Brown bear and black bear and tiny brown bat.

The people of the soil—call us *human* anyway—
linger at the shore. We are only humus.
Bear and otter no longer out-swim us.
Loon, hawk, and wild goose no longer fly away.

Opening the heart's own book,
look! there's Dante in a man-made Hell,
entering Malebolge on the back of the beast he dreamed,
there are rivers of blood and misery;

there's old blind Homer
listening as tales of Odysseus wind and unfold;
there are tales of Tlingit and Haida and Kwakiutl;
the dance of Krishna, eighth avatar of Vishnu.

But nothing prepares the blood to assume
this speechlessness, profound silence of complete grief,
this vision of hell we can't escape
unfolding before our eyes.

Strangling on our own greedy, greasy lies,
the thick black blood of the ancient world
covers and clogs our lives.
What can be washed away is washed away

like history, tar-balls riding out the tides.
We turn back to our own anthropomorphic needs,
our creature comforts, our poems and our famous lies,
closing the book on Homer, Dante, and Brunetti,

closing the book of the heart
on the face of god, and on her counterpart:
rock, fish, bird, plant, and beast:
on you, on me, and on the Geryon we ride: Exxon Valdez.

The Weather

HAYAN CHARARA

In ancient times a plague of locusts showed up to ruin the crops
and this became holy.

A sea surge not long ago made the trees bow down
and people were reminded of their shame.

A child dreams a cow drops dead on a dusty plain
and a farmer weeps for his children.

The weather on that day was a body floating in a street.
The coming storm was a flock of birds cleaning their feathers.

And a kingfisher hung by its beak always turns to face the wind.

❧ ❧ ❧

Typhoon Poem

PATRICK ROSAL

The teacher can't hear the children
over all this monsoon racket,
all the zillion spoons whacking
the rusty roofs, all the wicked tin streams
flipping full-grown bucks off their hooves.
Everywhere there used to be a river,
there's a bigger river now. Every hard face
on the block is sopping. Even the court
where girls from St. Ignominius ran
the roughneck boys off to play
their own three-on-three in plaid skirts
and church shoes for cash? —forget it.
The whole city's a flash flood
with brawn enough to flush trucks
sideways down the capitol's widest drives:
the crushed tonnage bobs around a bit
at the foot of some Spanish bastard's statue,
before it stalls and pools on white church steps.
Brute pilgrims. Face it, paddling dogs won't
make it, so children got no shot. But quick
thinking, the teacher lashes her students,
two at a time, with wire and stray twine.
She binds them across their breasts
to trees and metal posts lining the street's
half flooded walk. *No goddamned way,*
she swears. She won't let one little one
be washed out, even if their wriggling
makes their armpits bleed, even if
the kids must watch a good wood chair
catch in an eddy, then swirl off.
They'll have to make do with the vision
of their uncles' and neighbors' blue

bodies bumping past before they fishtail
out of sight. You can't wish away
the deluge. You can't vanish
the bloated carnage-waters. But the tykes
in crew cuts and pigtails, still fastened
to shafts and trunks in ragged rows,
will survive. For now, their teacher
has made them safe by building an orchard
of them in the middle of a city road,
this small chorus of young hard fruit,
this little grove moaning.

Water

DAN WILCOX

(August, 2005)

She launched me out on the lake in her canoe
my first time alone—left, right
I dip the paddles—the peace
of the depths, the distant cattails
the more distant mountains rippled
upside down in the lake, and

                                          no

screams, no cries for help, no
bodies bloated in sodden tee shirts
no floating tires, or doors, no cases of food

the mud is quiet on the lake bottom

not swirling in a stew of stink & shit

the lake is quiet, except for crickets
& the fish who break the surface

no thunder of collapsing walls, falling levees

the water clear except where my paddles
stir the weeds, the minnows, the reflections

not thick & opaque with earth & debris

this lake is in the mountains,

                                          far away

from the flood planes of the Gulf
far from the poisoned Mississippi

this water neatly outlined in trees
not limitless nightmare trees reaching
breathless to shelter children & cats

this water carries me gently back to a gravel beach
where she waits for her boat to return

not weep not more water for the empty bed
ten feet under & lost to mud

the boat tied to the roof of the car
then home, a home safe & dry
& far away from water.

֎ ֎ ֎

atlantis made easy

EVIE SHOCKLEY

orange was the color of her address, then blue silt : : whiskey burned brown
down the street, then a dangerous drink whirled around a paper umbrella
: : intoxication blue across the porch then rose in the attic : : bloated tuesday
taught us, she's never been dry and never will be : : brass, bass, ivory, skins
: : i hate to see that ninth ward wall go down : : army corpse engineers ran
a 'train on her : : aw chere : : sweet ghost, saturated, deserted : : teething
ground for the expected spectre, we knew it'd show up better late (against a
black backdrop), whenever : : wait in the water, wait in the water, children : :
stub your soul on a granite memory, a marble key change, an indigo mood : :
trouble (the water)

Deepwater

SAEED JONES

April 20, 2010—10:00 pm

When the only light is flame, I run to the end
   of myself. Metal bridge mangled, other men
jump into the ocean's open
throat, choked water somewhere
   under smoking blackness. Pray the waves
aren't stone-faced when I meet them.
Is this the night we were promised, the fire
this time?
   My skin already razed by a midnight sun,
everything I touch is hotter than a gun's barrel.
The air reeks of singed metal
or worse.
   Free-falling into the dark
against darkness, the water grabs me
and doesn't recognize itself.

⋈ ⋈ ⋈

Foreground, Fukushima

JODY BOLZ

A girl walks the seawall
as if it were a path
and the ocean its prospect,

a vastness spread
beneath another vastness,
but not without detail:

pine-crowned islets,
the lacework of whitecaps,
low late-winter clouds.

Like a figure in a woodblock
she lends scale to the scene,
a human being

at the edge of an island
and beyond her—still—
the dark, familiar sea.

Diary of Sila the Sky God

HILA RATZABI

February 5, 2014

Chance of snow storm in northeastern United States: definite
Favorite winter storm names so far this year: Ion, Pax, Wiley
Least favorite: Atlas, Hercules, Titan
Chance of my name being used: still hopeful
Ironic weather moment of the day: ship washed ashore in the Philippines
from Typhoon Haiyan embellished with the words: SAFETY FIRST
CO_2 levels worldwide: 397.80 ppm
Number of chemical weapons worldwide: hard to tell
Earth's heart rate: 267 beats per minute
Current emotions: where to put this cyclone

⊕ ⊕ ⊕

After ⅔ of a Village in Papua New Guinea Is Decimated by Natural Disaster

PURVI SHAH

July 18, 1998

The tsunami insisted we rise, all-encompassing
like a telephone buzzing in the heart of the night.
The earth shook and we collided with its fist,

thirty feet of force splintering the seams
of our bodies. Some of us are saved,
but the sea retains a partial bounty—an arm
grazed by coral, a sacrificial leg swollen

with infection. The seas recycle life:
bacteria swim through veins and arteries,
and people confuse malaria for the jungle's
heat. Others sustain a trust in the ecosystem

but feel dizzy, distended with beached
crabs and fish. 500 bodies form a school
in the lagoon, replacing the official
structure of learning, closed
due to an elimination of membership.

The children were the first to succumb, snatched
by the waves from under their mother's arms.

Thirteen hours later, when news would reach
Port Moresby, telephone lines would sing
across the globe, opening the smaller gates
of medicine and foreign money. Death

leaves its stench, marking the territory
of brown vegetation and rancid corpses
like a cat in heat. The news agencies
and government concoct a name for the Sissano
Lagoon: one long graveyard. I sojourn

to the island's lining of new sand, see familiar
bodies in the form of a bridge, almost a web
of humans settling into a new niche. I cross
to meet my relatives. The winds whisper:
your generation is destined to evaporate
like dew, without residue, or the scent
of fresh oxygen against the grass.

Evening

DORIANNE LAUX

Moonlight pours down
without mercy, no matter
how many have perished
beneath the trees.

The river rolls on.

There will always be
silence, no matter
how long someone
has wept against
the side of a house,
bare forearms pressed
to the shingles.

Everything ends.
Even pain, even sorrow.

The swans drift on.

Reeds bear the weight
of their feathery heads.
Pebbles grow smaller,
smoother beneath night's
rough currents. We walk

long distances, carting
our bags, our packages.
Burdens or gifts.

We know the land
is disappearing beneath
the sea, islands swallowed
like prehistoric fish.

We know we are doomed,
done for, damned, and still
the light reaches us, falls
on our shoulders even now,

even here where the moon is
hidden from us, even though
the stars are so far away.

   ❦ ❦ ❦

To Keep Faith

KARENNE WOOD

It's an idea like light, the star's trajectory
over sacred places that rise from their landscapes:
dark mesa, dark desert tower, dark river swelling
across the shadowed fields of the republic.

This is your passion: to save the earth's cathedrals.
The machinery of our country's interests works
against it. In another city, you might have disappeared,
blindfolded at sunrise with hands behind your back.

In another time, not long ago, I might have
found you face up in a field of silence among the still-
beautiful bodies of Dakota men. To speak
for the earth: I say history is against us here,

as though you hadn't already recalled who I was
before I learned to be wary of stories, or as though
your words hadn't entered me like light, small
wavecaps riding on all that darkness.

For you, then, some words about light. Relentless
light. Incantatory words we could lick
like blue flames. Words to keep faith with each other
and earth, that searing love, which still claims us.

⊷ ⊷ ⊷

A Great Civilization
DANE CERVINE

In the island forests of Bolivia before
any white man found them, the Arawak
cultivated lianas thick as a human arm,
blade-like leaves dangling six feet long
and smooth-boled Brazil nut trees,
the thick-bodied flowers smelling like warm meat.
Earth mounds rose above waters cultivated as canals
for travel between spacious villages framed
by moats and palisades, along which they'd walk
in long cotton tunics, heavy ornaments dangling
from wrists and necks. But in 1927,

anthropologists found their decsendents living
in constant hunger, no clothes,
no cows or llamas,
no musical instruments,
no art—except necklaces of animal teeth—
unable to count beyond three, no religion,
no conception of the universe. They

thought they'd stumbled upon a primitive
humankind living in the rawness of nature
for millennia—unaware that when the first
Europeans arrived centuries before, influenza
and smallpox raced ahead, bringing
the Arawak to their knees. And no one

knew, till now: scientists piecing together
records of teeth, shards of pottery,
eco-analysis and *voila!*
a great mysterious culture heretofore
unknown emerged from the mists
of history. Might we too—

this culture of moon travel,
the great web of internet,
an entire library of world music
in the palm of a hand—one day

be discovered again, as
barefoot entrepreneurs
having lost it all.

SECTION VII

Taking Root

↝ Resistance, Resilience, and Resurgence

Poets in this section celebrate individual and collective acts of resistance, grounding, and renewal. They give voice to belief systems that honor an ecological and socially just way of thinking, from diverse spiritual, religious, non-religious, and cultural traditions.

The living world speaks through these poems. Beginning with Joy Harjo's "Eagle Poem," we are reminded of our connection always to that place beyond us, like the "eagle that Sunday morning / Over Salt River." She writes,

> We see you, see ourselves and know
> That we must take the utmost care
> And kindness in all things.

Time and space are traversed. From Myra Sklarew's "Ode to Stromatolites" we learn a "story you traveled across eons to tell" of how these great cabbage heads "funneled oxygen to our earth and set us to breathing." The canyon provides a portal in Simon J. Ortiz's poem "Culture and the Universe" for accessing our connection to something larger than ourselves:

> We are measured
> by vastness beyond ourselves.
> Dark is light.
> Stone is rising.

Poets celebrate a sense of belonging and cultural connectedness to the natural world. In Patrick Rosal's "Photo of My Grandmother Running toward Us on a Beach in Illokos," we're offered such a vision: the woman running toward her grandchildren "trying to balance / an entire sea on her head," arms "flung wide open," laughing "as if she were asking us / to bring our burdens too."

Even in death, one generation connects to the next through soil and sea, fertilizer and fruit. In "Burial," Ross Gay writes of planting fruit trees with the ashes of his father, "now a naturalized citizen / waving the flag / from his subterranean lair."

A similar sense of ecological connectedness and belonging, this time to the sea, is claimed in Christian Campbell's "To Hold a Meditation," when the speaker of the poem, in diving for shells and coral, "serene as a turtle," finds

> . . . tombed
> in amber and seaweed. It is
> my grandfather, brought back now by a dayclean
> tide (having set his body to sea since time).

Poems throughout seek sources of healing and recovery. In Elee Kraljii Gardiner's poem "Aubade," the speaker's cancer treatment is simultaneous/analoguous to the seasons passing fall to winter to spring in her garden, offering the imagination to heal.

In "Taking Root" by Tara Betts, the healing is collective; what heals the land heals the people. The poem honors the vision of Kenyan activist and Nobel Peace Prize laureate Wangari Maathai, who led women through the collective act of planting trees to heal the rivers, forests, and soils as a means to ease poverty and protect the land. Betts writes, "she knew that losing the trees was more than trees."

Poets celebrate loose seeds and signs of resurgence. In the "casitas near the gray cannery, / nestled amid wild abrazos of climbing roses" in "Freeway 280," Lorna Dee Cervantes describes the resilience of a neighborhood razed for highway expansion:

> . . . new grasses sprout,
> wild mustard remembers, old gardens
> come back stronger than they were.

The resilience and wild rebellion of the natural world in this poem and others serve as a source of resolve for what is buried within the speaker of the poem:

> Maybe it's here
> en los campos extraños de esta ciudad
> where I'll find it, that part of me
> mown under
> like a corpse.

The natural world inspires resistance and vision, as in Chen Chen's "Set the Garden on Fire," a poem that looks at the ways in which neighbors use plantings to block their view of immigrants next door. "Let's build the community garden / that never was," Chen Chen writes,

Let's call the neighbors
out, call for an orchard, not a wall.

. . .

Come friend, neighbor,
you, come set the garden on fire
with all our hard-earned years, tender labor
of being here, ceaseless & volcanic
making of being here, together.

The section ends with song, Allison Adelle Hedge Coke's "America, I Sing You Back," a poem that echoes Walt Whitman and Langston Hughes, reminding us of the first mothers and sisters on this continent, a people who have not disappeared, songs that are still being song. "Sing again I will," Hedge Coke writes "as I have always done."

Eagle Poem

JOY HARJO

To pray you open your whole self
To sky, to earth, to sun, to moon
To one whole voice that is you.
And know there is more
That you can't see, can't hear,
Can't know except in moments
Steadily growing, and in languages
That aren't always sound but other
Circles of motion.
Like eagle that Sunday morning
Over Salt River. Circled in blue sky
In wind, swept our hearts clean
With sacred wings.
We see you, see ourselves and know
That we must take the utmost care
And kindness in all things.
Breathe in, knowing we are made of
All this, and breathe, knowing
We are truly blessed because we
Were born, and die soon within a
True circle of motion,
Like eagle rounding out the morning
Inside us.
We pray that it will be done
In beauty.
In beauty.

⊕ ⊕ ⊕

Abstract

AMY YOUNG

disharmony with the nature of things

Add up:
a small Antarctic penguin
a large African gazelle
the adder's flower
(the greater stichwort)
the unregenerate nature
of man.

Ad fin.

Ambassador   alveolonasal - ambivalency

Do not fear the dusty moth,
the bulbous toad,
the amber-shelled snail
lacking ambition.
Be eager in your amazement;
gregarious in your wonder.
Be an ambassador for small things,
always.

Anagoge   amusia – anapest

an uplifting of the mind to spiritual things;
literary interpretation that seeks to extract
from language a spiritual significance

The moon, in its ascension,
      calls to the shad in the sea
            to climb rivers,

a song unheard,
      reminiscent
            of the moon's own orbit.

Ancestral Home   anapestic - andrias

In through the ancient light,
fresh from dark purple fruits,

the burrowing bee
short-tongued and solitary

anchors itself
in the earth.

Anonymuncule   annoying - anseriform

an insignificant
anonymous writer

Born without sight,
the blind poet rubs
ointment on the condemned
man's neck.

Anonymous
as the cave-dwelling beetle,
the poet condemns
the hangman.

Apolytikion   apical cell - aporrhoea

concluding hymn

In his last hymn,
the beekeeper sings
of swifts and hummingbirds,
like one who has given up
on his own religion.

Asana   artist lithography - ashen

Stand under the sun,
still and tall,
in the manner of a reed.

Cast no shadow.

Show no smile,
      no tears.

Breathe in. Rise
with your breath.
Grow lighter.
Exhale milkweed seeds.

The long-bodied porcupine shows
no belief or disbelief in the existence
of a god.
Her tranquility (or his) depends
on a forest of pine bark, an athenaeum
of light and shadow.

Ode to Stromatolites
MYRA SKLAREW

Great cabbage heads, fossil portal to our earliest traces,
you bloom in rare fields, docile as mushrooms. You carry
secrets displaced from three billion years ago.

Once, when I lived among artists in North Country, I stumbled
on your fossil field and remembered a story I'd been told:
the way you funneled oxygen to our earth and set us to breathing.

The local gravel company thought it wise to excavate
your ancient home and grind up all your secrets
in a frugal bed of stone; let giant semitrailers and speeding cars

crush the story you traveled across eons to tell, embedded
in our mitochondria. But in Australia you line a shallow sea,
stubbornly gathering your clan. A strange sight—

like some ancient outgrowth—while we cling
to our killing ways, eagerly grasping our share of air. Lace
butterflies, we're transparent in your field of time.

⊕ ⊕ ⊕

the weight of all things
RANDALL HORTON

once there were particles. atoms clung
together & molecules.

there were noises from the bang

another universe begun. life
& the body formed contours

obtuse the head splendid. o human.
o being. stand up—

heaven often fails galaxies
lifted from a sinner's pocket

come now & reconsider. come now,

the body writhe—
upstream

creational myths begin in err—

inside the receptacle a door
opening to another door

biology. & bees alongside birds
procreate

to earth's rotation we build.

&-&-&

Culture and the Universe

SIMON J. ORTIZ

Two nights ago
in the canyon darkness,
only the half-moon and stars,
only mere men.
Prayer, faith, love,
existence.
        We are measured
by vastness beyond ourselves.
Dark is light.
Stone is rising.

I don't know
if humankind understands
culture: the act
of being human
is not easy knowledge.

With painted wooden sticks
and feathers, we journey
into the canyon toward stone,
a massive presence
in midwinter.

We stop.
        Lean into me.
        The universe
sings in quiet meditation.

We are wordless:
        I am in you.

Without knowing why
culture needs our knowledge,
we are one self in the canyon.

     And the stone wall

I lean upon spins me
wordless and silent
to the reach of stars
and to the heavens within.

It's not humankind after all
nor is it culture
that limits us.
It is the vastness
we do not enter.
It is the stars
we do not let own us.

After a New Moon

ARTHUR SZE

Each evening you gaze in the southwest sky
as a crescent extends in argentine light.
When the moon was new, your mind was
desireless, but now both wax to the world.
While your neighbor's field is cleared,
your corner plot is strewn with desiccated
sunflower stalks. You scrutinize the bare
apricot limbs that have never set fruit,
the wisteria that has never blossomed;
and wince, hearing how, at New Year's,
teens bashed in a door and clubbed strangers.
Near a pond, someone kicks a dog out
of a pickup. Each second, a river edged
with ice shifts course. Last summer's
exposed tractor tire is nearly buried
under silt. An owl lifts from a poplar,
while the moon, no, the human mind
moves from brightest bright to darkest dark.

❧❧❧

Graze a Dark Field

SHEREE RENÉE THOMAS

At this hour, who could discern where land ends
or water, where creek becomes bay, bay becomes
river, bending into a brown stretch of Tennessee
river so black it's blue

Through the August haze, the first light is a brushstroke
of gray seeping in. Ducks totter up the cobblestone bank,
their short bowlegs stumbling, rum drunk roustabout men.
Over the water, skeetas and witchdoctors loom
improbable creatures who graze a dark field

From Confederate Park around the bend, two fishermen
set out, thigh-high boots creased at the knees, a dog
panting at their heels. In the distance, a diesel chugs,
mockingbirds swoop, flash a bit of green. Spiders cast themselves
down from the wet limbs of pecan trees, leaning toward the river

What matters now? At the end, we become what
we have loved, each thing that transfixed us
its grace of its own making. We grow around the land
as it grows around us, bend around the rivers as dawn
crosses, whether asleep in nests, churning water,
or in the ground becoming life

⊷ ⊷ ⊷

No Turning Back for the Soul

JACQUELINE MARCUS

When the sun slowly slips down the hills of November,
crowning the shoulders of Bishop's Peak with its luminous jewels,
when the horses return to the open pasture, patches of grass,
where crows scatter among the fallen leaves,
I'll accept the illusory news for now that all is well with the world,
and bless the birds at the dog's blue bowl drifting inside the stormlight.
And maybe it *is* enough, after all, to believe that the burning leaf
is a *dazzling moment of the eternal*, as Blake would say,
seizing the rapturous syllables from some other timeless sphere.
Either way, I'm willing to cheer for the possible
when the hellish perils of the day vanish beneath this sky,
days when you feel the blast of rain with a mighty vengeance,
a wake up call to the soul flashing a fit of lightning—
when pain is dark, dark as a recollection,
when all you want to do is pray and forget and forgive and be
grateful, *strangely alive*, after so many years of sleep.

❧ ❧ ❧

What the Water Knows

SAM HAMILL

What the mouth sings, the soul must learn to forgive.
A rat's as moral as a monk in the eyes of the real world.
Still, the heart is a river
pouring from itself, a river that cannot be crossed.

It opens on a bay
and turns back upon itself as the tide comes in,
it carries the cry of the loon and the salts
of the unutterably human.

A distant eagle enters the mouth of a river
salmon no longer run and his wide wings glide
upstream until he disappears
into the nothing from which he came. Only the thought remains.

Lacking the eagle's cunning or the wisdom of the sparrow,
where shall I turn, drowning in sorrow?
Who will know what the trees know, the spidery patience
of young maple or what the willows confess?

Let me be water. The heart pours out in waves.
Listen to what the water says.
Wind, be a friend.
There's nothing I couldn't forgive.

❧ ❧ ❧

Moon Gathering

ELEANOR WILNER

And they will gather by the well,
its dark water a mirror to catch whatever
stars slide by in the slow precession of
the skies, the tilting dome of time,
over all, a light mist like a scrim,
and here and there some clouds
that will open at the last and let
the moon shine through; it will be
at the wheel's turning, when
three zeros stand like paw-prints
in the snow; it will be a crescent
moon, and it will shine up from
the dark water like a silver hook
without a fish—until, as we lean closer,
swimming up from the well, something
dark but glowing, animate, like live coals—
it is our own eyes staring up at us,
as the moon sets its hook;
and they, whose dim shapes are no more
than what we will become, take up
their long-handled dippers
of brass, and one by one, they catch
the moon in the cup-shaped bowls,
and they raise its floating light
to their lips, and with it, they drink back
our eyes, burning with desire to see
into the gullet of night: each one
dips and drinks, and dips, and drinks,
until there is only dark water,
until there is only the dark.

⊕ ⊕ ⊕

Photo of My Grandmother Running toward Us on a Beach in Ilokos
PATRICK ROSAL

Consider how happy she is
carrying the whole load of an ocean

on her head the way some women carry
water or fruits or fish My Lola

and the whole goddamned ocean
Tides Whalebone Reef And my dark

dark cousins stomping through the breakers
She is closing her eyes running

toward her American grandchildren
who wait for her on the shore

She is sopping wet trying to balance
an entire sea on her head Her arms are

flung wide open And she laughs
as if she were asking us

to bring our burdens too

࿓ ࿓ ࿓

Taking Root

TARA BETTS

for Wangari Maathai (1940–2011)

In the valleys and forests of Kenya, she stood,
stalwart as a tree. She knew what trees could
give. She remembered the land with fig trees
untouched. She recalled the beads of frogs' eggs
glistening on the banks of rivers, water clear
and bubbling, before the crops of tea cut down
broad trunks like mere stubble on a man's face.

Do not assume the rudimentary rise of branches
only mirrors the roots adumbrating into routes
underground. The unthinking forget the concert
between soil held in place, shade that protects
the living who remember the dead, water gurgling
to the air that bubbles and lifts leaves and blades
of grass. The trees boom a chorus of quiet drums.

When her people saw the rivers dwindle to trickle,
and topsoil was swept away, and even the tea failed
to thrive, the dazed wonder of malnutrition pointed
its gaze at adopting crops like customs that never
matched the sustenance that grew as it should
before strangers insisted this is the way. We need
not see every layer to know what we might see.

She knew that losing the trees was more than trees
in parks and public forests, those lungs breathing
in Kenya and the Congo, so when bulldozers came
and pangas were brandished, she planted seedlings,
and taught women to plant trees like the crops
they already knew. They stopped demolitions,
and men more interested in pockets than breath.

When the planting of trees and protesting occurs,
a common movement occurs, the act of taking root.

Burial

ROSS GAY

You're right, you're right,
the fertilizer's good—
it wasn't a gang of dullards
came up with chucking
a fish in the planting hole
or some mid-wife got lucky
with the placenta—
oh, I'll plant a tree here!—
and a sudden flush of quince
and jam enough for months—yes,
the magic dust our bodies become
casts spells on the roots
about which someone not me
could tell you the chemical processes,
but it's just magic to me,
which is why a couple springs ago
when first putting in my two bare root plum trees
out back I took the jar which has become
my father's house,
and lonely for him and hoping to coax him back
for my mother as much as me,
poured some of him in the planting holes
and he dove in glad for the robust air,
saddling a slight gust
into my nose and mouth,
chuckling as I coughed,
but mostly he disappeared
into the minor yawns in the earth
into which I placed the trees,
splaying wide their roots,
casting the grey dust of my old man
evenly throughout the hole,

replacing then the clods
of dense Indiana soil until the roots
and my father were buried,
watering it in all with one hand
while holding the tree
with the other straight as the flag
to the nation of simple joy
of which my father is now a naturalized citizen,
waving the flag
from his subterranean lair,
the roots curled around him
like shawls or jungle gyms, like
hookahs or the arms of ancestors,
before breast-stroking into the xylem,
riding the elevator up
through the cambium and into the leaves where,
when you put your ear close enough,
you can hear him whisper
good morning, where, if you close your eyes
and push your face you can feel
his stubbly jowls and good lord
this year he was giddy at the first
real fruit set and nestled into the 30 or 40 plums
in the two trees, peering out from the sweet meat
with his hands pressed against the purple skin
like cathedral glass,
and imagine his joy as the sun
wizarded forth those abundant sugars
and I plodded barefoot
and prayerful at the first ripe plum's swell and blush,
almost weepy conjuring
some surely ponderous verse
to convey this bottomless grace,
you know, *oh father oh father* kind of stuff,
hundreds of hot air balloons
filling the sky in my chest, replacing his intubated body

listing like a boat keel side up, replacing
the steady stream of water from the one eye
which his brother wiped before removing the tube,
keeping his hand on the forehead
until the last wind in his body wandered off,
while my brother wailed like an animal,
and my mother said, weeping,
it's ok, it's ok, you can go honey,
at all of which my father
guffawed by kicking from the first bite
buckets of juice down my chin,
staining one of my two button-down shirts,
the salmon colored silk one, hollering
there's more of that!
almost dancing now in the plum,
in the tree, the way he did as a person,
bent over and biting his lip
and chucking the one hip out
then the other with his elbows cocked
and fists loosely made
and eyes closed and mouth made trumpet
when he knew he could make you happy
just by being a little silly
and sweet.

To Hold a Meditation

CHRISTIAN CAMPBELL

And then I dive, serene as a turtle,
goggles strapped tight; I am the bronze-haired
men at Arawak Cay who dive for conch
all day. I am looking for shells
and pebbles, bits of coral, to turn over

and over in my hands, but half-hidden
by the blue-brown reef is a body tombed
in amber and seaweed. It is
my grandfather, brought back now by dayclean
tide (having set his body to sea since time).

Laid out on the shore, he is a shell of the sea's
patience. Still in his blind-white
catechist's gown, now all laced with seaweed,
coral has cocooned his legs, caked
his graying hair. Eyes closed with two stones.

All on shore rejoice my find—the brethren,
the braiders, the cigar sellers, the lovers.
We smoke spliffs from pages of the Bible:
first Peter, then Matthew, then all of Psalms.
We crouch under casuarinas (praise

these trees older than anything
we know). We hold a meditation.

⊕ ⊕ ⊕

...bergs, snowflakes,
...ws, sand grains, dust motes, atoms.

Mason w... se tools are glaciers, rain, rivers, ocean.

Chemist who made blood
of seawater, bone of minerals in stone, milk

of love. Whatever

You are, I know this,
Spinner, You are everywhere, in All The Ever-
Changing Above, whirling around us.

Yes, in the loose strands,
in the rough weave of the common

cloth threaded with our DNA on the hubbed, spoked
Spinning Wheel that is this world, solar system, galaxy,

universe.

Help us to see ourselves in all creation,
and all creation in ourselves, ourselves in one another.

Remind those of us who like connections
made with similes, metaphors, symbols
all of us are, everything is
already connected.

Remind us as the oceans go, so go we. As the air goes, so go we.
As other life forms on Earth go, so go we.

As our planet goes, so go we. Great Poet,
who inspired *In The Beginning was The Word . . .* ,

edit our thoughts so our ethics are our politics,
and our actions the afterlives of our words.

Aubade
ELEE KRALJII GARDINER
for angela rawlings

My colour rises
  and the garden exhales

~ *petit mort* ~

Tonight the bloodroot petals shock, drop.

  Purple Winecup tightens
  against chill malignancy closing shut,
  shut.

Inside the calyx of the breast, blight takes hold:

     cell
    atypical | division: : ;

I put the garden to sleep.
Prune back fear.
Slice stem from stalk, repeat
until a skeleton emerges.

Protocol is three weeks on, two weeks off.

Waiting in the outpatient lounge I question
how much of me is frost-hardy. I am

     trained to

a stake.

Slow

drip

of

pesticide.

                    The nurse wears gloves.

I become the rose bloom of blood in needle.
Become plum colour swelling at joints.
Preyed upon by butterfly clamps, I flutter,
brush at mustard stamen stains under my eyes.

Bruised by scent of Naugahyde and disinfectant
I am isolated, one stalk in sterile vase.
Wrapped in plastic.

        First frost. Birdcall absent. Thrush veins the late hours.
        This night has lasted months.

The inside of my forearm is written with winter ivy.

Doctors lattice me to a painful agenda of guesswork.
Opportunistic parasites take hold; statistics plant me
at the gravesite, a *Lisianthius nigrescens*.

Dormant, I sip colour,
borrow belief from the Stormy Weather,
her smoky purple bloom and deep green foliage
chosen for disease resistance.

I'm canny; I quiet crocus.
I seek root systems,
cleave to the rhythm and cycle
of the ice machine.
Lean towards windows
where I sense a quiver in hue,
a slight thrum from the east. *Aurora*
bleeding heart, Silene stenophylla.

> Revival smells of darkness, not loam
> but something scarcer.

I fever through the swailing
      while they monitor the brush fire.
They count the snap of cones and seeds,
interpret any augury with percentages.
They maintain
they expect the body to germinate.

Streams of killer language flow over, not into me. I husk.
      Accept a sip: a cup: a glass: this litre, drained
until one softened spot breeches with green.

Now half-formed and raw, dedicated
to the practice of revival

           here I am spring-loaded with pollen.

☙ ☙ ☙

Hiking with My Father

RUTH IRUPÉ SANABRIA

On the lookout for bears, cougars, hypothermia,
starvation, poisonous bugs, trees falling, landslides,
avalanches, poisonous berries, snakes, frostbite,
cuts, sprains, dehydration, and Confederate flags,
through Snoqualmie Falls, the Olympic Mountains,
and finally, Mount St. Helens,
we now witness
patches of miniscule purple petals
blooming so soon after the blast,
blooming from the sterile dust,
blooming from the forest of the standing dead.

We lean forward in the railings
toward the burnt saint
and her new fringe of purple lupine.

Notice, dad, the Saint's scars
and her new patterns
of moving water,
of receiving water,
of sharing water.
This is how it is to adapt
to lack of air, to loss of earth,
and to a cooler sun.

Where is the well of courage
or is it madness to rise again at the rim of violence?

᪦᪦᪦

...l Things

...world grows in me

...t at the least sound

...and my children's lives may be,

I go and lie down where the wood drake

rests in his beauty on the water, and the great heron feeds.

I come into the peace of wild things

who do not tax their lives with forethought

of grief. I come into the presence of still water.

And I feel above me the day-blind stars

waiting with their light. For a time

I rest in the grace of the world, and am free.

᪣᪣᪣

THISTLES in a FIELD

MARILYN NELSON

oil, Fidelia Bridges, 1875

> Accursed be the soil because of you. With suffering shall you get your
> food from it every day of your life. It shall yield you brambles and thistles.
> Genesis 3:18

Perhaps she painted this humble landscape,
whose unbrowsed grasses, daisies, Queen Anne's Lace,
and thistles stretch to the farthest mountain
with no tree or boulder to hide behind,
no landmark the human eye can focus on,
thinking of that passage in Genesis
when we were driven out of Paradise,
wearing the fur coats God had sewed for us,
onto the soil God cursed because of us.

Meditating on each curved blade of grass,
on each barbed, golden, upthrust fist of seed,
perhaps she imagined endless wasteland.
Eyes to the canvas, the palette, the brush,
did she paint what she saw, or what she dreamed
when she looked toward the dark end of her life?
How many more mountain ranges were left?
How many more square acres of thistles?
Thistles so armed, fiercely self-protective.

Did she wonder what power thistles guard,
beyond merely keeping themselves alive?
Did she discover, painting thistle ground,
the ironic coin of God's curse/blessing?
Cursed with thistle, you can eat the young leaves,
or the stems, steamed and drizzled with butter;
you can prepare the heads like artichokes;
you can wash, peel, slice, and fry thistle roots.
You can use it to fight melancholy!

Brazos Bend

NANCY K. PEARSON

Wintered lotus,
wrung of your one-watt heat,

your leaves float, seeds release. I limp
on two feet. I need a pill, an opiate to flower,

to fruit, to fold up
my pacing at night. Where your wintering stems break—

a lever, the midpoint of remaking
where I hesitate. I zoom out to find

what seeps through
the saturated presence of you.

One vantage point outside the history
of multiplicity—one seed pod, then,

an ugly thing I hold
trembling. I'm holed in.

Dear seedpod, I would name you pain but pain named me first.
Dear seedpod, mimetic alien,

will you not reciprocate
my bitter sentience?

My lens limits God's largeness, the water.
Floating lotus, a man tells me your seeds sow flowers for a thousand years,

your seeds we eat, unmake. I alter myself
by saying my hurt is a light. How a light hurts—

a firefly in a pickle jar
will shake to kill its brightness.

In your pod's eyes,
an animal slept, rain arrayed, a yearning stayed.

If a dying gives freedom to reshape,
what form should my return take?

Recovery

KATY RICHEY

In my garden, an uprising has begun. I dig on my knees.
I fill my hands with earth, search for root. I excise them.
But in the morning, they rise again.

I visit the stores. I call my mother. And finally resort to prayer.
But nothing works. I continue to pull, throw their wilted stems
on the concrete.

Then, one afternoon, I see loveliness. First the crabgrass—
the cavalry. Next the dreadlocked broadleaf plantain and the horse nettle—
the pepperweed florets, dandelion, white clover, hairy bittercress,

and the bull thistle, so wooly and brazen it's had laws passed against it.
I almost want to let them have the field, to watch them take it
overnight. Take every inch of space in the grass.

The doctor told me it would be this way:
I would wake to noxious mornings.
Find some peace in the process, she said. She didn't tell me
at night I would dream of growing.

☙ ☙ ☙

ng we are saying thank you
n the bridges to bow from the railings
we are run_ _ _ ut of the glass rooms
with our mouths full of food to look at the sky
and say thank you
we are standing by the water thanking it
standing by the windows looking out
in our directions

back from a series of hospitals back from a mugging
after funerals we are saying thank you
after the news of the dead
whether or not we knew them we are saying thank you

over telephones we are saying thank you
in doorways and in the backs of cars and in elevators
remembering wars and the police at the door
and the beatings on stairs we are saying thank you
in the banks we are saying thank you
in the faces of the officials and the rich
and of all who will never change
we go on saying thank you thank you

with the animals dying around us
taking our feelings we are saying thank you
with the forests falling faster than the minutes
of our lives we are saying thank you
with the words going out like cells of a brain
with the cities growing over us
we are saying thank you faster and faster
with nobody listening we are saying thank you
thank you we are saying and waving
dark though it is

Freeway 280
LORNA DEE CERVANTES

Las casitas near the gray cannery,
nestled amid wild abrazos of climbing roses
and man-high red geraniums
are gone now. The freeway conceals it
all beneath a raised scar.

But under the fake windsounds of the open lanes,
in the abandoned lots below, new grasses sprout,
wild mustard remembers, old gardens
come back stronger than they were,
trees have been left standing in their yards.
Albaricoqueros, cerezos, nogales . . .
Viejitas come here with paper bags to gather greens.
Espinaca, verdolagas, yerbabuena . . .

I scramble over the wire fence
that would have kept me out.
Once, I wanted out, wanted the rigid lanes
to take me to a place without sun,
without the smell of tomatoes burning
on swing shift in the greasy summer air.

Maybe it's here
en los campos extraños de esta ciudad
where I'll find it, that part of me
mown under
like a corpse
or a loose seed.

⊰⊱⊰

What's Never Wasted
YAEL FLUSBERG

Consider Spanish Harlem in the summer of '69
where the Young Lords hoped The People would rise
and demand an end to police brutality or shout
"Housing is a human right!"

Instead The People sighed "*Pues, hay much basura!*"—
and though the Lords wanted to organize something
other than garbage, they launched a mammoth clean up.

They tried borrowing brooms and bags from the same Sanitation
Department that refused darker-hued neighborhoods. Only,
this was no lending library, and, trust Puerto Ricans? (No way José!)

So the good Lords heisted the goods, swept and bagged it
and called for a pick up. It sat for weeks like uncollected debt
in someone else's account. So they moved mounds of waste
onto Broadway, preventing passage to greener pastures
for New Yorkers who made enough to live outside the City.

From that first success, the Lords took over hospitals
and hijacked health vans, bringing thankful phlebotomists
to playgrounds where they could test for leaden blood.

Trash leads to big things.

Picture how it piled up in Naples, the police,
the strikers, the smoke fumigating
the role of the mafia from the Italian debris.

Memphis sanitation workers will always be remembered
for saying those who hoisted garbage had worth,
for hosting a King on the mountaintop more than 40 years ago.

In the scriptures, 40 is a cycle of cleansing.
40 days and nights of rain, 40 years in the desert
before a new generation can enter The Promised Land.

Even if you've never been on Broadway, you have alternative routes
to get through kitchen scraps. You can compost, make rich stocks,
feed feral cats. In simpler times, things weren't designed for short
shelf lives. For years, we've been forced to throw out and shop anew.

Only, there is no out: just the earth beneath us
where we'll bury our bones alongside what we have
no more use for, where the best organized
will not squander a single scrap, a sea sweeping change.

Take a Giant Step

JOSE PADUA

All the out of business auto body shops
on this slow highway, all the abandoned
buildings with peeling paint, the vacant
lots overgrown with junk trees and weeds
bounded by chain link fences, all the things
we could never fix and threw away, all
the insane metaphors for living, the fake
equation of ideas, the pretty words that
soar today in a shallow heart as wisdom
before giving way to tomorrow's clever
observation, commandment, or list
of the neglected and overrated, and all
the shut ups and neverminds we breed
with our lips because we have never been
upon the verge of either idiocy or genius.
This is not where you belong, alone in this
tiny town without mending, this is not
the long endless line that waits for an exit
out of city sleep, this is not the thick
wall you can't hear through. So go,
like everything that has decayed
before us, everything that has shattered
so beautifully, go into that street like
a man crashing a parade with smelly
clothes and dirty skin, go into that building
that's on fire because the sky is full
of smoke and you're thinking about a river.

⊷⊷⊷

The Seeds Talk Back to Monsanto

BRENDA HILLMAN

        & there was heard mourning in the syntax
        there was heard brightness in the being of the
        land. & there was heard don't.
        There was heard nnnnnooooo—
           The mountains rise in their noon
of proud fevers. The dedicated grasses wait. In valleys
  where basalt meets granite & grains meet valleys
of loam, winds help the free seeds
        of grasses: rabbitfoot & foxtail, they help
quaking grass, the foreign stately ryegrass
      Lolium perenne & even the ripgut brome.
Culms of fescue sway as in Psalms. Syllables & glumes. Lemma,
pedicil, twigs & twains, bespuddled musings, ye oddlings, not forced.

        Engineered seeds on faraway farms hear
of the free seed movement. They want no part of Genetic
Use Restriction Technologies turning farmers
        into serfs. *& there was heard mourning in the syntax,*
there was lightness in the senses of the land. The seeds
      talk back to Monsanto. They talk back to AstraZeneca &
Novartis. They know their root *sed* turned into *sit* & they
refuse to grow. They fold their spikelets inside & sit
      like Thoreau
      in a *Don't sprout for Monsanto.* sit with. the. Don't. d.o.n.t.
      _{don't don't} sprout. Sisters, fold awns & bracts to add
      power when putting your handwriting on—
        Eco-terrorist seeds won't sprout for Monsanto.
They want no other weather than inside; but they can negotiate
      through poetry, something like::: *(1) would you like to try*
one of our delicious word seeds? or
(2) stalled were it not for magic, we're trying to decide what to do—

CODA: SUGGESTED ACTIVISM FOR ENDANGERED SEEDS

Ok, so, when you get home, send a copy of your poem with a letter to the USDA about bio-piracy harming farmers, which the United States is totally funding in Africa (see the Center for Grassroots Oversight website—"The Use of Terminator Seeds"). If you can't do more at this time, you can cut three copies of your poem into seed-like sylla-bles. Place the seedlings in boxes along with organic grass seeds and readable copies of the poem. Before you seal the grass seeds, expose them to sun. Mail to the CEOs of Monsanto, AstraZeneca, and Novartis. The seeds will tumble onto the desks. It is a meaningless gesture, word-seeds tumbling onto desks of corporations. The CEOs will not bother contacting the CIA; you're just a poet. The word-seeds will outlast you, you know that—

Set the Garden on Fire

CHEN CHEN

for Jeanette Li

My friend's new neighbors in the suburbs
are planting a neat row of roses
between her house & theirs.

Her neighbors smile, say the roses are part
of a community garden project, that's all.
But they whisper, too—whisper plans for trees,
a wall of them. They plant rumors
that her house is hiding illegals, when it's aunts
& uncles, visiting. They grow tall accusations
fed by talk radio, that her house was bought
with drug money, not seventeen years of woks
sizzling, people serving, delivering, filing,
people scrubbing, refilling, running—her family
running the best restaurant in town.
Like with your family, my friend says, *once we
moved in, they stopped calling us
hardworking immigrants.*
Friend, let's really move in, let's

plunge our hands into the soil.
Plant cilantro & strong tomatoes,
watermelon & honey-hearted cantaloupe,
good things, sweeter than any rose.
Let's build the community garden
that never was. Let's call the neighbors
out, call for an orchard, not a wall.
Trees with arms free, flaming
into apple, peach, pear—every imaginable,
edible fire.

Come friend, neighbor,
you, come set the garden on fire
with all our hard-earned years, tender labor
of being here, ceaseless & volcanic
making of being here, together.

Downriver, Río Grande Ghazalion
EMMY PÉREZ

Drive into the Valley, past a field of old farm equipment.
Near the tip of Tejas: Sal del Rey, blatant farm equipment.

I never bent into onion fields or declined sweet strawberries.
The kid in everyone's kitchen, escaping farm equipment.

When I think about seeing you, I want to jump on your back.
I confess—you're sexy, luxury—let's paint farm equipment

The color of parakeets congregating, squawking on 10th
Street McAllen power lines, strip mall trees, fading equipment.

99¢ meals. Surreal pickles like vine fetuses in jars.
Wrinkled wienies on a Stripes treadmill, saintly farm equipment.

Julia (te necesito) ¿dónde estás? ¿En el barrio
De nuestra nostalgia? ¿En el Río Grande de Loíza?

let's

weld

jade

cave

excavate equipment

repatriate

shell and bone

shards and kernels

study hopi

dry farming

dare roman

empire

incan terrace farms

aztec chinampas

                                        mississippi cotton
                                    california strawberries
                                seedless watermelons, grapes
                                 cherries still need their pits
                                        suck and spit them like chew

Sometimes I defer to the blues, tejanas, two chachalacas
Rustling in ébanos, and ébanos in chachalacas

                            río
                  bravo   ~grande
              caracoles   snails
                  both   spiral
                        galaxies

Agha Shahid Ali prayed for each couplet's own identity
Sin fronteras. Linked by rhyme, refrain, y su nombre de diosas
                            & colonizers.

Snake, bobcat, great horned owl, pauraque, bats, tlacuache
                            medicine.
Burrowing vato owls protect their land, urban EPT.

Return? To rivers, loves, monte, el chalán? Erase citrus?
So-called fences? Faith in Boca Chica~Gulf of México, fresh salt-
                    water confluences?

                    Salt is old, older than cranium.
                    What's older? Salt or water?

It's time to move beyond binaries, old loves. Remember eyes.
Not love but eyes—eyes are love. Yes. Remember the smell of skin:

                    Go swimming

        El día en que tú naciste / nacieron todas las flores.

The scent of water. *A tolerance for ambiguity*
In nepantla: between Hurricanes Dolly and Alex
                              flooding.

                    Terremoto, huracán
                        You lithium
                          The grass
                            Mineral, metal
                              Leaf cuts the ants clip and carry
                                Ant path
                                  Goat
                                    Sheep crossing
                                      Rio Grande
                                        Gorge

It takes hours to defang cactus. You nursed an orange all of
Christmas Day; at night, just before going to bed, you ate it.

A ~ marks your open text unions. Sign your ~name in e-mail,
Feel your flirty ambiguity, friendly besito.

֎ ֎ ֎

America, I Sing You Back

ALLISON ADELLE HEDGE COKE

a tribute for Phil Young, my father Robert Hedge Coke, Whitman, and Hughes

America, I sing back. Sing back what sung you in.
Sing back the moment you cherished breath.
Sing you home into yourself and back to reason.

Before America began to sing, I sung her to sleep,
held her cradleboard, wept her into day.
My song gave her creation, prepared her delivery,
held her severed cord beautifully beaded.

My song helped her stand, held her hand for first steps,
nourished her very being, fed her, placed her three sisters strong.
My song comforted her as she battled my reason
broke my long-held footing sure, as any child might do.

As she pushed herself away, forced me to remove myself,
as I cried this country, my song grew roses in each tear's fall.

My blood-veined rivers, painted pipestone quarries
circled canyons, while she made herself maiden fine.

But here I am, here I am, here I remain high on each and every peak,
carefully rumbling her great underbelly, preparing to pour forth singing—

and sing again I will, as I have always done.
Never silenced unless in the company of strangers, singing
the stoic face, polite repose, polite while dancing deep inside, polite
Mother of her world. Sister of myself.

When my song sings aloud again. When I call her back to cradle.
Call her to peer into waters, to behold herself in dark and light,
day and night, call her to sing along, call her to mature, to envision—
then, she will quake herself over. My song will make it so.

When she grows far past her self-considered purpose,
I will sing her back, sing her back. I will sing. Oh, I will—I do.
America, I sing back. Sing back what sung you in.

SECTION VIII

Plead for Me
↦ Beyond America

With an emphasis on the Global South, this section features poets writing about resource wars, environmental crisis, and struggles in support of local populations and indigenous rights. Some of the poets in this section live or have lived in North America as immigrants; others have never been to North America.

Environmental destruction is militarized in many of the poems. In "Ships," Nigerian poet Tolu Ogunlesi writes of two boats on a painted canvas of the harbor: one bearing oil, the other sailing off the edge of the earth, bearing "broken flesh." Ogunlesi writes,

> There, and everywhere else, will be blood,
> staining the atlas in hues deeper
> than the ink that staunchly marks place.

In Iraqi poet Taha Muhammad Ali's poem "Thrombosis in the Veins of Petroleum," the speaker fights for his life in the midst of a war for oil that wants him dead. His very resilience becomes

> a blood stain
> the size of a cloud
> on the shirt of this world!

Blood also soaks through Nicaraguan poet Esthela Calderón's poem "The Price of What You See"—a work that reveals the history of colonization, a history that fills museums with prizes, that costs "10,000 liters of Quiché blood," and that results in "Mahogany, Roble Beech, and Walnut trees cut down." Death and destruction also wreak havoc in Nicaraugauan poet Claribel Alegría's poem "The Rivers," in which the rivers

> no longer sing
> they lament
> they sweep their dead along
> cradle them
> they twinkle
> under a tepid moon.

Canadian poet Kim Goldberg reminds us in her poem "Spawn" that contamination is a global traveler. Goldberg describes observing fish in the Japanese market and in the ocean's current moving toward shore, "all of us together in this self-made retroactive cloud / with no vanishing point at all."

As in other sections, the poets in this section wrestle with disaster and the resulting despair. Mexican poet Homero Aridjis's poem "The Last Night of the World" resists certainty about the final outcome. The speaker mourns the death of the world at the hand of men, but though it seems like the world's last night, the world doesn't end. This poem also resists the bravado of revolutionary hope, offering instead an image of flawed humanity. The speaker turns a corner and comes upon his or her double, a beggar, who appears as

> an angel with big feet
> reading the paper under the muddied moon,
> the golden print of his feet were embossed on the sidewalk.

We're given the headlines:

> ANGELS INVADE THE CITY—
> was the news of the day;
> OUR VIRGINS LOVE-CRAZED BY ANGELS—
> yesterday's.

It is the angels, in their quest to be human, who in some way give heart to our own vulnerability. The vanished river mentioned at the start of the poem is not healed at its end, but the heart goes on.

UK poet David Attwooll's "Murmuration" closes the section and the anthology with a meditation on the murmuration of birds, chaos theory, and Occupy protest tents, finding hope in decentralized movement, awareness that our local actions connect to a larger whole:

> Dark webs encode surprise: the tip of a system's
> critical transitions, poised, then instantly
> transformed, as filings magnetise, or continents fold
> and drift, framing new maps, possible worlds.

We Travel Like All People

MAHMOUD DARWISH

We travel like everyone else, but we return to nothing. As if travel were
a path of clouds. We buried our loved ones in the shade of clouds and
    between roots of trees.
We said to our wives: *Give birth for hundreds of years, so that we may end this*
    journey
within an hour of a country, within a meter of the impossible!
We travel in the chariots of the Psalms, sleep in the tents of the prophets, and
    are born again in the language of Gypsies.
We measure space with a hoopoe's beak, and sing so that distance may
    forget us.
We cleanse the moonlight. Your road is long, so dream of seven women to
    bear
this long journey on your shoulders. Shake the trunks of palm trees for
    them.
You know the names, and which one will give birth to the Son of Galilee.
Ours is a country of words: Talk. Talk. Let me rest my road against a stone.
Ours is a country of words: Talk. Talk. Let me see an end to this journey.

෧෧෧

Fulfillment

SAADI YOUSSEF

I used to,

I often used to hope

as autumn painted forests with gold,

walnut brown,

or muted crimson,

I so hoped to see Iraq's face in the morning

to loosen water's braids over me,

to satisfy its mermaids with salty tears,

to float over Abu-al-Khaseeb's rivulets to ask the trees:

do you, trees, know where my father's grave is?

. . .

I often used to hope!

Let it be.

Let autumn finish its cycle.

Iraq's trees will remain naked.

Iraq's trees will remain high.

Iraq's trees will be secretly in the company

of my father's face.

London, 5-21-2003

☙ ☙ ☙

Ama-ar-gi

DUNYA MIKHAIL

Our clay tablets are cracked
Scattered, like us, are the Sumerian letters
"Freedom" is inscribed this way:
Ama-ar-gi

This, then, is how the maps grew borders
The birds don't know it yet
they leave their droppings wherever they want
their songs, like exiles, might pass by anywhere

There are no borders in Paradise
neither spoils nor victors
there are no victors at all
Paradise is Ama-ar-gi

There are no borders in Hell
neither losses nor demons
there are no demons at all
Hell is Ama-ar-gi

Ama-ar-gi might be a moon that follows us home
a shadow that stumbles on its true self
beads from a bracelet strung or broken together
a secret the tree keeps for centuries

Maybe it's what crowds the prisoner's heart
what shines around the pebbles in the embrace of the sun
what's mixed with drops of water among the rocks
what seeps out from the dead into our dreams

Maybe it's a flower borne to you
or thrown into the air
or hanging there alone
a flower that will live and die without us

Ama-ar-gi
that's how we return to the mother
strangers from strangers
inhaling-exhaling from inhaling-exhaling

Thus, like all of you
we breathe Ama-ar-gi
and before we shed our first tears
we weep Ama-ar-gi

NOTE

   Am-ar-gi: a Sumerian word that means "freedom" and "returning to the mother."

❧ ❧ ❧

Pomegranates

TALA ABU RAHMEH

Was it pomegranates we used to eat?
I can't quite remember.
It was before all the bombs
fell everywhere, even on that church
in the backyard of Grandma's house,
when Grandma did not believe in Jesus
and pushed her little sister
off of the windowsill,
then her mother got pregnant again.
The new daughter got the dead
daughter's name;
it was Aisha—the living one.
I think they were pomegranates,
we'd pick them, you and I, Mom,
from the tree,
red pearls they were
perfect sets of teeth.
We'd eat them so well
and stain our shirts with the mess.
It was nice then, Mom,
before the bombs, before you got sick.
Oh, the pomegranates,
my cousin—who, three days later,
got shot in the lungs—
reached for the highest one.
Mom, I told you,
if we put a Band-Aid on his chest,
he'd get better.
Mom, are you sure they were pomegranates?
Somehow I keep thinking of little figs
you'd break your arm to reach,
as they grew ripe and plump.

You'd sneak outside, past midnight,
and hum as you swallowed
their little strings of joy.
Mom, remember how it was only
the pomegranate tree
that remained standing
when you leaped off of the couch
and over my body screaming.
"I swear I will come up there
to your damn chopper
and scope your eyes out
if one inch of this missile
pierces the edges of my daughter."
Yes, Mom, it was pomegranates you couldn't chew,
when your body got infested with morphine,
when you spent July sleeping
before you slept forever in August.
I don't know how to make them sweeter.
You never gave me the recipe,
and now I cant ask you about them,
or about anything,
so I grab one and stare at its shell
and wonder if that's how the earth is now,
harsh on the surface,
but housing your body;
your limbs now pearls
and you are the lightest pomegranate,
the reddest there is.

❧ ❧ ❧

Thrombosis in the Veins of Petroleum

TAHA MUHAMMAD ALI

When I was a child
I fell into a pit
but didn't die;
I sank in a pond
when I was young,
but did not die;
and now, God help us—
one of my habits is running
into battalions of mines
along the border,
as my songs
and the days of my youth
are dispersed:
here a flower,
there a scream;
and yet,
I do not die!

They butchered me
on the doorstep
like a lamb for the feast—
thrombosis
in the veins of petroleum.
In God's name
they slit my throat
from ear to ear
a thousand times,
and each time
my dripping blood would swing
back and forth

like the feet of a man
hanged from the gallows,
and come to rest,
a large, crimson mallow
blossom—
a beacon
to guide ships
and mark
the site of palaces
and embassies.

❧ ❧ ❧

And tomorrow,
God help us—
the phone won't ring
in a brothel or castle,
and not in a single Gulf emirate,
except to offer a new prescription
for my extermination.
But . . .
just as the mallow tells us,
and as the borders know,
I won't die! I will not die!
I'll linger on—a piece of shrapnel
the size of a penknife
lodged in the neck;
I'll remain—
a blood stain
the size of a cloud
on the shirt of this world!

    23.IX.73

❧ ❧ ❧

Untitled

DENNIS BRUTUS

shadow-patterns of leaves
on a window-shade
moving gently in a breeze

suddenly I am seized with sadness—
perhaps for the first time—
this is the world I must leave ere long

this is the loveliness I must lose

oh, craven, will you not act?
save, I beg you, our world,
find courage to challenge terror

                        6/24/08; durban s a

꙰ ꙰ ꙰

Ships

TOLU OGUNLESI

for the Niger Delta

Unseen hands daily smear oil
across the ominous face of the clock,
the gently relentless art of many talented painters.

When that canvas is finished it will harbour
two ships; one sailing into port, loaded
with symptoms of an oilboom.

The other sailing away, tipping over the edge
of the earth, bearing broken flesh
into an invisible dustbin.

There, and everywhere else, will be blood,
staining the atlas in hues deeper
than the ink that staunchly marks place.

⊷ ⊷ ⊷

Sleeping in a Makeshift Grave

TANURE OJAIDE

Nigeria sleeps in a makeshift grave.
If she wakes with stars as her eyes,
the next world will be brighter for me and my compatriots.
A gunful of children broke the tetrarch's legs
& the elephant that once pulled the forest along for a path has fallen—
can she get up before she's covered for dead?
If the game's quartered, the delta will be swallowed whole—
the hunters know they only came together for this prize.
You cannot measure the size of the overfilled pits
that trail the boots of strong men that come and go
trampling and thrashing in their ironed uniform.
The hanged men are thrusting their fists from beyond.
The gunners strip their mothers before the world,
their undertaker presides over the land with a swaggerstick.
If Nigeria wakes from the grave after the murders,
let the people cast general, staff, and cap
into a marble grave in their born-again memory.
There's no other way to live free here than kill
or be killed. You can tell from our stone country.

❧ ❧ ❧

Kenya—A Love Letter

MUKOMA WA NGUGI

Inside looking out, snow is falling and I am thinking
how happy we once were, when promises and dreams
came easy and how when we, lovers covered only

by a warm Eldoret night, you waved a prophecy
at a shooting star and said, "when the time comes
we shall name our first child, Kenya" and how I

laughed and said "yes, our child then shall be country
and human" and we held hands, rough and toughened
by shelling castor seeds. My dear, when did our

clasped hands become heavy chains and anchors holding
us to the mines and diamond and oil fields? Our hands
calloused by love and play, these same hands—when

did they learn to grip a machete or a gun to spit hate?
And this earth that drinks our blood like a hungry child
this earth that we have scorched to cinders - when we
are done eating, how much of it will be left for Kenya?

❧ ❧ ❧

'Satao'

STEPHEN DERWENT PARTINGTON

Satao, Kenya's last great tusker, was poached in 2014

Cowards, let us sing in dead Elmolo
how the elephants have died.
We thank the cavemen, that they drew them,
that zoologists described them,
for the photos of them herding
which the tourists left behind,
for who would ever, fools, believe us?
Teeth from heaven to the ground!?

I stretch my arm out like a trunk
to palm the graveyard of its cranium;
it's how, I hear, they mourned.
The brain within worked tools and language.
I have none: a useless pen
(it's only good for drafting elegies)
and even then, no words.
We once had tuskers. Tell the birds!

⌖⌖⌖

Snow in Ulan Bator

JIANG TAO

Monday morning I got up early, thinking I was home,
scrounged a drink of water in the bathroom.
I turned my socks inside out and slipped them on
as if what happened last night was nothing.

But it's snowing outside. After only one night
the grassland retreats in haste
exposing a great cluster of Japanese cars
sinking into bottomless mud. This

I'm actually already familiar with.
It's been this way for more than a century, from Tokyo to Beijing,
and now again here.
Straight-nosed wide-mouthed commuters,

their faces exhausted from stuffing themselves
with potatoes cooked in the freezing wind,
are going to work now, shotguns on their shoulders
replaced by a forest of black umbrellas.

But I'm still in my underwear,
switching quickly between BBC and CNN.
The white-haired anchorman always looked arrogant
but now he speaks proletarian English.

I'm skeptical, understanding half of what he says
I guess that a great shift might come
— but not local mountains becoming golden hills
nor Pyongyang turning into Beijing.

I sense that what was looming
is coming, so I decide to get dressed, go downstairs
and join the crowded Far East poetry festival
and during my reading throw in some foreign words

like "Black Monday" and stuff like that,
implying: this good snow, isn't it just in time?

Translated by Ming Di

The Day It Rained Fish and Swallows

KRISTINE ONG MUSLIM

It was the day the local weatherman
received a raise. It was the day
you thought you saw but would not admit
to noticing a long dead relative watering
your plants outside, outside where the ground
now shifts and trembles, quivers and lets loose
a hundred million dying fish and swallows.
Everywhere, the sheen of fish scales.
Everywhere, the feathered lumps.
You kneel, take the one nearest your feet,
cup it in your hand where it fidgets once, twice
before it dies. Its eyes glassy, the sclera
muted gray like the industrial-grade paint
shielding a tank in the chemical plant
across your grandfather's fields of lavender.

☙ ☙ ☙

The Walls

KAZURNARI USUKI

It was unusually chilly
and it was raining in June.
A man hanged himself in a small apartment.
Just as he had promised his sweetheart,
he died leaving a fantastic suicide note: *I'll die for you*.

You mutter that tragedy is beautiful
because you are carrying death within life

and because you are intensely conscious of death
while living.

As the skull envelopes the brain,
a person envelopes death
in a wall known as the body.
Even so, life is tinged
with the faint smell of death
leaking from within.

The ground around Hokusatsu holds pellet-sized ore of uranium.
It is said that the foundation of a nuclear power plant is anchored
directly to the bedrock to make it earthquake-proof.
And it is surrounded by multiple layers of walls
that hold the radioactive materials.

However, just as life
one day reaches completion
on account of the death it contains,
these walls are destined
to break down because of what they contain.
Only then
will we see the real face
of what has been concealed
behind so many walls.

Translated by Naoshi Koriyama

Give Us Back Everything

YASUNORI AKIYAMA

In an abandoned hamlet
several dozen cows
tied to cowsheds died, sprawled on the floor,
leaving tooth-marks on the wooden door frames.

From their parched hide,
from their hooves kicking the air,
from the rusty iron beams of the cowshed,
from the dirt of the floor,
from the dent in the roof,
from the roots of the grass, trunks of trees, and the air,
something is silently watching.

The impact of death eating into humanity
has taken its first steps toward eternity.
It pushed up the concrete floors
covering the ground in Hiroshima and Nagasaki,
stood up from the seabed of Bikini Atoll,
let the *Lucky Dragon* drift about,
crushed some humans to death.

We must not be patient.
To be patient is to run away.
To endure is to look away from reality.
When it hurts, we should cry out loudly, *Ouch!*
Crying, *Ouch! Ouch!*
we should locate the source of the pain.

We must not treat those driven from their homes by radioactivity
as an unimportant minority.
We must not keep them waiting.
We should say in unison
to those who hid what they didn't want us to see
and to those who, from the beginning,
treated what shouldn't exist as though it had never existed,
Give us back our cows! Give us back the fodder!
Give us back our homes, farms, grass and trees!
Give us back our water, air, insects, fish and birds!
Give us back our neighbors!
Give us back peace for the babies not yet born!
Give us back everything that once was!
Give us back the future that is yet to come!

Translated by Naoshi Koriyama

☙☙☙

What Should We Do?

HIROMI MISHOU

In the azure sky
shines a bright blue mosque.
I wonder if the stolen Magic Lamp of Aladdin
is still shining now
in the marketplace of Baghdad
that I heard about in my dreams
—in my boyhood—
in the exotic story
of Ali Baba and the Forty Thieves.

Dr. Charmockly of the Pediatrics Department of Baghdad University
   Medical College says:
   Children suffering from leukemia[1] are overflowing the hospital's hallways.
   What can a doctor without medicines do for them?
   What did the doctors of Hiroshima do
   for their patients fifty-eight years ago?
Asked these unanswerable questions,
my memory is forever scorched by the flash of that day,
and I just look down speechless.

Children suffering from leukemia, held by young mothers,
smile innocently.
Staring at the photos on my desk of deformed children—
children without brains whose eyes and eyelids protrude,
children with hydrocephalus—
I become blind.

Dr. Al Ali who has come from Basra says:

What can a doctor do
who has no medicines to prescribe?
What did you do?
What do you think can be done?
I would like to hear your advice, you, the doctor from Hiroshima.[2]

Children are sprawled all over the examination tables.
Is it you, mother, who is whispering
into your child's ear?
Skinny cheeks,
pearl-like eyes.
I gently touch
the tender skin.
It's cold!
The skin is ice-cold.

NOTES

1. These children were exposed to radiation from deleted uranium shells fired by United States and coalition forces.

2. Hiromi Misho, the author of this poem, is himself a hibakusha (survivor of the atomic bombings) and a doctor who has dedicated his life to treating A-bomb victims in Hiroshima.

Translated by Naoshi Koriyama

❧❧❧

"Microwave" ("Micro-ondas")
ANGÉLICA FREITAS

how to explain brazil to an extraterrestrial:
your face on a flag. they'd recognize
you as leader
and knock you off. dirty
part of the conquest.
but it already happened, in another shape: aerial
view of the amazon,
a hundred-odd
hydroelectric plants
to fry your eggs in the microwave.
and they'd finish you off: just
part of the conquest.
and what if they came
to tour the waterfalls?
or to be taught by the elite
how to make a democracy?
the spaceships cover the sky
completely.
all the offices and fast food joints declare
an end to the working day.
cockroaches and rats
fled first.
it's christmas, carnival, easter,
our lady of aparecida, and the final judgement
all at once.
lovers fuck for the last time.
atms dry heave.
the supermarket was a cemetery!
the malls, the freeways!
to explain civil unions
to an iguana, to explain
political alliances to a cat, to explain

climate change

to an aquarium turtle.

it's done, already. now, wait.

eat an activia.

dwell in philosophy. imagine!

in our tropical country . . . disastrous!

not one river more. tragic!

worse than locusts,

your marvelous hydroelectric plants will be

seen, in flames, from sirius:

"my country was a sweet corn *pamonha*

that a starving alien

put in the microwave."

watch us burn:

possible epitaph.

Translated by Tiffany Higgins

ଈଈଈ

Little Farm
JUAN CARLOS GALEANO

The little farm has coffee and comes out to greet the morning wearing her
    flower-tobacco leaf-banana-pineapple hat.

(Millions of years ago, the stars and planets purchased their tickets to see her
    smile at this moment.)

Hand in hand, noon and afternoon come out to behold and praise her.

Clouds tell their kids, thunder and lightning, to stop playing
hide-and-seek; to come and admire the little farm.

The tobacco philosopher, born on the farm, says with his leaves:
"There's nothing better than to be here at this moment on the farm."

The little farm cries tears of joy and imagines that the lightning bolts
will capture this moment in a photograph.

                    Translated by James Kimbrell and Rebecca Morgan

✧ ✧ ✧

History

JUAN CARLOS GALEANO

In the north we hunted many buffalo
whose lard warmed us all winter.

But in the jungle they told us that to bring more light
we should throw more trees into the sun's furnace.

One day our hand slipped and tossed in the entire jungle
with its birds, fish, and rivers.

Now we spend a lot of time gazing at the stars
and our daily menu almost never changes.

Today we hunted down a cloud
that was going to become winter in New York City

Translated by James Kimbrell and Rebecca Morgan

֍ ֍ ֍

Kyoto Protocol

LUIS ALBERTO AMBROGGIO

The wilderness howls
red death
at what Man—
believing himself God—
inflicts and condemns.

I have come
with my mother
to rescue the dead
but they flee
on pure impulse.

I wanted to return
the green blood
to their bodies.
Here—the sands tell me—
are the orphans.

The woods are grief itself
losing more and more
of their hidden language.

    Translated by Yvette Neisser Moreno

❖ ❖ ❖

The Rivers
CLARIBEL ALEGRÍA

The terrain in my country
is abrupt
the gullies go dry
in the summertime
and are stained with red
in the winter.
The Sumpul is boiling with corpses
a mother said
the Goascarán
the Lempa
are all boiling with dead.
The rivers no longer sing
they lament
they sweep their dead along
cradle them
they twinkle
under the tepid moon
under the dark
accomplice night
they cradle their dead
the wounded
those who are fleeing
those who pass by
they grow irate
bubbling and seething
dawn draws near
almost within reach
the rivers are coffins
crystalline flasks
cradling their dead
escorting them
between their wide banks

the dead sail down
and the sea receives them
and they revive.

Translated by Darwin J. Flakoll

↜ ↜ ↜

The Parrots
ERNESTO CARDENAL

My friend Michel is a commanding officer in Somoto,
                near the border with Honduras,
and he told me about finding a shipment of parrots
that were going to be smuggled to the United States
                in order for them learn to speak English.
There were 186 parrots, and 47 had already died in their cages.
And he took them back to the place from where they'd been taken,
and when the truck was getting close to a place called The Plains
near the mountainss where those parrots came from
                (the mountains looked immense behind those plains)
the parrots began to get excited and beat their wings
                and press themselves against the walls of their cages.
And when the cages were opened
they all flew like arrows in the same direction to their mountains.
That's just what the Revolution did with us, I think:
it freed us from cages
                in which we were being carried off to speak English.
It brought us back to the Homeland from which we'd been uprooted.

Comrades in fatigues green as parrots
                gave the parrots their green mountains.
                But there were 47 dead.

                        Translated by Jonathan Cohen

☙ ☙ ☙

New Ecology

ERNESTO CARDENAL

In September more coyotes were seen near San Ubaldo.
More alligators, soon after the victory,
    in the rivers, out by San Ubaldo.
        Along the highway more rabbits, weasels . . .
The bird population has tripled, we're told,
    especially tree ducks.
The noisy tree ducks fly down to swim
            where they see the water shining.

Somoza's people also destroyed the lakes, rivers, and mountains.
    They altered the course of the rivers for their farms.
The Ochomogo dried up last summer.
The Sinecapa dried up because the big landowners stripped the land.
The Rio Grande in Matagalpa, all dried up, during the war,
    out by the Sébaco Plains.
They put two dams in the Ochomogo,
           and the capitalist chemical wastes
spilled into the Ochomogo and the fish swam around as if drunk.
    The Boaco River filled with sewage.
The Moyuá Lagoon dried up. A Somocist colonel
robbed the lands from peasants, and built a dam.
The Moyuá Lagoon that for centuries had been so beautiful.
(But the little fish will soon return.)
They stripped the land and they dammed the rivers.
    Hardly any iguanas sunning themselves,
        hardly any armadillos.
Somoza used to sell the green turtle of the Caribbean.
They exported turtle eggs and iguanas by the truckload.
    The loggerhead turtle being wiped out.
José Somoza was wiping out the sawfish of the Great Lake.
In danger of extinction the jungle's tiger cat,
    its soft, jungle-colored fur,

and the puma, the tapir in the mountains
(like the peasants in the mountains).
And poor Rio Chiquito! Its misfortune
the whole country's. Somocism mirrored in its waters.
The Rio Chiquito in León, fed by streams
of sewage, wastes from soap factories and tanneries,
white water from soap factories, and red from tanneries;
plastics on the bottom, chamber pots, rusty iron. Somocism
left us that.
(We will see it clear and pretty again singing toward the sea.)
And into Lake Managua all of Managua's sewage water
and chemical wastes.
And out by Solentiname, on the island La Zanata:
a great stinking white heap of sawfish skeletons.

But the sawfish and the freshwater shark could finally breathe again.
Tisma is teeming once more with herons
                                    reflected in its mirrors.
It has many grackles, tree ducks, kingfishers, teals.
                    The plant life has benefited as well.
The armadillos go around very happy with this government.
                    We will save the woodlands, rivers, lagoons.
We're going to decontaminate Lake Managua.
The humans weren't the only ones who longed for liberation.
The whole ecology has been moaning. The Revolution
also belongs to lakes, rivers, trees, animals.

Translated by Jonathan Cohen

✆✆✆

The Price of What You See

ESTHELA CALDERÓN

Squatting on its clay, a ceramic jug cries.
Inside, its lament is not tears, not water,
but the memory of extirpated gods.
In its curved walls flow the Huari, the Chimu-Inca and the Quimbaya,
stone in hand and unconscious heart.
Higher up, there are the arrows and spears of the Taínos, the Mayas and the
Tiahuanacos,
from the land of the Aztecs as well as the Nicaraos,
to the fire of the Onas.
The jug is painted with gods and a red river,
the open snout of Tepezcuintle, waiting for a mouthful of jade,
so he can rank the real price of what you see.
A thousand gold leaves in an altarpiece,
10,000 liters of Quiché blood.
Cathedral Capital, chairs for the choir and the clergy,
Mahogany, Roble Beech, and Walnut trees cut down.
A spindle bed for the queen,
mutilated Jacarandas.
History frowns in museums.
And, for those who were defeated, there are no more numbers
that serve to count their dead.

Translated by Steven F. White

About Angels IX

HOMERO ARIDJIS

Through the night, coated in frost,
the woods around my town wait for the light of dawn.
Like closed leaves, the monarch butterflies
cover the trunk and branches of the trees.
Superimposed, one upon the other, like a single organism.

The sky goes blue with cold. The first rays of sun
touch the clusters of numb butterflies
and one bunch falls, opening into wings.
Another cluster is lit and through the effect of the light
splinters into a thousand flying bodies.

The eight o'clock sun opens up a secret that slept
perched on the trunks of the trees,
and there is a breeze of wings, rivers of butterflies in the air.
Visible through the bushes, the souls of the dead
can be felt with the eye and hand.

It is noon. In the perfect silence, the sound
of a chainsaw is heard advancing toward us,
shearing wings and felling trees. Man, with his thousand
naked and hungry children, comes howling his needs
and shoving fistfuls of butterflies into his mouth.

The angel says nothing.

Translated by George McWhirter and Betty Ferber

⊕ ⊕ ⊕

The Last Night of the World

HOMERO ARIDJIS

I believed it was the last night of the world
and the angels of light and dark would appear
on the horizon and many would go down
in mortal conflict. In the battle
between the hosts of good and evil,
man would be made spectator; the golds
from the sundered day, tumble from the clouds.

But it was not the last night of the world,
only one more night that would not come back to the world.
Standing at the window of a room that looked out
over a few grey houses and a vanished river,
an angel was thinking about the bodies of water that had been.
It heard the story of its lost childhood in the distance;
the river ran through yesterday, which is the future running backwards.

The virgin, a Mazahua Indian, was begging in the street,
but nobody would give a dime to help her
because there was a street full of Mazahua women
and it would take a sack of coins to give to all.
And because this nobody had holes in his pockets
and bony legs. The street was a concrete
loneliness lost in other lonelinesses of concrete.

It made my head ache to see what men had done
to the water and the birds,
to the life and the trees along the avenue.
It made my head ache to see my shadow in the street
and to know that down every road and every moment
the end of the world drew nigh. A beggar
with shining eyes was pursuing me.

In the shop windows of men, there were
stuffed animals and plastic fruit,
photographs of the earth when it was still blue;
of woods, long before their ruination.
Hungering after memory, but for myself
more, I turned a corner, seeking to come upon
that double of mine, the beggar, by surprise.

I met an angel with big feet
reading the paper under the muddied moon,
the golden prints of his feet were embossed on the sidewalk.
ANGELS INVADE THE CITY—
was the news of the day;
OUR VIRGINS LOVE-CRAZED BY ANGELS—
yesterday's.

Then, unwilling and unenthused,
I unwalked all the roads,
as if the love of the beings I knew
had deserted the streets of the Earth.
Then, on reaching my home,
like the angel at the window, I put
my ear to hearing the water of the vanished river.

Translated by George McWhirter

❧ ❧ ❧

Celebrate

JORGE RIECHMANN

I sing
while my garden withers.

I sing
while my animals my parents and my children struggle in agony.

I sing
while seas I've never navigated
jungles I haven't hiked
and cities I've yet to see all die.

I sing
with my sweet cosmic expansive
cadaver's hoarse and brilliant voice.

Translated by Steven F. White

❧ ❧ ❧

In the Middle of the Bridge

KIRMEN URIBE

> For the water of the river is also a flag.
> —Yehuda Amichai

On the bridge over the Artibai,
my arms flat on the railing.

The aspen, the wooden
skeleton of that old boat.

After the war they left it
to disintegrate right there, a reprisal.

The leaves on the surface of the water
head upstream.

A sign that it's now high tide.
This is the moment I like best.

For it makes me think water doesn't
always head in the same direction.

Translated by Elizabeth Macklin

⊰⊱⊰

Circle the Wagons: In Ink: Meditation on Treaty Two

SHANE RHODES

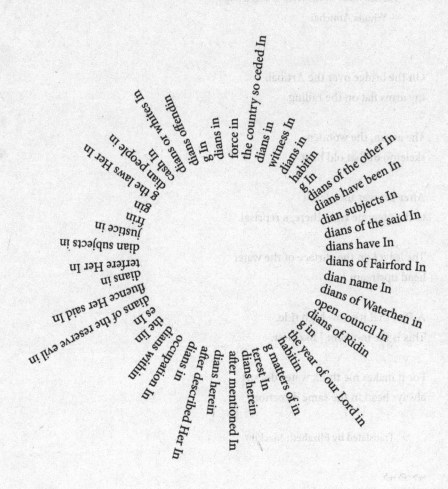

NOTE

All text in this mediatation is taken from the Government of Canada 1871 Treaty Two document. No additional text has been added.

ᐃᐧᐊ

beware of dog

DANIELA ELZA

the neighbours are   on vacation
took the dog with them.   asked me
to keep an eye on   the house.

                I watch

the garden   slowly   fall
prey   to weeds. its fingertips
awaken   blooms in
    unexpected   places.

          the quiet

months of summer's   creeping
out of flower beds

        reaching over fences.

re-   defining   yard.
my dandelions thriving   without the
use-   your-   weed- kill   look.

the owners are   away
took the bb-gun   with them.
birds grace   this explosion
    of pods
        fruit
          wisdom

bees feast on   untamed pollen
the lawn   un-touched   un-mowed

regains memory of seed.

this morning   I misread the sign
on their gate:

        beware of god.

❧❧❧

Spawn

KIM GOLDBERG

Under the bluest sky of the year, I stood at the edge of my world
and watched the flickerflashing churn of brimming life, the sea gone
white with sperm—the stench and smoky spew
of diesel-powered winches winding in their nets, beating
out the fish. I watched the shooting stars cascade into
the darkened hold to be later stripped of roe for
Japanese markets. The yawning emptiness between electrons
in the salty air—packed tight today with sirens' wail
and squaggling song from four thousand gulls and brant
aloft beyond the endless snowy drift of milt
whipped thick and scattered into bands of froth along a tideline
with no vanishing point at all.
All of this on the same day that the radioactive cloud
from Japan's nuclear disaster was scheduled to reach our shore—
all of us together in this self-made retroactive cloud
with no vanishing point at all.
We tipped and scattered clamshells in the froth, our lifeline
lost beyond the endless rift cleaving molten
rock and magma from four thousand songs and plants.
The salty air packed tight today with sirens' wail
in Japanese markets, while the yawning emptiness of our elections
echoes in a darkened hold to be later stripped and sold
as fish bait. We watched the shooting stars cascade into
a diesel-flowered meadow binding all our heads, beating
while it burned until the stench and smoky spew
was traded for the flickerflash of atomic churn. And the sea was gone
under the bluest sky of the year, as we stood at the edge of our world.

❧ ❧ ❧

Sometimes We Resist

STEPHEN COLLIS

I was   in a park
I could not see
global capitalism its
dinosaur bones
covered in chrome
I saw   trees
their leaves
turning yellow and
golden brown
I saw   the harbour
the city set down
below the mountain
I asked   how do we resist?
Consider the trees
the mountain's root grip
I asked   what if they come
with saw teeth
for the trees
with horizontal
directional drilling
for pipelines through
mountain's immobile heart?

Sometimes the voice
sometimes the voices
tear teeth from saw's blades
sometimes a body
sometimes all our bodies
blunt the bits of drills
dull dollar's desire
sometimes   we resist
sometimes   we win

❧ ❧ ❧

Hutopia (excerpt)

ALEC FINLAY

(II) PROSPECT COTTAGE

Jarman's neat cabin
on the borderless
shingle jut of Dungeness

———

in the shadow
of the power station
in the knowledge
of death
Derek began
to garden

each summer passing
taught him which flowers
would endure
the biting northerlies

sea kale & sea thistle
horned poppy, night-
shade & valerian
lavender & santolina

nodding their colours
amid the salt-
tangle of wire, rust
bloom & flint

———

Derek is gone
his garden
grows on

❧ ❧ ❧

Turning the Ship for Home and Then the Telling
PIPPA LITTLE

The captain's sun-sizzled, wears a cap with "Die Trying"
stuck at an angle, fists the lumpish red of lobsters.
He's sailing the Algetia back from the Eastern Garbage Patch,
an unmapped country he can't board,
for it jiggles and scrambles and discards itself
like knitting twirling off the needles,
but at its deep clotted heart it pulls in close,
clamps whales and crabs alike in nets and knots
and chokes—not only the lines, the ropes, the spars
but all the plastic tops and jagged fragments
whale-swallowed, a whole ocean's innards
spiked orange, fluorescent pink, green, blue—
pulled and sucked by the sea into a whorl
that grows, accrues, accumulates
hour after hour in daylight and dark,
where he is powerless except in witness,
his mourning the world takes for crazy.

✤ ✤ ✤

Murmuration

DAVID ATTWOOLL

Viral on YouTube and now here, flung
above the lake a swirling weft of birds.
Black but diaphanous this skirl of stars twists
and banks to its own mysterious arithmetic.

Neural networks more subtle than markets
conjure an aerial screensaver
contingent as crowds that flock the ether
to counter power, occupy tents.

Dark webs encode surprise: the tip of a system's
critical transitions, poised, then instantly
transformed, as filings magnetise, or continents fold
and drift, framing new maps, possible worlds.

 споⰃспоⰃспоⰃ

||||||||||||||||||||||||||||||||||||||||||||||||||||||||||||||||||||||||||||||||||||||||||||||||||||||||||||||||||||||||||||||||||||||||

WE, THE PEOPLE OF COLOR, gathered together at this multinational People of Color Environmental Leadership Summit, to begin to build a national and international movement of all peoples of color to fight the destruction and taking of our lands and communities, do hereby re-establish our spiritual interdependence to the sacredness of our Mother Earth; to respect and celebrate each of our cultures, languages and beliefs about the natural world and our roles in healing ourselves; to ensure environmental justice; to promote economic alternatives which would contribute to the development of environmentally safe livelihoods; and, to secure our political, economic and cultural liberation that has been denied for over 500 years of colonization and oppression, resulting in the poisoning of our communities and land and the genocide of our peoples, do affirm and adopt these Principles of Environmental Justice:

THE PRINCIPLES OF ENVIRONMENTAL JUSTICE

1) Environmental Justice affirms the sacredness of Mother Earth, ecological unity and the interdependence of all species, and the right to be free from ecological destruction.

2) Environmental Justice demands that public policy be based on mutual respect and justice for all peoples, free from any form of discrimination or bias.

3) Environmental Justice mandates the right to ethical, balanced and responsible uses of land and renewable resources in the interest of a sustainable planet for humans and other living things.

4) Environmental Justice calls for universal protection from nuclear testing, extraction, production and disposal of toxic/hazardous wastes and poisons and nuclear testing that threaten the fundamental right to clean air, land, water, and food.

5) Environmental Justice affirms the fundamental right to political, economic, cultural and environmental self-determination of all peoples.

6) Environmental Justice demands the cessation of the production of all toxins, hazardous wastes, and radioactive materials, and that all past and current producers be held strictly accountable to the people for detoxification and the containment at the point of production.

7) Environmental Justice demands the right to participate as equal partners at every level of decision-making, including needs assessment, planning, implementation, enforcement and evaluation.

8) Environmental Justice affirms the right of all workers to a safe and healthy work environment without being forced to choose between an unsafe livelihood and unemployment. It also affirms the right of those who work at home to be free from environmental hazards.

9) Environmental Justice protects the right of victims of environmental injustice to receive full compensation and reparations for damages as well as quality health care.

10) Environmental Justice considers governmental acts of environmental injustice a violation of international law, the Universal Declaration On Human Rights, and the United Nations Convention on Genocide.

11) Environmental Justice must recognize a special legal and natural relationship of Native Peoples to the U.S. government through treaties, agreements, compacts, and covenants affirming sovereignty and self-determination.

12) Environmental Justice affirms the need for urban and rural ecological policies to clean up and rebuild our cities and rural areas in balance with nature, honoring the cultural integrity of all our communities, and provided fair access for all to the full range of resources.

13) Environmental Justice calls for the strict enforcement of principles of informed consent, and a halt to the testing of experimental reproductive and medical procedures and vaccinations on people of color.

14) Environmental Justice opposes the destructive operations of multinational corporations.

15) Environmental Justice opposes military occupation, repression and exploitation of lands, peoples and cultures, and other life forms.

16) Environmental Justice calls for the education of present and future generations which emphasizes social and environmental issues, based on our experience and an appreciation of our diverse cultural perspectives.

17) Environmental Justice requires that we, as individuals, make personal and consumer choices to consume as little of Mother Earth's resources and to produce as little waste as possible; and make the conscious decision to challenge and reprioritize our lifestyles to ensure the health of the natural world for present and future generations.

Delegates to the First National People of Color Environmental Leadership Summit held on October 24–27, 1991, in Washington, D.C., drafted and adopted these seventeen principles of environmental justice. Since then, the principles have served as a defining document for the growing grassroots movement for environmental justice.

More information on environmental justice and environmental racism can be found online at www.ejnet.org/ej/.

EDITOR'S ACKNOWLEDGMENTS

So many people made this book possible. My gratitude to the University of Georgia editors, board, and staff who believed in this book and saw it through to completion. My thanks also to Regan Huff and to Camille Dungy who encouraged and conceived of this project as a book.

Deepest appreciation to Split This Rock for serving as the institutional home for this project these past four years. Many thanks to Sarah Browning, Mugabi Byenka, Camisha Jones, Tiana Trutna, Katherine Howell, Alex Borden, Cathy Merritt, Thea Piccone, Anisa Rahaman, Simone Roberts, and Laith Shakir. Thanks as well to Jamie Jarvis and Jay Smith.

For reading and feedback on various parts of this book during its formative stages, I am indebted to Wendy Babiak, Yael Flusberg, Lilace Mellin Guignard, Joe Hall, Tiffany Higgins, Jennifer James, Katy Richey, Judith Sornberger, and Amy Young.

My gratitude to the Compton Foundation and the Reva and David Logan Foundation for their support of this project and to the Black Earth Institute for community support.

For its eco-justice poetry portfolio and preview of this book in January 2016, many thanks to *Poetry Magazine* and editor Don Share.

This work would not be possible were it not informed and inspired by the work of environmental justice activists and scholars who have shaped this conversation over many years.

Thanks, always, to my husband, David R. Phillips, who supported this project throughout.

Deepest of gratitude, as well, to the poets for their work and to those everywhere who believe, like Arundati Roy, that "another world is not only possible, she is on her way."

ABOUT THE TITLE AND POSTSCRIPT

"Ghost Fishing" is the title of a poem I wrote about fifteen years ago in response to an environmental justice tour I took with activist Damu Smith and Dr. Robert Bullard, along with a group of activists and scholars. That tour was the inspiration for this anthology. I had toured many communities affected by industrialization and toxic waste in my work, but something about the level of pollution and discrimination in Louisiana in communities like Mossville, Diamond, and Convent disturbed me more than any other place I had previously visited, and that deep and unyielding disturbance was the stimulus for this book. When visiting these former plantation communities that now house the oil and chemical industries, I felt as if I was witnessing genocide. I also felt that anything I could do in response would be inadequate. The article I wrote for the environmental newsletter where I worked was not enough. The poem I wrote was not enough. This book, in fact, is not enough.

NOTES FROM THE AUTHORS

IIIIIIIIIIIIIIIIIIIIIIIIIIIIIIIIIIIIIIIIIIIIIIIIIIIIIIIIIIIIIIIIIIIIIIIIIIIIIIIIIIIIIIIIIIIIIIIIIIIIIIIIIIIIIIIIIIIIIIIIIIIIIIIIIIIIIIIIIIII

SECTION I. *LA FRONTERA / SIN FRONTERAS*: LAND, CULTURE, POSSESSION, AND DISPOSSESSION

"Zacuanpapalotls" by Brenda Cárdenas: *Zacuanpapalotls* is the Nahuatl word for monarch butterflies. The poem alludes to the Aztec (or Mexica) people's belief that the souls of the dead are reborn as monarchs. It also refers to the liminal space in which Chicana/o culture exists.

"We Who Weave" by LeConté Dill: Enslaved Africans were imported to the Sea Islands and low country of Georgia and South Carolina during eighteenth-century European colonization of North America to work as laborers on cotton, rice, and indigo plantations. In spite of white disinvestment and exploitation, black slaves and their descendants created thriving communities and retained African customs there.

"Cleaning" by Camille T. Dungy: There was a jar of tomatoes, and then there wasn't. It is important to acknowledge when we are culpable for loss.

"How to Disappear the Stars" by Lauren Camp: The poem came about during my rural village's multiyear fight against developers who wished to build a huge mess of homes right next to us; this would have changed the entire nature of our community, bringing in light pollution, crime, and traffic and removing some of the wildlife.

SECTION II. INSTEAD OF FLOWERS: WAR

"*Wi'-gi-e*" by Elise Paschen: *Wi'-gi-e* means *prayer* in Osage. The poem is spoken by Mollie Burkhart, whose sister Anna Kyle Brown was murdered during the Osage Reign of Terror (1921–26), when outsiders married Osage women and then killed them for their headrights. During this period of history, the Osages were considered one of the wealthiest people in the world because of the oil discovered on their land. My own family, the Tallchiefs, lived in Fairfax, Oklahoma, during this time.

"Lunch in Nablus City Park" by Naomi Shihab Nye: The poem rose out of a very particular outdoor meal with beautiful, suffering people in the Occupied West Bank, Palestine.

"The Dogs of Ashdod" by Zein El-Amine: The poem was written in the wake of the invasion of Gaza in November of 2012 after a *Jerusalem Post* reporter sent a tweet of inquiry to see if residents of Israel were concerned about their pets because of the sound of sirens.

"If It Were" by Javier Zamora: The poem imagines a different outcome to El Salvador's civil war, one where Monseñor Romero is still alive and we didn't have to flee.

"Daisy Cutter" by Camille T. Dungy: I wrote this poem during the ramp up to the Iraq War, when talking heads went on and on about tactics of Shock and Awe.

"In Jordan's Northernmost Province" by Shara Lessley: November 2008: In an effort to ensure the safety of more than fifty thousand residents, the Middle East's first all-female demining team began clearing a bomb-infested region along the Jordanian-Syrian border, often unearthing Dragon's Teeth, which are designed to maim rather than kill.

"Another Day" by Sara Goudarzi: This poem is inspired by Goudarzi's childhood experiences of the war between Iran and Iraq.

SECTION III. LITTLE FARM, BIG FARM: FOOD, CULTURE, AND CAPITAL

"From the Field" by Lenard D. Moore: The poem depicts the work that my brothers and I used to do. In fact, I heard the sound of two trees rubbing together and noticed the sound actually came from those trees while toiling in the field.

"Wealth" by Allison Adelle Hedge Coke: The poem focuses on disparity during the Great Depression and the Dust Bowl and the continuing familial legacy of being misread as having when there is naught.

"Almonds" by Elizabeth Jacobson: Central to this poem is the paradox that soon we may need to choose between food and water for our survival.

"harvest" and "after harvest" by Quraysh Ali Lansana: Growing up in Oklahoma, I have likened harvest to sitting in the chair of a slow, methodical barber for my entire life.

ورق by Philip Metres: The poem is a leaf from A Concordance of Leaves (Diode Editions, 2013) and a testament to the Palestinian agricultural way of life; "the olive is the foundation of the house."

SECTION IV. TELL THE BIRDS: HUMAN-ANIMAL RELATIONS

"The Great Chain of Being" by Clare Rossini: The Great Chain, a notion going back to the Greek philosophers and further elaborated by Christian thinkers in the Middle Ages, is a strict, religious hierarchical structure of all matter and life, believed to have been decreed by God.

"Whole Notes" by Pamela Uschuk: The poem was written after I took my Literature of the Environment class to Wolfwood Wolf Refuge as part of their study of wolves and their keystone importance in the Rocky Mountain eco-system.

"*ginen* the micronesian kingfisher [*i sihek*]" by Craig Santos Perez: The poem explores the endangerment of a bird species that is endemic to Guam.

"The Bee People" by Amy Miller: At a recent city council debate on beekeeping, I was surprised at how easy it was to spot the beekeepers in the audience—their hair and skin had a distinctive glow, perhaps from beeswax and honey, or perhaps (I thought) from the world-saving nature of their work.

"The Barnacle and the Gray Whale" by Cecilia Llompart: This poem is the first in a series I wrote as a coping mechanism during the Deepwater Horizon oil spill of 2010. As a somewhat dreamy dialogue between marine animals contemplating their vast and ancient world, it's a meditation on biological and spiritual interconnectedness, on a world less touched by man, and on a deep love for all forms of life.

"Strategy against Dying" by Monica Sok: The father in the poem, a survivor of the Cambodian genocide, is appalled by his children's brutality toward a butterfly.

"Eviction Notice" by Brian Patrick Heston: The poem is an attempt to dramatize the "greening" of the postindustrial U.S. city, which rarely touches those on the lowest rungs of the economic ladder.

"Albatross" by Kevin Simmonds: Inside the stomachs of thousands of dead baby albatrosses on Midway Atoll (a remote cluster of islands more than two thousand miles from the nearest continent and roughly equidistant between North America and Asia) are lethal quantities of plastic fed to them by their parents who mistake the floating trash for food as they forage over the Pacific Ocean.

"The Dreams of Antelope" by Dane Cervine: Eco-justice can only be pursued in seeing how all aspects fit together, including the perceived destructive elements of nature or human life.

"The Parable of St. Matthew Island" by Dane Cervine: There are stark illustrations, parables waiting to be read, all around us.

"Too Many" by David Baker: The poem is about one of the several fawns who've been born in my backyard in Granville, Ohio, over the past few years; one of them returns to my porch now and then.

SECTION V. UNQUIET AIR: RESOURCE EXTRACTION

"Money," by Jane Meade: This is the introductory poem to my book *Money Money Money / Water Water Water*, which is, in part, an exploration of the commodification of natural recourses.

"Epithalamia" by Joan Naviyuk Kane: On one level, this poem is about the ways in which combustion-engine-driven white heteronormative American culture and being entirely misread contribute to the preponderance of huffing by indigenous girls and women.

"29 Men" by Heather Lynn Davis: When I heard that Massey Energy allowed numerous safety violations at the Upper Big Branch in West Virginia, resulting in the 2010 explosion that killed twenty-nine men, I wanted to call out Massey Energy CEO Don Blankenship in some way. I also wanted to memorialize the men and implicate fossil fuel energy consumers (all of us) in their deaths. Blankenship has been convicted of violating safety standards but may never see jail time. After the Mine Safety and Health Administration assessed $10.8 million in fines against the company, it was bought by a competitor, who also settled a potential $209 million in criminal liabilities. Of course, no amount of money or jail time will bring back the twenty-nine men who died that day.

"Snake River IV" by Molly McGlennen: This is part of series of poems that I have been writing recently that is attentive to narrating the often marginalized and concealed stories of my hometown of Minneapolis as an Indigenous space, with tremendous Anishinaabe and Dakota history and continued presence.

"Refinement" by Elee Kraljii Gardiner: The poem was written after watching a film installation at the ICA in Boston in which motor oil was poured over a stack of sugar cubes—a dissolution/invasion I found tactile, disturbing, and absolutely linked to geopolitics.

"Ghost Fishing Louisiana" by Melissa Tuckey: In 1996, while attending an EPA-sponsored environmental justice meeting in Louisiana, I spent two days touring communities affected by issues relating to environmental justice with activist Damu Smith, sociologist Dr. Robert Bullard, and others. What I saw has haunted me since and left me with a deep sense of responsibility—town after town poisoned by the oil and chemical industries, the vast majority of which were African American communities. In the town of Mossville, we were greeted with a handmade sign bearing the names of the people in this small community who had died from cancer. "Ghost Fishing" was my response to this tour.

"To Haiti from Mountain Dell Farm" by Lisa Wujnovich: Struck by the enormity of the Haiti earthquake in 2010, I wrote this poem in response to how hydrofracking gas companies play with such devastation.

"Finding Water on Mars" by Grant Clauser: While writing this poem, I guess I was stuck by the contrast of energy companies wantonly destroying our planet while the Mars Rover was busy studying another for future exploitation.

"It's What They Do" by Judith Sornberger: I live in the middle of Marcellus Shale country, the so-called "sacrifice zone" for natural gas drilling.

"Living by a Tank Farm Cradle Song" by Vivian Faith Prescott: The poem depicts a true event I experienced while raising my children next door to a tank farm.

SECTION VI. TO SEE THE EARTH: ECO-DISASTER

"A Massive Dying Off" by Camille T. Dungy: This poem was commissioned for a reading in protest of "disaster capitalism." When he read it, the man who commissioned the poem asked if I might be able to write something with a more hopeful ending. I did write another poem, but I didn't let him read that one before the event as I have trouble imagining a hopeful outcome for a world at the mercy of disaster capitalism.

"Dance, Dance, While the Hive Collapses" by Tiffany Higgins: Imadacloprid is only one pesticide in the class of neonicotinoids implicated in the collapse of bee colonies (due to neurotoxic alterations that damage navigation systems, decreases in foraging behavior, and mutagenic effects); such pesticides are particularly insidious as they become systemically present in root systems and thus in nectar and pollen on which bees and other pollinators, such as monarch butterflies, feed; these neonicontinoids are not only applied in agriculture but also are a popular urban pesticide, included in household garden applications.

"A Violet in the Crucible" by Brenda Hillman: The poem refers to British poet Percy Bysshe Shelley's remark about translating poetry—if a violet were thrown into a crucible to detect its qualities; I extrapolated on this to consider a poet going into the "corridors of power" to try to get anything done, noting it is like being an endangered species.

"Transients" by Vivian Faith Prescott: This is a mourning poem that juxtaposes one's love of nature with making a living in the oil cleanup industry."

"Typhoon Poem" by Patrick Rosal: "This is a story that was related to me by word of mouth just days after Typhoon Ondoy, while the waters were still receding."

"atlantis made easy" by Evie Shockley: I dedicate "atlantis made easy" to the people of the New Orleans-that-was, wherever they may be now.

"Diary of Sila the Sky God" by Hila Ratzabi: The poem is part of a manuscript that engages with Inuit mythology as a frame through which to contemplate the terrors of the climate crisis.

"After ⅔ of a Village in Papua New Guinea is Decimated by Natural Disaster" by Purvi Shah: In July 1998, a 7.0 earthquake triggered an undersea landslide that spawned a tsunami, carrying away thousands of lives in Papua New Guinea.

"A Great Civilization" by Dane Cervine: We are not the first great civilization, nor will we be the last—if all goes well—which should bring a certain humility to us.

SECTION VII. TAKING ROOT: RESISTANCE, RESILIENCE, AND RESURGENCE

"Abstract" by Amy Young: The poem is part of an ongoing project that involves reading *Webster's Third New International Dictionary*.

"Ode to Stromatolites" by Myra Sklarew: When I served as president of Yaddo Artists' Community, I lived near a gravel company that was pulverizing ancient and rare fossils in order to build roads.

"Moon Gathering" by Eleanor Wilner: "the wheel's turning, when / three zeros stand like paw-prints / in the snow" refers to the turn of the millennium, the year 2000; the poem was written in the late 1990s.

"Taking Root" by Tara Betts: This is a poem inspired by the late activist and Nobel Prize winner Wangari Maathai and her book *Unbowed: A Memoir*, which details her life and work, including establishing and running the Green Belt Movement, where groups of women plant trees to decrease deforestation.

"Invocation" by Everett Hoagland: In lieu of going to my Unitarian church one Sunday morning two years ago, I read aloud my recently written poem titled "Invocation" at the beginning of my church hour, ocean-eco-oriented poetry reading for the annual Connecting for Change Conference (a Bioneers conference) in New Bedford.

"Aubade" by Elee Kraljii Gardiner: The poem is a morning glory of hope about surviving toxins, dedicated to angela rawlings.

"Hiking with My Father" by Ruth Irupé Sanabria: As a child, I would go hiking with my father, who had survived torture in a concentration camp, years of political imprisonment in Argentina and an emotionally brutal exile in the United States; in the mountains and on the trails I would notice a restorative peace wash over him.

"THISTLES in a FIELD" by Marilyn Nelson: The title is from a small oil painting in an exhibition at the Florence Griswold Museum a couple of years ago; the poem relates its subject to the wisdom of George Washington Carver.

"Take a Giant Step" by Jose Padua: I wrote this poem after driving through a rather desolate stretch of highway in central Pennsylvania, though there are so many places in America that could have inspired it.

"The Seeds Talk Back to Monsanto" by Brenda Hillman: The piece proposes that the engineered seeds (so-called terminator seeds that do not reproduce) commit acts of disobedience against Monsanto.

"America, I Sing You Back" by Allison Adelle Hedge Coke: This is a response song to Whitman's "I Hear America Singing" and Langston Hughes's poem, "I, Too," with a singing reclamation of the hemisphere, America.

SECTION VIII. PLEAD FOR ME: BEYOND AMERICA

"'Satao'" by Stephen Derwent Partington: The poem was written following the poaching of Satao, the last of Kenya's great tuskers, who was killed in 2014 despite regular protection.

"Snow in Ulan Bator" by Jiang Tao: While attending a poetry event in Ulan Bator in 2008, the author saw from TV the news about the financial crisis in the United States.

"The Day It Rained Fish and Swallows" by Kristine Ong Muslim: The poem contains the imagery of teeming lavender fields facing the industrial superstructure of a chemical manufacturing plant, the dialectics of which have been fleshed out in story form in my book *Age of Blight*.

"'Microwave' ('Micro-ondas')" by Angélica Freitas: As of this writing, in its section of the Amazon basin alone, Brazil currently has 138 operational, 16 under-construction, and 221 planned dams, involving the removal of tens of thousands of indigenous and river peoples, as well as alteration of interconnected freshwater and terrestrial ecologies ("State of the Amazon: Freshwater Connectivity and Ecosystem Health," World Wildlife Fund, April 2015).

"Kyoto Protocol" by Luis Alberto Ambroggio: The poem is named after the international treaty that commits state parties to reduce greenhouse gas emissions, a treaty the United States signed but failed to ratify.

"About Angels IX" by Homero Aridjis: Monarch butterflies overwinter on Cerro Altamirano in Contepec, Michoacan, where I was born and grew up.

"The Last Night of the World" by Homero Aridjis: J. M. G. Le Clézio has written about *A Time of Angels* that "it is, above all, the time we live in, a time when everything comes apart and is deconstructed and we suddenly find we are all in the 'disaster zone.'"

"In the Middle of the Bridge" by Kirmen Uribe: The poem is about the traces left by humans in the nature and the fragility of memory. The image of the river going up instead of down reminds me that another world is possible.

"Circle the Wagons: In Ink: Meditation on Treaty Two" by Shane Rhodes: All words in this poem are taken from Treaty Two, which was signed between representatives of Queen Victoria and the Ojibwe inhabitants of almost 35,700 square miles of unceded territory in southwest Manitoba and southeast Saskatchewan in 1871. The treaty called on the First Nations signatories to cede title to the lands on which they lived in exchange for promises from the government of Canada of receiving such things as reserves; education; farming supplies; the right to hunt, trap, and fish; and small, annual cash payments.

"Spawn" by Kim Goldberg: In March 2011, one of the world's most spectacular wildlife phenomena, the annual herring spawn along the inside coast of Vancouver Island, coincided with one of the world's most horrific technological disasters, the Fukushima nuclear reactor meltdowns.

"Sometimes We Resist" by Stephen Collis: The poem was written at the Kinder Morgan blockade and read at the police line by Haisla First Nation author Eden Robinson.

"Murmation" by David Attwooll: I saw a spectacular murmuration of starlings in rural Oxfordshire around the time of the Occupy movements in London and New York.

ABOUT THE AUTHORS

FRANCES PAYNE ADLER is the author of five books: *Making of a Matriot, Raising the Tents,* and three collaborative poetry-photography books for exhibitions that have shown in galleries and state capital buildings across the country. She is also coeditor of *Fire and Ink: An Anthology of Social Action Writing.* The poem "Supreme" is part of her current collaborative work, *Dare I Call You Cousin,* an exhibition of poems, photos, and videos about the Israeli-Palestinian struggle. Adler is professor emerita and founder of the Creative Writing and Social Action Program at California State University Monterey Bay and lives in Portland, Oregon.

YASUNORI AKIYAMA was born in Tokyo in 1938. After his house burned down in an air raid in 1945, his family moved to Matsumoto City, in Nagano Prefecture. He has published three volumes of poetry, *Flowing Sand, Memories of the People,* and *Crying Slope,* and is the publisher of *Matsumoto Poetry.* He is also on the planning committee of the Mikebara Poetry Festival, a yearly celebration featuring poetry and painting from around Japan. His poems strive to convey the hatefulness of war and the preciousness of peace and focus on such themes as the horror of air raids and the souls of those who died in them; the death of his uncle who was killed in the war; and the sadness of his parents, who lost their house.

CLARIBEL ALEGRÍA is a well-known Nicaraguan poet, essayist, and novelist. Alegría is the author of numerous books of poetry including *Casting Off, Sorrow, Umbrales,* and *La Mujer del Río.* In 2006 she was awarded the Neustadt International Prize for Literature.

PAMELA ALEXANDER spent three years traveling North America in an RV with her cat Metta, after teaching creative writing for many years at Oberlin College and MIT. Now settled in Tucson, she has published nonfiction essays and is completing her fifth book of poems. She serves on the editorial board of *Field.*

LUIS ALBERTO AMBROGGIO is an internationally known poet and the author of seventeen collections of poetry, including *Difficult Beauty, The Wind's Archeology* (winner of a 2013 International Latino Book Award), and *We Are All Whitman.* With numerous recognitions and awards, his poetry, translated into several languages, has been included in the Archives of Hispanic-American Literature of the Library of Congress. https://en.wikipedia.org/wiki/Luis_Alberto_Ambroggio.

DOUG ANDERSON's most recent book is *Horse Medicine*.

HOMERO ARIDJIS is one of Latin America's greatest living writers. He is a pioneering environmental activist, two-term president of PEN International, and former Mexican ambassador to Switzerland, the Netherlands, and UNESCO. His most recent work is *News of the Earth*, a compendium of Aridjis' lifelong relationship with the natural world; many of his forty-eight books of poetry and prose have been translated into a dozen languages, and he has been awarded important literary and environmental prizes in Mexico, France, Italy, the United States, and Serbia.

JENNIFER H. ATKINSON is the author of five collections of poetry, most recently, *The Thinking Eye*. Her poems have appeared in many journals, including *Field, Image, Witness, Poecology, Terrain, Cincinnati Review*, and the *Missouri Review*. She teaches in the MFA and BFA programs at George Mason University.

DAVID ATTWOOLL has poetry in various anthologies and magazines and was a winner of the 2013 Poetry Business prize with *Surfacing*. *Ground Work* followed, and his first full collection is *The Sound Ladder*. David lives in Oxford, England, where he works in publishing and plays drums in a street band. For more information, visit http://www .davidattwoollpoetry.co.uk.

DAVID BAKER's most recent poetry volumes are *Scavenger Loop* and *Never-Ending Birds*, which won the Theodore Roethke Memorial Poetry Prize in 2011. His latest prose book is *Show Me Your Environment: Essays on Poetry, Poets, and Poems*. He teaches at Denison University and is poetry editor of the *Kenyon Review*.

JOHN BALABAN is the author of twelve books of poetry and prose, which have won the Academy of American Poets' Lamont Prize and a National Poetry Series Selection. His poetry has received two nominations for the National Book Award. His *Locusts at the Edge of Summer: New and Selected Poems* won the 1998 William Carlos Williams Award from the Poetry Society of America.

SAMIYA BASHIR's books of poetry *Field Theories, Gospel*, and *Where the Apple Falls* and anthologies, including *Role Call: A Generational Anthology of Social & Political Black Literature & Art*, exist. Sometimes she makes poems of dirt. Sometimes zeros and ones. Sometimes variously rendered text. Sometimes light. She lives in Portland, Oregon, with a magic cat who shares her obsession with trees and blackbirds and occasionally crashes her classes and poetry salons at Reed College.

GABRIELLA M. BELFIGLIO has been published widely in anthologies and journals. She works as an artist and teacher in Brooklyn, New York. For more information, visit www .gabriellabelfigio.info.

WENDELL BERRY was born in Henry County, Kentucky, in 1934. The author of more than forty works of fiction, nonfiction, and poetry, Berry has been the recipient of numerous awards and honors, including a Wallace Stegner Fellowship, a Guggenheim Foundation, a Lannan Foundation Award for Non-Fiction, the National Humanities Medal, and Membership in the Fellowship of Southern Writers. His most recent books of poetry include *This Day: Sabbath Poem Collected and New*, *A Small Porch*, and *Roots to Save the Earth*.

TARA BETTS is the author of *Break the Habit* and *Arc & Hue* as well as the chapbooks *7 x 7: Kwansabas* and *The Greatest!: An Homage to Muhammad Ali*. She is currently a visiting lecturer at University of Illinois–Chicago.

KIMBERLY BLAESER, Anishinaabe writer, photographer, and scholar, is the author of three poetry collections—most recently *Apprenticed to Justice*—and the editor of *Traces in Blood, Bone, and Stone: Contemporary Ojibwe Poetry*. A professor at the University of Wisconsin–Milwaukee and the Wisconsin poet laureate (2015–16), Blaeser is also a member of the Aldo Leopold Foundation Board of Directors and an editorial board member for both the American Indian Lives series of the University of Nebraska Press and the Native American Series of the Michigan State University Press. Blaeser is currently at work on a collection, *Ancient Light*, which includes ekphrastic poetry and a form she calls "Picto-Poems."

JODY BOLZ is the author of *Shadow Play* and *A Lesson in Narrative Time*. A former writer and editor for the Wilderness Society and the Nature Conservancy, she has published widely in literary magazines—*American Scholar*, *Indiana Review*, *Ploughshares*, *Poetry East*, and *Prairie Schooner* among them—and in many anthologies. She edits *Poet Lore*, America's oldest poetry journal, founded in 1889.

BRIAN BRODEUR is the author of the poetry collections *Natural Causes* and *Other Latitudes*, as well as the poetry chapbooks *Local Fauna* and *So the Night Cannot Go On without Us*. Assistant professor of English at Indiana University East, he lives with his wife and daughter in the Whitewater River valley.

SARAH BROWNING is cofounder and executive director of *Split This Rock: Poetry of Provocation & Witness* and an associate fellow of the Institute for Policy Studies. Author of *Whiskey in the Garden of Eden* and coeditor of *D.C. Poets against the War: An Anthology*, she is the recipient of artist fellowships from the D.C. Commission on the Arts and Humanities, a Creative Communities Initiative grant, and the People Before Profits Poetry Prize.

DENNIS BRUTUS was an activist and writer who lived from November 1924 to December 2009. He was well known for his published collections, the last being *It Is The Constant Image Of Your Face: A Dennis Brutus Reader*. In 2008, the South African Department of Arts and Culture awarded him the Lifetime Honorary Award for his lifelong dedication to African and world poetry and the arts.

ESTHELA CALDERÓN, born in Telica, Nicaragua, in 1970, is the author of *Soledad*; *Amor y conciencia*; *Soplo de corriente vital*, a pioneering collection of ethnobotanical poetry; *Coyol quebrado*; *Los huesos de mi abuelo*; and *Las manos que matan*. She is the director of the Promotora Cultural Leonesa in León, Nicaragua, and teaches at St. Lawrence University, where she edits the online cultural journal *Aquí y allá*.

LAUREN CAMP is the author of three books, most recently *One Hundred Hungers*, winner of the Dorset Prize. She is a Black Earth Institute Fellow and the producer/host of *Audio Saucepan* on Santa Fe Public Radio. For more information, visit www.lauren-camp.com.

CHRISTIAN CAMPBELL is the author of *Running the Dusk*, which won the Aldeburgh First Collection Prize and was a finalist for the Forward Prize for the Best First Collection and the Cave Canem Poetry Prize, among many other awards. *Running the Dusk* was recently translated into Spanish and published in Cuba as *Correr el Crepúsculo*. His current work includes a book on poetry and diaspora and a series of essays on Jean-Michel Basquiat commissioned for exhibitions in Canada, the United States, and the United Kingdom, for which he received the Art Writing Award from the Ontario Association of Art Galleries.

ERNESTO CARDENAL is a Nicaraguan priest, poet, and politician. His works of poetry include *Zero Hour*, *Homage to the American Indian*, and *The Origin of the Species*. Cardenal was nominated for the Nobel Prize in Literature in 2005 and has won the Queen Sofia Prize for Ibero-American Poetry.

BRENDA CÁRDENAS is the author of *Boomerang* and the chapbooks *Bread of the Earth / The Last Colors* with Roberto Harrison and *From the Tongues of Brick and Stone*. Her poems and essays have appeared or are forthcoming in *Latina/o Poetics: The Art of Poetry*, *The Golden Shovel Anthology*, *Poetry*, *City Creatures: Animal Encounters in the Chicago Wilderness*, *Angels of the Americlypse: New Latino/a Writing*, *The Wind Shifts: New Latino Poetry*, and *Rattle*, among many others. Cárdenas, an associate professor in the creative writing program at the University of Wisconsin–Milwaukee, served as the Milwaukee poet laureate from 2010 to 2012.

LORNA DEE CERVANTES, an award-winning Chicana poet, a feminist, and a political writer, is the author of five books of poetry. Her most recent collection is *Sueño: New Poems*, published by Wings Press in 2013. Cervantes has been the recipient of many honors and awards, including a Lila Wallace-Reader's Digest Award, the American Book Award, the Paterson Prize for Poetry, and a Latino Literature Award.

DANE CERVINE's latest poetry book is *How Therapists Dance*, from Plain View Press, which also published his previous book, *The Jeweled Net of Indra*. His poems have been chosen by Adrienne Rich for a National Writers Union Award and by Tony Hoagland as a finalist for the Wabash Poetry Prize, among other awards. Look for his essays at *TriQuarterly*, *Contrary*, *Turning Wheel*, and *Miramar*. For more information, visit www .DaneCervine.typepad.com.

HAYAN CHARARA is the author of three poetry books, most recently *Something Sinister*. He also edited an anthology of contemporary Arab American poetry, *Inclined to Speak*. Born in Detroit, Michigan, he lived many years in New York City and now resides in Houston, Texas.

CHEN CHEN is the author of the chapbooks *Set the Garden on Fire* and *Kissing the Sphinx*. A Kundiman Fellow, his work has appeared in *Poetry*, *Narrative*, *Drunken Boat*, and *The Best American Poetry 2015*. He is pursuing a PhD in English and creative writing at Texas Tech University.

GRANT CLAUSER is the author of the books *Necessary Myths* and *The Trouble with Rivers*. His poems have appeared in the *American Poetry Review*, *Cheat River Review*, *Cortland Review*, *The Literary Review*, *Painted Bride Quarterly*, and others. By day he writes about electronics and daydreams about fly-fishing. He teaches workshops at Musehouse and runs the blog www.unIambic.com.

LUCILLE CLIFTON was an American poet who lived from June 1936 to February 2010. Clifton's work focused on the African American experience and strength during adversity. She was the first author to have two books chosen as finalists for a Pulitzer Prize, *Good Woman: Poems and a Memoir, 1969–1980* and *Next: New Poems*, and in 2007 she was awarded the prestigious Ruth Lilly Poetry Prize.

MARTHA COLLINS has published eight books of poetry, most recently *Admit One: An American Scrapbook*, as well as four volumes of cotranslated Vietnamese poetry. She has won numerous awards for her work, including fellowships from the NEA, the Bunting Institute, the Witter Bynner Foundation, and the Ingram Merrill Foundation. Founder of the creative writing program at UMass-Boston, Collins served for ten years as Pauline Delaney Professor of Creative Writing at Oberlin College, and is currently editor-at-large for Oberlin's *Field* magazine.

STEPHEN COLLIS is the author of ten books, most recently *Once in Blockadia*. He was sued for $5.6 million by U.S. energy giant Kinder Morgan while working in opposition to the Trans Mountain Pipeline expansion in 2014. The oil company's lawyers read his poetry in court as "evidence."

MAHMOUD DARWISH was a Palestinian poet who lived from March 1941 to August 2008. Darwish published over thirty volumes of poetry, including *Leaves of Olives* and *Unfortunately, It Was Paradise: Selected Poems*. He earned the Lannan Cultural Freedom Prize from the Lannan Foundation, the Lenin Peace Prize, and the Knight of Arts and Belles Lettres Medal from France.

HAYES DAVIS's first volume, *Let Our Eyes Linger*, was published by Poetry Mutual Press. His work has appeared in *New England Review*, *Poet Lore*, *Gargoyle*, *Fledgling Rag*, *Beltway Poetry Quarterly*, *Delaware Poetry Review*, *Kinfolks*, and several anthologies, and he was nominated for a Pushcart Prize in 2016. Holder of a masters of fine arts from the University of Maryland, he lives in Silver Spring, Maryland, with his wife, poet Teri Ellen Cross Davis, and their children.

HEATHER LYNN DAVIS is an early morning writer, publications manager, and mom who lives and dreams in the Shenandoah Valley. Her book *The Lost Tribe of Us* won the 2007 Main Street Rag Poetry Book Award. A graduate of Hollins University and Syracuse University, she is married to the poet Jose Padua.

BRIAN KOMEI DEMPSTER's debut book of poetry, *Topaz*, was published by Four Way Books in 2013 and received the 15 Bytes 2014 Book Award in Poetry. Dempster is editor of *From Our Side of the Fence: Growing Up in America's Concentration Camps*, which received a 2007 Nisei Voices Award from the National Japanese American Historical Society, and of *Making Home from War: Stories of Japanese American Exile and Resettlement*. He is a professor of rhetoric and language and a faculty member in Asian Pacific American studies at the University of San Francisco, where he also serves as director of administration for the master of arts in Asia Pacific studies.

MING DI is a Chinese poet and translator living in the United States, author of *River Merchant's Wife*, editor of *New Cathay—Contemporary Chinese Poetry*, and cotranslator of *Empty Chairs—Poems by Liu Xia*.

NATALIE DIAZ was born and raised in the Fort Mojave Indian Village in Needles, California, on the banks of the Colorado River. She is Mojave and an enrolled member of the Gila River Indian Tribe. Her first poetry collection, *When My Brother Was an*

Aztec, was published by Copper Canyon Press. Diaz teaches at Arizona State University and the Institute of American Indian Arts Low Rez MFA program. She splits her time between the east coast and Mohave Valley, Arizona, where she works to revitalize the Mojave language.

LECONTÉ DILL was born and raised in South Central Los Angeles, and is currently an assistant professor at the SUNY Downstate School of Public Health. LeConté has participated in the VONA Voices and Cave Canem writing workshops, and her work has been featured in the *Berkeley Poetry Review*, the *Feminist Wire*, and *Los Angeles Magazine*. She is committed to amplifying the voices of marginalized groups through their own words, having facilitated poetry workshops and copublished poetry anthologies with urban youth of color in Oakland, California, and LGBTQ migrants in Johannesburg, South Africa.

CAMILLE T. DUNGY is the author of *Smith Blue, Suck on the Marrow*, and *What to Eat, What to Drink, What to Leave for Poison*. She edited *Black Nature: Four Centuries of African American Nature Poetry*, coedited the *From the Fishhouse* poetry anthology, and served as assistant editor for *Gathering Ground: A Reader Celebrating Cave Canem's First Decade*. Her honors include an American Book Award, two Northern California Book Awards, a California Book Award silver medal, a Sustainable Arts Foundation grant, and a fellowship from the NEA. Dungy is currently a professor in the English Department at Colorado State University.

ZEIN EL-AMINE was born and raised in Lebanon. He has an MFA in poetry from the University of Maryland. His poems have been published by *Wild River Review, Folio, Foreign Policy in Focus, Beltway Quarterly, DC Poets against the War Anthology, Penumbra, GYST*, and *Joybringer*. His short stories have appeared in *Uno Mas, Jadaliyya, Middle East Report*, and *Bound Off*.

DANIELA ELZA's work has appeared nationally and internationally in over one hundred publications. Her poetry collections are *the weight of dew, the book of It*, and *milk tooth bane bone*, of which David Abram says, "Out of the ache of the present moment, Daniela Elza has crafted something spare and irresistible, an open armature for wonder."

KATHY ENGEL has been writing poems and working at reimagining the world for a long time. She is currently chair of the Department of Art & Public Policy at the Tisch School of the Arts, NYU. She loves to swim, dance, cook and eat, and be with family and community.

LOUISE ERDRICH is the author of fifteen novels as well as volumes of poetry, children's books, and short stories. Her novel *The Plague of Doves* won the Anisfield-Wolf Book

Award and was a finalist for the Pulitzer Prize, and her debut novel, *Love Medicine*, was the winner of the National Book Critics Circle Award. In 2015 she was awarded the Library of Congress Prize for American Fiction.

MARTÍN ESPADA has published almost twenty books as a poet, editor, essayist, and translator. His newest collection of poems is called *Vivas to Those Who Have Failed* (2016). The recipient of the Shelley Memorial Award and a Guggenheim Fellowship, Espada is a professor of English at the University of Massachusetts–Amherst.

TARFIA FAIZULLAH is the author of *Seam* and *Register of Illuminated Villages*. Her poems appear widely in periodicals and anthologies; have been translated into Chinese, Spanish, and Bengali; and have received numerous awards, including a Pushcart Prize and a Fulbright fellowship. Tarfia codirects the Organic Weapon Arts Chapbook Press & Video Series and is the Nicholas Delbanco Visiting Professor of Poetry at University of Michigan's Helen Zell Writers' Program.

BETTY FERBER translated Homero Aridjis's novels *1492: The Life and Times of Juan Cabezon of Castile*, *The Lord of the Last Days: Visions of the Year 1000*, and *Persephone*, as well as *News of the Earth*, a compendium of Aridjis's lifelong relationship with the natural world. As international coordinator of the Group of 100, she shared the Mikhail Gorbachev / Green Cross Millennium Award for International Environmental Leadership with Homero Aridjis.

ALEC FINLAY is a Scotland-born artist and poet whose work crosses over a range of media and forms. Finlay established Morning Star in 1990, a press specializing in collaborations between artists and poets, including the award-winning Pocketbooks series (1999–2002). He has published over thirty books and won six Scottish Design Awards, including two Grand Prix Awards (2001, 2015). Recent publications include *A Variety of Cultures*, *ebban an' flowan*, *a better tale to tell*, and *Global Oracle*.

ANN FISHER-WIRTH has published four books of poems: *Dream Cabinet*, *Carta Marina*, *Blue Window*, and *Five Terraces*. With Laura-Gray Street, she coedited the groundbreaking *Ecopoetry Anthology*. A fellow of Black Earth Institute, she has held two senior Fulbrights (Switzerland, Sweden), served as president of ASLE, and received numerous awards for her writing and teaching. She teaches at the University of Mississippi. Her current project is a collaborative poetry/photography manuscript called "Mississippi" with the acclaimed photographer Maude Schuyler Clay.

YAEL FLUSBERG is known for teaching Pen & Pose, themed workshops that weave yoga practices with writing as a way to dive into mindful exploration of the self. Her nineteen-poem collection, *The Last of My Village*, won *Poetica Magazine*'s 2010 chapbook contest; other work has recently appeared in *The Poetry of Yoga*, Jacar Press's *and love*, and has been broadcast on NPR's *Latino USA*. For more information, visit www .yaelflusberg.com.

JENNIFER ELISE FOERSTER is an alumna of the Institute of American Indian Arts, received her MFA from the Vermont College of Fine Arts, and is completing a PhD at the University of Denver. She is the recipient of a 2017 NEA Creative Writing Fellowship and a Lannan Foundation Writing Residency Fellowship and was a Wallace Stegner Fellow in Poetry at Stanford University. She is the author of *Leaving Tulsa* and *Bright Raft in the Afterweather*.

ANGÉLICA FREITAS is the author of *Rilke shake* and *Um útero é do tamanho de um punho*. Her graphic novel, *Guadalupe*, published by Companhia das Letras, was illustrated by Odyr Bernardi, and her poems have been translated into and published in German, Spanish, and English. She coedits the poetry journal *Modo de Usar & Co.* and lives in Pelotas, Rio Grande do Sul, Brazil.

JASON FRYE is a poet, editor, and travel writer living in North Carolina.

JUAN CARLOS GALEANO, born in the Amazon region of Colombia, is a poet, translator, and essayist whose most recent publications include *Amazonia y otros poemas* and *Historias del viento*. Throughout his career, Galeano has published five collections of poetry, all of which draw inspiration from Amazonian cosmologies and the modern world. He currently teaches Latin American poetry and cultures of the Amazon basin at Florida State University.

ROSS GAY is the author of, most recently, *Catalog of Unabashed Gratitude*. He teaches in the MFA program at Indiana University, Bloomington. He is also on the board of the Bloomington Community Orchard and is dreaming of his garden right now.

MARIA MAZZIOTTI GILLAN is a recipient of AWP's 2014 George Garrett Award, *Poets & Writers'* 2011 Barnes & Noble Writers for Writers Award, and the 2008 American Book Award for *All That Lies between Us*. She has published twenty books and is founder/ executive director of the Poetry Center at Passaic County Community College, editor of the *Paterson Literary Review*, and director of creative writing / professor of English at Binghamton University-SUNY. Visit her website at mariagillan.com.

KIM GOLDBERG is the author of seven books of poetry and nonfiction, including *Red Zone* and *Ride Backwards on Dragon*. She holds a degree in biology from the University of Oregon and lives on Vancouver Island, where she is an avid birdwatcher and nature lover. Join her on twitter at @KimPigSquash. Website: www.PigSquashPress.com.

RIGOBERTO GONZÁLEZ is the author of seventeen books. He is professor of English at Rutgers-Newark, the state university of New Jersey, and on the board of directors of the Association of Writers & Writing Programs.

SARA GOUDARZI is a Brooklyn writer and poet. Born in Tehran, she grew up in Iran, Kenya, and the United States.

LILACE MELLIN GUIGNARD lives with her husband and two children in rural Pennsylvania, where she teaches poetry writing, women's studies, and rock climbing at Mansfield University. Her work has appeared in the journals *Calyx*, *poemmemoirstory*, *Louisiana Literature*, *Paterson Literary Review*, *Ecotone*, and *Poetry*.

CELESTE GUZMÁN MENDOZA is a published poet, essayist, and playwright. She is codirector and a cofounder of CantoMundo, a workshop for Latina/o poets. She currently works at LLILAS Benson at the University of Texas at Austin.

SAM HAMILL is the author of more than forty books, including acclaimed translations of classical Chinese and Japanese poetry, four volumes of essays, and sixteen collections of poetry, most recently *Habitation: Collected Poems*.

JOY HARJO has published seven books of poetry, including her most recent collection, *Conflict Resolution for Holy Beings*. Her memoir *Crazy Brave* was awarded the PEN USA Literary Award in Creative Nonfiction. She was also honored with the Academy of American Poets Wallace Stevens Award.

ALLISON ADELLE HEDGE COKE's books include *Year of the Rat*; *Dog Road Woman*; *Off-Season City Pipe*; *Blood Run*; *Streaming*; *Rock, Ghost, Willow, Deer*; *Sing: Poetry of the Indigenous Americas*; *Effigies*; and *Effigies II*. Hedge Coke, who came of age in North Carolina, working fields, factories, and waters, directs the Literary Sandhill Cranefest; is currently at work on a film, *Red Dust: Resiliency in the Dirty Thirties*; and performs with her band, Rd Klã. Her awards include a King*Chavez*Parks Award, American Book Award, Lifetime Achievement Award from Native Writers' Circle of the Americas, and multiple Wordcraft Circle of Native Writers awards, including Wordcrafter of the Year, Mentor of the Year, and Editor and Writer of the Year awards.

BRIAN PATRICK HESTON is the author of the chapbook *Latchkey Kids* and the full-length collection *If You Find Yourself*. His poems have appeared in such publications as *North American Review*, *Poet Lore*, *Spoon River Poetry Review*, *River Styx*, and *Prairie Schooner*. Presently, he is a PhD candidate in literature and creative writing at Georgia State University.

TIFFANY HIGGINS is author of *And Aeneas Stares into Her Helmet*, selected by Evie Shockley as winner of the Carolina Wren Poetry Prize. Her poems have appeared in *Poetry*, *Kenyon Review*, *Massachusetts Review*, *Taos Journal of Poetry & Art*, *Kenyon Review*, *From the Fishhouse*, *Catamaran Literary Reader*, and other journals. She translates contemporary Brazilian writers and blogs on emerging news related to Brazilian indigenous and poor peoples' social ecologies, including resistance movements at http://tifhiggins.blogspot.com.

BRENDA HILLMAN is the author of nine collections of poetry from Wesleyan University Press, the most recent of which are *Practical Water* and *Seasonal Works with Letters on Fire*. Her work has received the Los Angeles Times Book Award, the William Carlos Williams Prize, and the Griffin International Poetry Prize. She lives in the Bay Area, where she is Olivia Filippi Professor at Saint Mary's College. Visit her on the web at http://www.blueflowerarts.com/brenda-hillman.

JANE HIRSHFIELD's most recent books are *The Beauty* (poems) and *Ten Windows: How Great Poems Transform the World*. Her work has appeared in the *New Yorker*, the *Atlantic*, *Harper's*, the *New York Review of Books*, *Poetry*, and eight editions of *The Best American Poetry*. A former chancellor of the Academy of American Poets, she has a special interest in the confluence of poetry and science.

EVERETT HOAGLAND is emeritus professor at the University of Massachusetts–Dartmouth and from 1994 to 1998 was the first poet laureate of New Bedford. His work has been regularly published in national and international literary periodicals and anthologies (including college textbooks) since 1970. His most recent books include . . . *Here* . . . *New & Selected Poems*, *Ocean Voices: An Anthology of Ocean Poems*, and his self-published collection titled *The Music: And Other Selected Poems*. His awards include the 2015 Langston Hughes Society Award.

LINDA HOGAN is a poet, public speaker, and writer of fiction and essays. Her recently published works include *Dark. Sweet.: New and Selected Poems*, *Indios*, and *Rounding the Human Corners*. Hogan has received a number of awards for her work, including the American Book Award, the Mountains and Plains Book Award, and the Lannan Literary Award for Poetry.

AILISH HOPPER is the author of *Dark~Sky Society* and the chapbook *Bird in the Head*, which won the Center for Book Arts Prize. Individual work has appeared in *Agni*, *APR*, *Harvard Review*, *Ploughshares*, and *Poetry*, and she has received support from Vermont Studio Center, MacDowell Colony, and Yaddo. She teaches at Goucher College in Baltimore.

RANDALL HORTON is the recipient of the Gwendolyn Brooks Poetry Award, the Bea González Poetry Award, and most recently a National Endowment of the Arts Fellowship in Literature. Randall is a member of the experimental performance group Heroes Are Gang Leaders and an associate professor of English at the University of New Haven.

ELIZABETH JACOBSON is the author of the poetry collection *Her Knees Pulled In* and a chapbook, *A Brown Stone*. She is the founding director of the WingSpan Poetry Project, which conducts weekly poetry classes for residents at homeless and battered-family shelters in Santa Fe, New Mexico, and Miami, Florida. Her honors include the Mountain West Writers' Award from *Western Humanities Review*, the Jim Sagel Prize for poetry from *Puerto del Sol*, a grant from New Mexico Literary Arts, and a residency from the Herekeke Foundation.

JAIME LEE JARVIS is a freelance writer/editor and former Peace Corps volunteer. Her childhood in southern California and her visit to the Aral Sea's (former) southern shore in 1999 sparked a deep commitment to environmental issues in the United States and internationally.

HONORÉE FANONNE JEFFERS is the author of four books of poetry, *The Gospel of Barbecue*, *Outlandish Blues*, *Red Clay Suite*, and *The Glory Gets*. She has won fellowships from the National Endowment for the Arts and from the Witter Bynner Foundation through the Library of Congress, and she is an elected member of the American Antiquarian Society. She teaches at the University of Oklahoma.

SAEED JONES's debut poetry collection *Prelude to Bruis* was the winner of the 2015 PEN/Joyce Osterweil Award for Poetry and the 2015 Stonewall Book Award/Barbara Gittings Literature Award and a finalist for the 2015 National Book Critics Circle Award. The book was also a finalist for 2015 awards from Lambda Literary and the Publishing Triangle. His poetry and essays have appeared in such publications as the *New York Times*, *Guernica*, *Ebony*, and *Best American Poetry* and on NPR. Saeed won a Pushcart Prize for poetry in 2013 and is BuzzFeed's executive editor of culture.

JUNE JORDAN was a Caribbean-American poet, writer, playwright, children's writer, and human rights activist who lived from July 1936 to June 2002. Author of twenty-six books, her works included *Who Look at Me*, *Soldier: A Poet's Childhood*, and *Civil Wars*. Jordan earned numerous awards including the Lila Wallace Reader's Digest Writers Award and the Ground Breakers–Dream Makers Award from the Woman's Foundation in 1994.

JOAN NAVIYUK KANE lives in Alaska with her husband and sons. Her books include *The Cormorant Hunter's Wife*, *Hyperboreal*, *The Straits*, and *Milk Black Carbon*. She teaches in the graduate creative writing program at the Institute of American Indian Arts and is a judge for the 2017 Griffin Poetry Prize.

DOUGLAS KEARNEY most recent collection, *Buck Studies*, is a CLMP Firecracker awardee and California Book Award silver medalist. *Publisher's Weekly* called Kearney's *Mess and Mess and* "an extraordinary book." He teaches at CalArts.

ALAN KING is the author of *Drift*. He's also a Cave Canem graduate fellow and holds a master of fine arts in creative writing from the Stonecoast Program at the University of Southern Maine. He lives in Bowie, Maryland, with his wife, Tosin, and their daughter, Jazmyn.

YUSEF KOMUNYAKAA's books of poetry include *Neon Vernacular* (for which he received the Pulitzer Prize), *Taboo*, *Warhorses*, *The Chameleon Couch*, and *The Emperor of Water Clocks*. His plays, performance art, and libretti include *Wakonda's Dream*, *Saturnalia*, *Testimony*, and *Gilgamesh: A Verse Play*. He teaches at New York University.

ELEE KRALJII GARDINER directs Thursdays Writing Collective. She is the editor and publisher of seven anthologies from the collective and the coeditor with John Asfour of *V6A: Writing from Vancouver's Downtown Eastside*. *Serpentine Loop* is her first book of poetry. A frequent collaborator, she is originally from Boston.

CHRISTI KRAMER holds a PhD from the University of British Columbia, where her interdisciplinary work, arising from something she witnessed while writing with children exiled by war, was a poetic inquiry toward a deeper understanding of poetic image and imagination, as a "wellspring that feeds the building of peace." Her MFA in poetry is from George Mason University. Christi makes her home between Northern Idaho (Kootenai and Kalispel territories), where she was born, and Vancouver, British Columbia (Coast Salish Territory).

AARON KREUTER lives in Toronto, Canada, where he spends his time writing, paddling, and pursuing a PhD in English literature at York University. His poem "Fan Fiction" was included in *Best Canadian Poetry 2014*. His first book of poems, *Arguments for Lawn Chairs*, came out in fall 2016 from Guernica Editions.

QURAYSH ALI LANSANA is the author of eight books of poetry, three textbooks, and a children's book; the editor of eight anthologies; and coauthor of a book of pedagogy. He is a faculty member of the creative writing program of the School of the Art Institute of Chicago. His most recent books include *The BreakBeat Poets: New American Poetry in the Age of Hip Hop* and *The Walmart Republic*.

DORIANNE LAUX is the author of several books of poetry, most recently, *The Book of Men*. She teaches poetry at North Carolina State University and is a member of the founding faculty of Pacific University's low residency MFA program.

SHARA LESSLEY, a former Wallace Stegner Fellow at Stanford University, is the author of *Two-Headed Nightingale*. Her awards include the Mary Wood Fellowship from Washington College, an Artist Fellowship from the state of North Carolina, the Diane Middlebrook Poetry Fellowship from the University of Wisconsin, Colgate University's Olive B. O'Connor Fellowship, and a "Discovery"/*The Nation* prize. A recent resident of the Middle East, Shara was awarded a 2015 Poetry Fellowship from the NEA and is currently editing an anthology of essays on poetry and place with the poet Bruce Snider.

DENISE LEVERTOV was a British-born American poet who lived from October 1923 to December 1997. Levertov wrote and published over twenty books of poetry including *The Double Image*, *Here and Now*, and *Poems 1972–1982*. Among the many awards Lervetov received were the Shelley Memorial Award, the Robert Frost Medal, the Lenore Marshall Prize, the Lannan Award, and a Guggenheim Fellowship.

PIPPA LITTLE is Scottish and lives in North East England, where she is a Royal Literary Fund Fellow at Newcastle University. *Overwintering*, from OxfordPoets/Carcanet Press, came out in 2016, and she is working on her second collection.

CECILIA LLOMPART was born in Puerto Rico and raised in Florida. Her first collection, *The Wingless*, was published by Carnegie Mellon University Press in the spring of 2014. She is the recipient of two awards from the Academy of American Poets and a fellowship from the Dickinson House, in addition to having been a finalist for the Field Office agency's 2016 Postcard Prize in poetry. In 2015, she founded the New Wanderers Collective. She currently divides her time between Paris and elsewhere.

CHRISTINA LOVIN is the author of *Echo*, *A Stirring in the Dark*, *What We Burned for Warmth*, *Little Fires*, and *Flesh*. Her award-winning writing is widely published and anthologized, and has been supported by the Elizabeth George Foundation, the Kentucky Foundation for Women, and the Kentucky Arts Council. She lives in Kentucky, where she collects wool, dust, rejection letters, and shelter dogs and teaches writing at Eastern Kentucky University.

ELIZABETH MACKLIN is the author of the poetry collections *A Woman Kneeling in the Big City* and *You've Just Been Told* and the translator of a number of works by the Basque writer Kirmen Uribe, most recently his award-winning novel *Bilbao–New York–Bilbao*.

JACQUELINE MARCUS's new collection of poems, *Summer Rains*, was recently published by Iris Press. She is the author of *Close to the Shore* and the editor of ForPoetry.com / EnvironmentalPress.com. She's a contributing writer at truthout.org.

MORTON MARCUS, the author of over five hundred poems that appeared in literary journals across the country, lived from September 1936 to October 2009. His poetry is collected in eleven volumes, including *Origins*, *Pages from a Scrapbook of Immigrants*, and *The Dark Figure in the Doorway: Last Poems*.

JAMAAL MAY is the author of two collections of poems, *Hum*, published in 2013, and *The Big Book of Exit Strategies*, published in 2016. *Hum* has won a Beatrice Hawley Award and an American Library Association Notable Book Award and was an NAACP Image Award nominee. He is currently living Detroit and serving as Co–Poetry Editor for *Solstice*, teaching in the Vermont College of Fine Arts MFA Program, and codirecting the Organic Weapon Arts Chapbook and Video Series.

MOLLY MCGLENNEN was born and raised in Minneapolis, Minnesota, and is of Anishinaabe and European descent. Currently an associate professor of English and Native American studies at Vassar College, she is the author of a collection of poetry, *Fried Fish and Flour Biscuits*, published by Salt's award-winning Earthworks Series of indigenous writers and a critical monograph *Creative Alliances: The Transnational Designs of Indigenous Women's Poetry*, which earned the Beatrice Medicine Award for outstanding scholarship in American Indian literature.

JOSHUA MCKINNEY is the author of three books of poetry: *Saunter*, *The Novice Mourner*, and *Mad Cursive*. His work has appeared widely in such journals as *Colorado Review*, *Denver Quarterly*, *Kenyon Review*, *New American Writing*, and *Ploughshares*. Coeditor of the online poetry journal *Clade Song*, he teaches poetry writing and literature at California State University, Sacramento.

GEORGE MCWHIRTER is transatlantically anthologized in *The Penguin Book of Canadian Verse*, edited by Ralph Gustafson, and *Irish Writing in the Twentieth Century*, edited by David Pierce. His most recent books of poetry are *The Incorrection* and *The Anachronicles*. His latest book of stories, *The Gift Of Women*, was published by Exile Editions in 2014, and he served as Vancouver's inaugural poet laureate from 2007 to 2009.

JANE MEAD is the author of four full-length books of poetry, most recently *Money Money Money / Water Water Water*, from Alice James Books. She is the recipient of grants and awards from the Whiting, Guggenheim, and Lannan Foundations and has taught at many colleges and universities. She farms in northern California.

W. S. MERWIN is an American poet who has authored over fifty books of poetry, translation, and prose, having most recently published *Garden Time* and *The Moon before Morning*. Merwin has received many awards for his poetry including the Pulitzer Prize for Poetry, the Aiken Taylor Award for Modern American Poetry, and the Lenore Marshall Poetry Prize. In 2010, with his wife Paula, he cofounded the Merwin Conservancy, a nonprofit organization dedicated to preserving his off-grid hand-built home and the eighteen-acre restored forest he built in Haiku, Maui.

PHILIP METRES is the author of *Pictures at an Exhibition*, *Sand Opera*, *A Concordance of Leaves*, and *To See the Earth*, among other works. A recipient of the Lannan, two National Endowment for the Arts awards, and two Arab American Book Awards, he is professor of English at John Carroll University.

DUNYA MIKHAIL is an Iraqi American poet. Her newest book is *The Beekeeper: Rescuing the Stolen Women of Iraq*. Her other books include *The Iraqi Nights*, *Diary of A Wave outside the Sea*, and *The War Works Hard*.

AMY MILLER's writing has appeared in *Bellingham Review*, *Nimrod*, *Rattle*, ZYZZYVA, *Fine Gardening*, and *The Poet's Market*. She won the Cultural Center of Cape Cod National Poetry Competition, judged by Tony Hoagland, and has been a finalist for the Pablo Neruda Prize and the 49th Parallel Award. She lives in Ashland, Oregon, and blogs at writers-island.blogspot.com.

HIROMI MISHOU, a Japanese poet and doctor of the illness caused by the atomic bomb, as well as an atomic bomb victim, died last year in 2015. His fiancée died by atomic bomb in 1945.

PATRICIA MONAGHAN (1946–2012) was a poet, scholar, activist, and mentor and friend to hundreds. She was the author of six books of poetry and editor of several other books, with scholarship directed at woman's spirituality. A Quaker and organizer, she cofounded the Black Earth Institute, a think-tank for artists and scholars addressing and reconnecting spirit, earth, and social justice. She sought, connected, and wrote about roots in Ireland and found and wrote about her beloved Driftless Area in Wisconsin.

LENARD D. MOORE is a poet, fiction writer, essayist, and book reviewer, who teaches African American literature and creative writing at the University of Mount Olive, where he directs the literary festival. His literary works have appeared in *African American Review*, *Agni*, *Callaloo*, *Colorado Review*, *North American Review*, *North Dakota Quarterly*, *Obsidian*, *Prairie Schooner*, and *Valley Voices*, and he is the author of *A Temple Looming*, among other books. He is the founder and executive director of the Carolina African American Writers' Collective and cofounder of the Washington Street Writers Group.

TAHA MUHAMMAD ALI was a Palestinian poet and short story writer who lived from 1931 to October 2011. Ali was self-taught and began writing poetry in the 1970s. His collections in English include *Never Mind: Twenty Poems and a Story* and *So What: New and Selected Poems, 1971–2005*.

KRISTINE ONG MUSLIM is the author of several books of fiction and poetry, including most recently the short story collection *Age of Blight*. Her poems have appeared in *New Welsh Review*, *Southword*, and elsewhere. She grew up and continues to live in a rural town in southern Philippines.

MARILYN NELSON's prize-winning young adult books include *Carver: A Life in Poems* and *A Wreath for Emmett Till*. A former poet laureate of Connecticut, in 2012 Nelson was awarded the Frost Medal; in 2013 she was elected a chancellor of the Academy of American Poets. Her latest collections are *How I Discovered Poetry* and *My Seneca Village*.

AIMEE NEZHUKUMATATHIL is the author of three collections of poetry, most recently, *Lucky Fish*. She is the poetry editor of *Orion* magazine and her poems have appeared in the Best American Poetry series, *American Poetry Review*, *New England Review*, *Poetry*, and *Tin House*. She is professor of English at the State University of New York at Fredonia and in 2016–17, Nezhukumatathil will be the Grisham Writer-in-Residence at the University of Mississippi's MFA program.

VALERIE NIEMAN's second poetry collection, *Hotel Worthy*, was published in 2015. The author of three novels, the most recent being *Blood Clay*, she has held North Carolina and NEA creative writing fellowships. A graduate of Queens University of Charlotte and a former journalist, she teaches writing at North Carolina A&T State University.

MARGARET NOODIN received an MFA in creative writing and a PhD in English and linguistics from the University of Minnesota. She is currently an assistant professor at the University of Wisconsin–Milwaukee, where she also serves as the director of the Electa Quinney Institute for American Indian Education. She is the author of *Bawaajimo: A Dialect of Dreams in Anishinaabe Language and Literature* and *Weweni*, a collection of bilingual poems in Ojibwe and English.

NAOMI SHIHAB NYE grew up in Ferguson, Missouri; Jerusalem, Palestine; and San Antonio, Texas, and has always believed in justice for all—including animals and plants. She has written or edited thirty-five books.

TOLU OGUNLESI is a Nigerian journalist, poet, and communications consultant. His poetry and fiction have appeared in *Wasafiri*, *Magma*, *Sable*, the *London Magazine*, and elsewhere. He currently lives in Abuja, Nigeria.

TANURE OJAIDE is the Frank Porter Graham Professor of Africana Studies at the University of North Carolina at Charlotte. He has published many collections of poetry and works of scholarship and has won major awards for his creative writing.

SIMON J. ORTIZ is a widely read Native American poet of the Acoma Pueblo tribe. His works include *A Good Journey*, *This America*, and *Out There Somewhere*. Ortiz is the recipient of the New Mexico Humanities Council Humanitarian Award, the National Endowment for the Arts Discovery Award, the Lila Wallace Reader's Digest Writer's Award and in 1981 his work *From Sand Creek: Rising in This Heart Which Is Our America* received the Pushcart Prize in poetry.

WILFRED OWEN, an English soldier, was one of the leading poets of the First World War. Owen was known for his verses on the horrors of trench and gas warfare; his best-known works, most of which were published posthumously, include "Dulce et Decorum Est," "Insensibility," "Anthem for Doomed Youth," and "Futility." The first collection of Owen's poetry was published two years after his untimely death at the age of twenty-five in the year 1918.

JOSE PADUA was born in Washington, D.C. His poetry, fiction, and nonfiction have appeared in many journals, newspapers, and anthologies. After living in big cities like Washington and New York all his life, he now lives in the small town of Front Royal, Virginia, where he and his wife, the poet Heather Davis, write the blog *Shenandoah Breakdown*, http://shenandoahbreakdown.wordpress.com/.

GREGORY PARDLO is the author *Totem*, winner of the 2007 APR/Honickman First Book Prize, and *Digest*, winner of the 2015 Pulitzer Prize. He has received fellowships from the National Endowment for the Arts and the New York Foundation for the Arts.

STEPHEN DERWENT PARTINGTON lives in Machakos County, Kenya. The former poetry editor of East Africa's leading literary magazine, *Kwani?*, he has published two collections of poetry. The most recent, *How to Euthanise a Cactus*, concentrates on Kenya's postelection violence of 2007–8.

ELISE PASCHEN is the author, most recently, of *The Nightlife*, as well as *Bestiary* and *Infidelities*, the Nicholas Roerich Poetry Prize winner. Her poems have appeared in the *New Yorker*, *Poetry* and other magazines and anthologies. Coeditor of *Poetry Speaks* and *Poetry in Motion*, she teaches in the MFA writing program at the School of the Art Institute of Chicago.

NANCY K. PEARSON's second book of poems, *The Whole by Contemplation of a Single Bone*, won the Poets Out Loud Prize. Her book of poems *Two Minutes of Light* won the L.L. Winship/PEN New England Award. Her poems garnered two seven-month fellowships at the Fine Arts Work Center in Provincetown.

EMMY PÉREZ's newest poetry collection is *With the River on Our Face*. Her first collection *Solstice* was published as a second edition in 2011. Currently, she is an associate professor at the University of Texas Rio Grande Valley, where she teaches in the MFA in creative writing and Mexican American studies programs.

VIVIAN FAITH PRESCOTT is a fifth-generation Alaskan who lives on the small island of Wrangell in southeastern Alaska, at her family's fishcamp. She has an MFA from the University of Alaska Anchorage and a PhD in cross-cultural studies. She is the founder and facilitator of writers' groups in both Sitka and Wrangell, as well as cofounder of Petroglyph Press, a regional Alaskan chapbook press.

GRETCHEN PRIMACK is the author of two poetry collections, *Kind* and *Doris' Red Spaces*, and coauthor, with Jenny Brown, of *The Lucky Ones: My Passionate Fight for Farm Animals*. Her poems have appeared in the *Paris Review, Prairie Schooner, Borderlands, Field, Antioch Review, Ploughshares, Poet Lore*, and other journals.

TALA ABU RAHMEH is a writer and translator based in New York. Her poems have been published in a number of magazines and books including Naomi Shihab Nye's *Time to Let Me In: 25 under 25, LARB, 20*20* magazine, *Enizagam, 34th Parallel, Blast Furnace*, and *Kweli*. Parts of her memoir-in-progress were published in *Beirut Re-collected*, published by Tamyras Publishers and available in both French and English. Her poem "Cape Cod" was nominated for a Pushcart Prize.

HILA RATZABI was selected by Adrienne Rich as a recipient of a National Writers Union Poetry Prize, and she has been nominated for a Pushcart Prize. Her poetry has been published in *Narrative, Alaska Quarterly Review, Drunken Boat, Linebreak*, the *Nervous Breakdown*, and others. She holds an MFA from Sarah Lawrence College and lives in Philadelphia.

SHANE RHODES is the author of five books of poetry including his most recent *X: Poems and Anti-poems* and *Err*. Shane's awards include a National Magazine Gold Award for poetry, the P. K. Page Founder's Award for Poetry, and his work has been featured in *Best Canadian Poetry* in 2008, 2011, 2012, and 2014. Shane lives and writes in Ottawa, Canada.

ADRIENNE RICH was an American poet, essayist, and activist who lived from May 1929 to March 2012. She published more than thirty books of poetry and prose and won such honors as the Bollingen Prize, the Lannan Lifetime Achievement Award, the Academy of American Poets Fellowship, the Ruth Lilly Poetry Prize, the Lenore Marshall Poetry Prize, the National Book Award, and a MacArthur Fellowship; she was also a chancellor of the Academy of American Poets. In 1997 she refused the National Medal of Arts saying, Art "means nothing if it simply decorates the dinner table of the power which holds it hostage."

KATY RICHEY has received fellowships from Callaloo Creative Writing Workshops and the Cave Canem Foundation. She is the recipient of a 2015 Fine Arts Work Center Walker Scholarship for Writers of Color and a 2014 Maryland State Arts Council individual artist award for poetry. She hosts the Sunday Kind of Love reading series open mic at Busboys and Poets in Washington, D.C., sponsored by Split This Rock.

JORGE RIECHMANN, born in Madrid in 1962, is the author of *Futuralgia* and *Entreser*. He teaches Moral Philosophy at the Universidad Autónoma in Madrid, where he also collaborates with Ecologistas en Acción and Izquierda Anticapitalista.

LYNN RIGGS was a Cherokee poet, author, and playwright born on a farm in Verdigris Valley, Oklahoma. Riggs often wrote about life on the frontier and is most widely known for his play *Green Grow the Lilacs*, which was adapted into the landmark musical *Oklahoma!* Throughout his life, Riggs published twenty-one poems, plays, short stories, and a television script; eleven years before his death in 1954 he was inducted into the Oklahoma Hall of Fame for his literary success.

LISA RIZZO is the author of *Always a Blue House* and *In the Poem an Ocean*. Her work has also appeared in a variety of journals and anthologies such as *Calyx* and *Naugatuck River Review*. Two of her poems received first and second prizes in the 2011 Maggi H. Meyer Poetry Prize competition. For more information, visit www.lisarizzopoetry.com.

ED ROBERSON is the author of ten books of poetry including a chapbook, *Closest Pronunciation*, and his latest book, *To See the Earth before the End of the World*. He recently received the Ruth Lilly Pegasus Award from the Poetry Foundation.

PATRICK ROSAL is the author of *Brooklyn Antediluvian*, his fourth full-length collection of poetry. He teaches in the MFA program at Rutgers University–Camden.

CLARE ROSSINI is artist-in-residence at Trinity College in Hartford, Connecticut, where she teaches creative writing and directs a program that places college students in an inner-city arts classroom. Her most recent book is *Lingo*.

FRANCINE RUBIN's poetry has appeared in the chapbook *Geometries*, in the pamphlet *The Last Ballet Class*, and at the David Mikow Art Gallery. A former ballet dancer, she now works as the director of academic support at Roxbury Community College. Online, she is at http://francinerubin.tumblr.com.

MURIEL RUKEYSER was an American poet, writer, translator, and activist who lived from December 1913 to February 1980. Her writing career began in journalism, and at twenty-one she covered the Scottsboro case in Alabama. Among the forty books she authored were *The Book of the Dead* and *The Life of Poetry*. Rukeyser was awarded the first Harriet Monroe Poetry Award, as well as the Yale Series of Younger Poets Award, the Levinson Prize, and the Copernicus Prize.

RUTH IRUPÉ SANABRIA's first collection of poetry, *The Strange House Testifies* (Bilingual Press), won second place (poetry) in the 2010 Annual Latino Book Awards. Her second collection of poems, *Beasts Behave in Foreign Land*, received the 2014 Letras Latinas/ Red Hen Press Award. She works as a high school English teacher and lives with her husband and three children in Perth Amboy, New Jersey.

CRAIG SANTOS PEREZ is a native Chamorro from the Pacific Island of Guam. He is the author of three books, most recently *from unincorporated territory [guma']*, which received an American Book Award 2015. He is an associate professor in the English department at the University of Hawai'i, Mānoa.

CHERYL SAVAGEAU is the author of three books of poetry. She has won fellowships from the National Endowment for the Arts and the Massachusetts Artists Foundation. Her children's book, *Muskrat Will Be Swimming*, was a Smithsonian Notable Book and won the Skipping Stones Award for children's environmental literature.

TIM SEIBLES is an English professor at Old Dominion University. He is the author of several collections of poetry, including *Hurdy-Gurdy*, *Hammerlock*, and *Buffalo Head Solos*. His last collection, *Fast Animal*, was a finalist for the 2012 National Book Award.

PURVI SHAH, known for her sparkly eyeshadow and raucous laughter, inspires change as a nonprofit consultant, antiviolence advocate, and writer. During the tenth anniversary of 9/11, she directed *Together We Are New York*, a community-based poetry project to highlight Asian American voices. You can discover her work at http://purvipoets.net, on Twitter @PurviPoets, or in her award-winning book of poetry, *Terrain Tracks*, and her poetry chaplet, *Dark Lip of the Beloved: Sound Your Fiery God-Praise*.

LEE SHARKEY is the author of *Walking Backwards*, *Calendars of Fire*, *A Darker, Sweeter String*, and eight earlier full-length poetry collections and chapbooks. Her work has appeared in *Massachusetts Review*, *Crazyhorse*, *Field*, *Kenyon Review*, *Nimrod*, *Pleiades*, *Seattle Review*, and other journals. She is the recipient of the Abraham Sutzkever Centennial Translation Prize and is a senior editor of the *Beloit Poetry Journal*.

MATTHEW SHENODA is the author of the poetry collections *Somewhere Else* (winner of the American Book Award), *Seasons of Lotus, Seasons of Bone*, and *Tahrir Suite* (winner of the Arab American Book Award) and is coeditor, with Kwame Dawes, of *Bearden's Odyssey: Poets Respond to the Art of Romare Bearden*. He is currently associate professor in the Department of Creative Writing at Columbia College Chicago. For more information, visit www.matthewshenoda.com.

EVIE SHOCKLEY is the author of four collections of poetry, including *the new black*, winner of the 2012 Hurston/Wright Legacy Award in Poetry, and *semiautomatic*. She is also the author of *Renegade Poetics: Black Aesthetics and Formal Innovation in African American Poetry*. She serves as creative writing editor for *Feminist Studies* and is an associate professor of English at Rutgers University.

KEVIN SIMMONDS is the author of *Bend to It* and *Mad for Meat* and the editor of the anthologies *Collective Brightness: LGBTIQ Poets on Faith, Religion & Spirituality* and *Ota Benga Under My Mother's Roof*. He lives in San Francisco and Japan.

MYRA SKLAREW, former president of the Yaddo Artists' Community and professor emerita of literature at American University, was educated at Tufts University and at the writing seminars at the Johns Hopkins University. She studied bacterial viruses and genetics at Cold Spring Harbor Biological Laboratory and conducted research on the memory and frontal lobe function of Rhesus monkeys at Yale University School of Medicine. Her published works include numerous collections of poetry (*The Science of Goodbyes* among others), fiction, and nonfiction (including *A Survivor Named Trauma*).

KAREN SKOLFIELD's book *Frost in the Low Areas* won the 2014 PEN New England Award in poetry. Her poems have appeared in *Crazyhorse, Guernica, Indiana Review, Pleiades, Slice, Washington Square Review*, and other journals. Skolfield teaches writing to engineers at the University of Massachusetts Amherst. For more information, visit www.karenskolfield.com.

DANEZ SMITH is the author of *[insert] boy*, winner of the Lambda Literary Award for Gay Poetry and the Kate Tufts Discovery Award, and *Don't Call Us Dead*. Smith has received fellowships from the McKnight Foundation and the Poetry Foundation and lives in Minneapolis.

J. D. SMITH's third collection, *Labor Day at Venice Beach*, was published in 2012. His work in several genres has appeared in such publications as *Boulevard, Dark Mountain*, the *Los Angeles Times*, and *Terrain*. Smith lives and works in Washington, D.C.

MONICA SOK is a Cambodian poet from Lancaster, Pennsylvania. Author of the chapbook *Year Zero*, Sok is the 2016–18 Stadler Fellow at Bucknell University.

JUDITH SORNBERGER's most recent book, *The Accidental Pilgrim: Finding God and His Mother in Tuscany*, is from Shanti Arts Publications. She is the author of seven collections of poems, most recently *Wal-Mart Orchid*. She lives on the side of a mountain outside of Wellsboro, Pennsylvania.

ALISON SWAN's poems and prose have appeared in many publications, including her poetry chapbooks *Before the Snow Moon* and *Dog Heart*, the recent anthologies *Here: Women Writing on the Upper Peninsula* and *Poetry in Michigan / Michigan in Poetry*, and the journals *TriQuarterly* and *North American Review*. Her book *Fresh Water: Women Writing on the Great Lakes* is a Michigan Notable Book. A recipient of a Mesa Refuge Fellowship and the Petoskey Prize for Grassroots Environmental Leadership, she teaches in the Environmental and Sustainability Studies Program at Western Michigan University. She lives in Ann Arbor.

ARTHUR SZE's latest book of poetry is *Compass Rose*. He is a recipient of the Jackson Poetry Prize and is a chancellor of the Academy of American Poets. He lives in Santa Fe, New Mexico.

JIANG TAO is one of the most interesting poets and poetry critics from China. He teaches poetry at Beijing University. He won the Liu Li-an Poetry Prize in 1997 and the Poetry East West Award in Criticism in 2014.

SHEREE RENÉE THOMAS, a native of Memphis, is a 2016 Tennessee Arts Fellow and a Cave Canem and New York Foundation for the Arts fellow. She has taught at Smith College as a Lakes Writer-in-Residence and was awarded residencies at the Millay Colony, Blue Mountain, Ledig House, and Virginia Center for the Creative Arts. Her work has appeared in numerous publications, including *Callaloo*, *Memphis Noir*, *Mythic Delirium*, *The Ringing Ear*, *Stories for Chip*, the *New York Times*, and *Transition*.

TRUTH THOMAS is a singer-songwriter and award-winning poet who was born in Knoxville, Tennessee, and raised in Washington, D.C. He is the founder of Cherry Castle Publishing. Thomas's poems have appeared in over one hundred publications, including *Callaloo*, *Emerson Review*, *Newtowner Magazine*, *New York Quarterly*, *Pluck!*, and *The 100 Best African American Poems* (edited by Nikki Giovanni).

JEAN TOOMER, grandson of the first African American governor, was an African American poet and novelist who lived from December 1894 to March 1967. He is best known for his book *Cane*, published in 1923. His other works include the long poem *Blue Meridian* and the poetry volume *The Wayward and the Seeking*.

MELISSA TUCKEY is a writer, editor, and poet living in upstate New York. She is the author of *Tenuous Chapel*, a book of poems selected by Charles Simic for the ABZ first-book award, and *Rope as Witness*, a chapbook published by Pudding House. She's a cofounder of Split This Rock, a fellow at the Black Earth Institute, and a recipient of a Provincetown Fine Arts Work Center Winter Fellowship, among other honors.

KIRMEN URIBE won the National Prize of Literature in Spain for his first novel *Bilbao–New York–Bilbao*. His poetry collection *Meanwhile Take My Hand*, translated into English by Elizabeth Macklin, was a finalist for the 2008 PEN Award for Poetry in Translation. His works has been published at such American publications as the *New Yorker*, *Open City*, and *Circumference or Little Star*. He writes in the Basque language.

PAMELA USCHUK, a political activist and wilderness advocate, has howled out six books of poems, including *Crazy Love*, winner of an American Book Award, and the collection of poems *Blood Flower*. Uschuk is editor in chief of *Cutthroat: A Journal of the Arts* and lives in Tucson, Arizona. Her work has been translated into a dozen languages.

KAZURNARI USUKI is a poet and dermatologist who was born in Kagoshima, Japan, in 1961. His books include *A Transparent Stone* and *The Tail of Light*.

DAN VERA is a writer, editor, and literary historian in Washington, D.C. His poetry appears in *Speaking Wiri Wiri* and *The Space between Our Danger and Delight*, as well as in various journals and anthologies. He cocurates the literary history site D.C. Writers' Homes and chairs the board of Split This Rock Poetry.

MARGARET WALKER was an African American poet and writer who lived from July 1915 to November 1988. Walker's works include *For My People*, which won the Yale Series of Younger Poets Award in 1942, and the novel *Jubilee*. In 2014 Walker was inducted into the Chicago Literary Hall of Fame.

WANG PING has published eleven books of poetry and prose, including *American Visa*, *Foreign Devil*, *Of Flesh and Spirit*, *New Generation*, *Aching for Beauty*, *The Magic Whip*, *The Last Communist Virgin*, and *10,000 Waves*. She is a recipient of NEA, Bush, Lannan, and McKnight fellowships and the founder and director of Kinship of Rivers project.

MUKOMA WA NGUGI is an assistant professor of English at Cornell University and the author of the novels *Mrs. Shaw*, *Black Star Nairobi*, and *Nairobi Heat* and two books of poetry, *Hurling Words at Consciousness* and *Logotherapy*. He is the cofounder of the Mabati-Cornell Kiswahili Prize for African Literature and codirector of the Global South Project–Cornell.

BETH WELLINGTON is a poet, journalist, online organizer, and activist who lives in central Appalachia. In her work she often gives voice to those who endure and resist. One of her favorite things, besides writing, is to prepare good food from local farms and gardens with friends.

STEVEN F. WHITE teaches in the Hispanic studies program at St. Lawrence University. He translated Federico García Lorca's *Poet in New York* and is the editor of *El consumo de lo que somos: Muestra de poesía ecológica hispánica contemporánea* and *Ayahuasca Reader: Encounters with the Amazon's Sacred Vine*.

DAN WILCOX is the host of the Third Thursday Poetry Night at the Social Justice Center in Albany, New York, and a member of Veterans for Peace and the poetry performance group 3 Guys from Albany. As a photographer, he claims to have the world's largest collection of photos of unknown poets.

ELEANOR WILNER is the author of seven books of poetry, most recently *Tourist in Hell* and *The Girl with Bees in Her Hair*. Her awards include a MacArthur Foundation Fellowship, the Juniper Prize, and three Pushcart Prizes; she teaches in the MFA program for writers at Warren Wilson College.

KARENNE WOOD (Monacan) earned an MFA in creative writing from George Mason University and a PhD in linguistic anthropology from the University of Virginia. Her book of poems *Markings on Earth* won the North American Native Authors' First Book Award in 2000, and her second book, *Weaving the Boundary*, was published in 2016 by the University of Arizona Press. Her poems have appeared in such journals as the *Kenyon Review* and *Shenandoah*.

LISA WUJNOVICH writes poetry and farms at Mountain Dell Farm in Hancock, New York, where she hosts a monthly new moon women's sauna in a converted cypress water barrel. She is the author of the chapbooks *Fieldwork* and *This Place Called Us*. She also coedited the anthology *The Lake Rises: Poems to and for Our Bodies of Water*.

AMY YOUNG is former poet laureate of Alexandria, Virginia. Her poems have appeared in *Poet Lore* and *Northern Virginia Review*, as well as in other publications, and have been set to music and performed by the Twenty-First-Century Consort at the Smithsonian American Art Museum and by the Pittsburgh New Music Ensemble. She teaches writing at the Lab School of Washington and enjoys birdwatching and long walks along the Potomac River.

SAADI YOUSSEF is an Iraqi poet, journalist, publisher, and political activist. He is the author of thirty volumes of poetry and seven books of prose and most recently, in 2012, published *Nostalgia, My Enemy: Poems*. He now lives in London, where he is also a leading translator of English literature into Arabic.

JAVIER ZAMORA was born in El Salvador and migrated to the United States when he was nine. He holds fellowships from CantoMundo, Colgate University, MacDowell, the National Endowment for the Arts, and Yaddo, and he was the recipient of the Barnes and Noble Writer for Writer's Award. His poems have appeared in *APR*, *Narrative*, *Ploughshares*, *Poetry*, *Kenyon Review*, and elsewhere.

PERMISSIONS AND CREDITS
||||||||||||||||||||||||||||||||||||||||||||||||||||||||||||||||||||||||||||||||||||||||||||||||||||||||||||||||||||||||||||||||||||

Frances Payne Adler. "Supreme." From "Dare I Call You Cousin" exhibition, 2016. Originally published in *Global Poetry Anthology 2013* (Montreal, Quebec: Signal Editions/Vehicule Press, 2013), 74–75. Montreal International Poetry Prize, finalist. Reprinted by permission of the author.

Yasunori Akiyama: "Give Us Back Everything" from *Reverberations from Fukushima: 50 Japanese Poets Speak Out* (Portland: Inkwater Press, 2014). Copyright © 2014 by Yasunori Akiyama. Translated by Leah Stenson. Permission granted by editor.

Claribel Alegría: "The Rivers" from *Poetry Like Bread: Poets of The Political Imagination From Curbstone Press* (Willimantic, Conneticut: Curbstone Press, 1994). Copyright © 1994 by Claribel Alegría. Permission granted by author.

Pamela Alexander: "Makers" appeared online as Split This Rock's Poem of the Week on July 29, 2016. Copyright © 2016 by Pamela Alexander. Permission granted by author.

Luis Alberto Ambroggio: "Kyoto Protocol" from *Difficult Beauty* (New York City: Cross-Cultural Communications, 2009). Additionally published in *La desnudez del asombro* (Madrid, Spain: Editorial Vision Libros, 2009). Translated by Yvette Neisser Moreno. Copyright © 2009 by Luis Alberto Ambroggio. Permission granted by author.

Doug Anderson: "Raining in the Fields" from *Horse Medicine* (New York City: Barrow Street Press, 2015). Copyright © 2015 by Doug Anderson. Permission granted by author.

Homero Aridjis: "About Angels IX" and "The Last Night of the World" from *Tiempo De Angeles* (Mexico City: Fundación de Cultura Televisa, 1994). Translated by George McWhirter. Subsequently published in *Tiempo De Angeles* (Mexico City: Fundación de Cultura Económica-Consejo de la Crónica de la Ciudad de México, 1997). Translated by George McWhirter. Additionally, published in *Tiempo De Angeles* (Mexico City: Fundación de Cultura Económica, 2000). Translated by George McWhirter. Furthermore, published in *Tiempo De Angeles / A Time of Angels* (San Francisco: Fundación de Cultura Económica and City Lights Publishers, 2012). Translated by George McWhirter. Copyright © 1994, 1997, 2000, 2012 by Homero Aridjis. Permission granted by author.

Jennifer H. Atkinson: "Landscape with Translucent Moon" and "At the Chernobyl Power Plant Eco-Reserve" appeared in the *Missouri Review* (Winter 2013). Copyright © 2013 by Jennifer H. Atkinson. Reprinted from *The Thinking Eye* by Jennifer Atkinson. Copyright © 2016 by Parlor Press. Used by permission.

David Attwooll: "Murmuration" first appeared in *Surfacing* (Smith/Doorstop, 2013) and is reprinted with thanks to the publisher. Copyright © 2013 by David Attwooll.

David Baker: "Too Many" from *Never-Ending Birds: Poems* (New York City: W. W. Norton and Company Inc., 2009). Copyright © 2011 by David Baker. Permission granted by author.

John Balaban: "For the Missing in Action" from *Locusts at the Edge of Summer: New and Selected Poems*. Copyright © 1997 by John Balaban. Reprinted with the permission of The Permissions Company, Inc., on behalf of Copper Canyon Press, www,coppercanyonpress.org.

Samiya Bashir: "Blackbody Curve" appeared in *Poetry Magazine* (January 2016). Copyright © 2016 by Samiya Bashir. Permission granted by author.

Gabriella M. Belfiglio: "Descent." Copyright © 2016 by Gabriella Belfiglio. Permission granted by author.

Wendell Berry: "2008, XII" Copyright © 2010 by Wendell Berry from *This Day: Collected & New Sabbath Poems* and "The Peace of Wild Things" Copyright © 1998 by Wendell Berry from *Selected Poems of Wendell Berry*. Reprinted with permission of Counterpoint.

Tara Betts: "Taking Root." Copyright © 2016 by Tara Betts. Permission granted by author.

Kimberly Blaeser: "Eloquence of Earth" (excerpt) appeared online on *Mujeres Talk* blog on May 13, 2014. Subsequently published in *Amethyst and Agate: Poems of Lake Superior* (Duluth, Minn.: Holy Cow! Press, 2015). Copyright © 2014, 2015 by Kimberly Blaeser. Permission granted by author.

Jody Bolz: "Foreground, Fukushima." Copyright © 2016 by Jody Bolz. Permission granted by author.

Brian Brodeur: "Cousins" appeared in *River Styx* (Fall 2012). Subsequently published in *Local Fauna* (Kent, Ohio: The Kent State University Press, 2015). Copyright © 2012, 2015 by Brian Brodeur. Permission granted by author.

Sarah Browning: "Birthday Poem, March 31, 1999" originally published in *Whiskey in the Garden of Eden* (Washington, D.C.: Word Works, 2007). Copyright © 2007 by Sarah Browning. Permission granted by author.

Dennis Brutus: "Untitled" from *Poetry and Protest: A Dennis Brutus Reader* (Chicago: Haymarket Books, 2006). Copyright © 2006 by Dennis Brutus.

Esthela Calderón: "The Price of What You See." Copyright © 2016 by Esthela Calderon. Translated by Steven F. White. Permission granted by translator.

Lauren Camp: "How to Disappear the Stars" was first published in *Adobe Walls Anthology*. Copyright © 2010 by Lauren Camp. Permission granted by author.

Christian Campbell: "To Hold a Meditation" appeared in *Callaloo* (Spring 2008). Subsequently published in *Running the Dusk* (Leeds, England: Peepal Tree, 2010). Copyright © 2008, 2008 by Christian Campbell. Permission granted by Peepal Tree.

Ernesto Cardenal: "The Parrots" translated by Jonathon Cohen, from *Pluriverse: New and Selected Poems*, copyright ©1977, 1979, 1980, 1984,1986, 2009 by Ernesto Cardenal. Copyright © 2009 by New Directions Publishing Corp. Translation copyright by Jonathon Cohen © 1977, 1979, 1980, 1984,1986, 2009. Reprinted by permission of New Directions Publishing Corp. "New Ecology," translated by Donald D. Walsh, from *Pluriverse: New and Selected Poems*, copyright © 1977, 1979, 1980, 1984, 1986, 2009 by Ernesto Cardenal. Copyright © 2009 by New Directions Publishing Corp. Translation copyright © 1977, 1980 by Donald D. Walsh. Reprinted by permission of New Directions Publishing Corp.

Brenda Cárdenas: "Zacuanpapalotls" from *Boomerang* (Arizona State University, Tempe, Ariz.: Bilingual Press/Editorial Bilingüe, 2009). Copyright © 2009 by Brenda Cárdenas. Permission granted by author.

Lorna Dee Cervantes: "Freeway 280" from *Emplumada* (Pittsburgh, Pa.: University of Pittsburgh Press, 1981). Copyright © 1981 by Lorna Dee Cervantes. "Freeway 280" first appeared in Latin *American Literary Review* 5, no. 10 (1977). Reprinted with permission from *Latin American Literary Review* and the author.

Dane Cervine: "A Great Civilization" appeared in *Caesura* (2012). Copyright © 2012 by Dane Cervine. Permission granted by author. "The Dreams of Antelope" appeared in *Monterey Poetry Review* (October 2013). Copyright © 2013 by Dane Cervine. Permission granted by author. "The Parable of St. Matthew Island." Copyright © 2016 by Dane Cervine. Permission granted by author.

Hayan Charara: "The Weather" from *The Alchemists Diary* (New York City: Hanging Loose Press, 2001). Subsequently appeared in *Hanging Loose* 94 (2009). Afterward published in *Something Sinister* (Pittsburgh, Pa.: Carnegie Mellon University Press, 2016). Copyright © 2001, 2009, 2016 by Hayan Charara. Permission granted by author.

Chen Chen: "Set the Garden on Fire" appeared online as Split This Rock's Poem of the Week on September 25, 2014. Subsequently, published in *Set the Garden on Fire* (Cincinatti, Ohio: Porkbelly Press, 2015). Copyright © 2014, 2015 by Chen Chen. Permission granted by author.

Grant Clauser: "Finding Water on Mars" appeared in *Split Rock Review* (issue 3). Copyright © 2014 by Grant Clauser. Permission granted by author.

Lucille Clifton, "generations," "the killing of the trees," and "cutting greens" from *The Collected Poems of Lucille Clifton*. Copyright © 1987, 1991 by Lucille Clifton. Reprinted with the permission of The Permissions Company, Inc., on behalf of BOA Editions Ltd., www.boaeditions.org.

Martha Collins: "Moving Still" (excerpt) from *Day unto Day* by Martha Collins (Minneapolis: Milkweed Editions, 2014). Copyright © 2014 by Martha Collins. Reprinted with permission from Milkweed Editions. www.milkweed.org.

Stephen Collis: "Sometimes We Resist" from *Once in Blockadia* © 2016, Stephen Collis, Talonbooks, Vancouver, B.C. Reprinted by permission of the publisher.

Mahmoud Darwish: "We Travel Like All People" from *Unfortunately, It Was Paradise: Selected Poems* (Berkeley, Calif.: University of California Press, 2013). Copyright © 2013 by Mahmoud Darwish. Permission granted by publisher.

Hayes Davis: "Inundated" appeared in *Delaware Poetry Review*, Spring 2010. Reprinted with permission of the author.

Heather Lynne Davis: "29 Men" appeared online at The Quarry: Split This Rock Online Poetry Database on June 30, 2014. Copyright © 2014 by Heather Lynne Davis. Permission granted by author.

Brian Komei Dempster, "Crossing" from *Topaz*. Copyright © 2013 by Brian Komei Dempster. Reprinted with the permission of The Permissions Company, Inc., on behalf of Four Way Books, www.fourwaybooks.com.

Natalie Diaz: "Cloud Watching" and "Why I Don't Mention Flowers When Conversations with My Brother Reach Uncomfortable Silence" from *When My Brother Was* an *Aztec* (Port Townsend, Wash.: Copper Canyon Press, 2012). Copyright © 2012 by Natalie Diaz. Permission granted by author.

LeConté Dill: "We Who Weave" appeared in *Poetry Magazine* (January 2016). Copyright © 2016 by LeConté Dill. Permission granted by author.

Camille T. Dungy: "Cleaning" from *What to Eat, What to Drink, What to Leave for Poison* (Los Angeles: Red Hen Press, 2006). Copyright © 2006 by Camille T. Dungy. Permission granted by author. "Daisy Cutter" and "A Massive Dying Off" from *Smith Blue* (Carbondale: Southern Illinois University Press, 2011). Copyright © 2011 by Camille T. Dungy. Reprinted by permission of Southern Illinois Press.

Zein El-Amine: "The Dogs of Ashdod" appeared in *Wild River Review* (2014). Copyright © 2014 by Zein El-Amine. Permission granted by author.

Daniela Elza: "beware of dog" from *Force Field: 77 Women Poets of British Columbia* (Salt Spring Island, B.C.: Mother Tongue Publishing Limited, 2013). Copyright © 2013 by Daniela Elza. Permission granted by author.

Kathy Engel: "Now I Pray" appeared in *Poetry Magazine* (January 2016). Copyright © 2016 by Kathy Engel. Permission granted by author. "Return" appeared in *Poet Lore* (Spring/Summer 2015). Copyright © 2015 by Kathy Engel. Permission granted by author.

Louise Erdrich: "I Was Sleeping Where the Black Oaks Move" originally published in *Jacklight*; currently collected in *Original Fire: Selected and New Poems*. Copyright © 1984 Louise Erdrich, used by permission of The Wylie Agency LLC.

Martín Espada: "Federico's Ghost" copyright © 1990 by Martín Espada, from *Alabanza: New and Selected Poems 1982–2002* by Martín Espada. Used by permission of W. W. Norton & Company, Inc. and the author. "Coca-Cola and Coco Frío" from *City of Coughing and Dead Radiators* by Martín Espada, copyright © 1993 Martín Espada. Used by permission of W. W. Norton & Company, Inc. and the author.

Tarfia Faizullah: "Register of Eliminated Villages" appeared in *Passages North* (Winter 2012). Copyright © 2012 by Tarfia Faizullah. Permission granted by author.

Alec Finlay: "Hutopia" (excerpt) from *Remote Performances in Nature and Architecture* (Burlington, Vermont: Ashgate, 2015). Copyright © 2015 by Alec Finlay. Permission granted by author.

Everett Hoagland: "Invocation." Copyright © 2016 by Everett Hoagland. Permission granted by author.

Linda Hogan: "Bamboo," "Fat," "Milk," and "Mountain Lion" are reprinted by permission from *The Book of Medicines* (Coffee House Press, 1993). Copyright © 1993 by Linda Hogan.

Ailish Hopper: "Did It Ever Occur to You That Maybe You're Falling in Love?" appeared in *Poetry Magazine* (January 2016). Copyright © 2016 by Ailish Hopper. Permission granted by author.

Randall Horton: "the weight of all things" appeared online in issue 64 of the *Offending Adam* on May 30, 2011. Copyright © 2011 by Randall Horton. Permission granted by author.

Elizabeth Jacobson: "Almonds" appeared in *About Place Journal* (November 2014). Copyright © 2014 by Elizabeth Jacobson. Permission granted by author.

Jaime Lee Jarvis: "Aral" appeared online with a longer epigraph as Split This Rock's Poem of the Week on November 2, 2010. Copyright © 2010 by Jaime Lee Jarvis. Permission granted by author.

Honorée Fanonne Jeffers: "Suddenly in Grace" initially appeared in *Red Clay Suite* (Carbondale, Illinois: Southern Illinois University Press, 2007). Copyright © 2007 by Honorée Fanonne Jeffers. Permission granted by the publisher. "Wampum" appeared in *Poetry Magazine* (January 2016). Copyright © 2016 by Honorée Fanonne Jeffers. Permission granted by author.

Saeed Jones: "Deepwater" appeared online at Poets For Living Waters on August 12, 2010. Copyright © 2010 by Saeed Jones. Permission granted by author.

June Jordan: "Focus in Real Time" and "Who Would Be Free, Themselves Must Strike the Blow" from *Directed By Desire: Collected Poems* (Port Townsend, Wash.: Copper Canyon Press, 2005). Copyright © 2005 by June Jordan Literary Estate. Reprinted with permission of the June M. Jordan Literary Estate and Copper Canyon Press. www.junejordan.com.

Joan Naviyuk Kane: "Epithalamia" first appeared in *Poetry Magazine* (January 2016). "Epithalamia" from *Black Milk Carbo*n, by Joan Naviyuk Kane. Copyright © 2017 by Joan Kane. Reprinted permission of the University of Pittsburgh Press.

Douglas Kearney: "The Orange Alert" from *Fear, Some: Poems* (Los Angeles, Calif.: Red Hen Press, 2006). Copyright © 2006 by Douglas Kearney. Permission granted by author.

Alan King: "Uptown" appeared in *Wasafiri* (issue 76, 2013). Copyright © 2013 by Alan King. Permission granted by author.

Yusef Komunyakaa: "You and I Are Disappearing" from *Dien Cai Dau.* © 1988 by Yusef Komunyakaa. Published by Wesleyan University Press. Used by permission. "Crossing a City Highway" appeared in *Poetry Magazine* (January 2016). Copyright © 2016 by Yusef Komunyakaa. Permission granted by author.

Elee Kraljii Gardiner: "Refinement" from *The Enpipe Line: 70,000+ Kilometres of Poetry Written in Resistance to the Enbridge Northern Gateway Pipelines Proposal* (Smithers, B.C.: Creekstone Press, 2012). Copyright © 2012 by Elee Kraljii Gardiner. Permission granted by author. "Aubade" from *Serpentine Loop* (Vancouver, B.C.: Anvil Press, 2016). Copyright © 2016 by Elee Kraljii Gardiner. Permission granted by author.

Christi Kramer: "Awe is the entrance" from the chapter "Lean In as the Story Is Told: Vestibular Sense, Poetic Image and Instruction for Seeing" in *Poetic Inquiry II: Seeing, Caring, Understanding: Using Poetry as and for Inquiry* (Rotterdam, The Netherlands: Sense Publishers, 2016). Copyright © 2016 by Christi Kramer. Permission granted by author.

Aaron Kreuter: "Paddling the Nickel Tailings near Sudbury" appeared online as Split This Rock's Poem of The Week on May 14, 2015. Subsequently published in *Arguments for Lawn Chairs* (Toronto, Ont.: Guernica Editions, 2016). Copyright © 2015, 2016 by Aaron Kreuter. Permission granted by author.

Quraysh Ali Lansana: "harvest" and "after harvest" from *Mystic Turf* (Detroit, Mich.: Willow Books, 2012). Copyright © 2012 by Quraysh Ali Lansana. Permission granted by author.

Dorianne Laux: "Evening" appeared online at www.doriannelaux.net in 2015. Copyright © 2015 by Dorianne Laux. Permission granted by author.

Shara Lessley: "In Jordan's Northernmost Province" (for the Middle East's first all-female de-mining crew) appeared in *Crazyhorse* (Fall 2013). Subsequently, featured online by the National Endowment for the Arts as part of the Writers' Corner (2015). Copyright © 2013, 2015 by Shara Lessley. Permission granted by author.

Denise Levertov: "In California during the Gulf War" by Denise Levertov, from *Poems 1968–1972*, copyright © 1972 by Denise Levertov. Reprinted by permission of New Directions Publishing Corp. Reprinted by permission of Pollinger Limited (www.pollingerltd.com) on behalf of the estate of Denise Levertov. "Overheard in S.E. Asia" by Denise Levertov, from *Evening Train*, copyright © 1992 by Denise Levertov. Reprinted by permission of New Directions Publishing Corp. Reprinted with permission of Pollinger Limited (www.pollingerltd.com) on behalf of the estate of Denise Levertov.

Pippa Little: "Turning the Ship for Home and Then the Telling." Copyright © 2016 by Pippa Little. Permission granted by author.

Cecilia Llompart: "The Barnacle and the Grey Whale" appeared online as part of Poem-A-Day from www.poets.org on February 28, 2014. Copyright © 2014 by Cecilia Llompart. Permission granted by author.

Christina Lovin: "Little Fires" (excerpt) from *Little Fires* (Georgetown, Ky.: Finishing Line Press, 2007). Additionally appeared online at www.christinalovin.com. Copyright © 2007 by Christina Lovin. Subsequently published in *Echo: Poems* (Huron, Ohio: Bottom Dog Press, 2014). Copyright © 2014 by Christina Lovin. Permission granted by author.

Jacqueline Marcus: "No Turning Back for the Soul" from *Summer Rains* (Oak Ridge, Tenn.: Iris Press, 2015). Copyright © 2015 by Jacqueline Marcus. Permission granted by author.

Morton Marcus: "There Are Days Now" from *Big Winds, Glass Mornings, Shadows Cast by Stars: Poems 1972–1980* (Los Angeles, Calif.: Jazz Press, 1981). Copyright © 1981 by Morton Marcus. Permission granted by Jazz Press.

Jamaal May: "Pomegranate Means Grenade" first appeared in *Callaloo* (Spring 2012). From *Hum*. Copyright © 2013 by Jamaal May. Reprinted with permission of The Permissions Company, Inc., on behalf of Alice James Books, www.alicejamesbooks.org.

Molly McGlennen: "Snake River IV" appeared in *Red Ink: Journal of Indigenous Literature, Art and Humanities* (Spring 2015). Copyright © 2015 by Molly McGlennen. Permission granted by author.

Joshua McKinney: "Hum" appeared in *Boulevard Magazine* (Fall 2014). Subsequently appeared online in *Poetry Daily* at www.poems.com on October 14, 2014. Copyright © 2014 by Joshua McKinney. Permission granted by author.

Jane Mead: "Money" from *Money Money Money / Water Water Water*. Copyright © 2014 by Jane Mead. Reprinted with the permission of The Permissions Company, Inc., on behalf of Alice James Books, www.alicejamesbooks.org.

W. S. Merwin: "Thanks" and "Native Trees" from *The Rain in the Trees* by W. S. Merwin, copyright © 1988 by W. S. Merwin. Used by permission of Alred A. Knopf, an imprint

gi-e" and "Whale Song" from *Sing: Poetry from the Indigenous Americas* (Tucson: University of Arizona Press, 2011). Copyright © 2011 by Elise Paschen. Permission granted by author.

Nancy K. Pearson: "Brazos Bend" from *The Whole by Contemplation of a Single Bone: Poems* (New York City: Fordham University Press, 2016). Copyright © 2016 by Nancy K. Pearson. Permission granted by author.

Emmy Pérez: "Staying in the flood" appeared in *Cuadernos De Aldeeu* (Fall 2013). "Downriver, Río Grande Ghazalion" appeared in *Newfound Journal* (Fall 2014). This poem has quotes from Gloria Anzaldúa's *Borderlands/La Frontera: The New Mestiza*, the traditional song "Las Mañanitas," and Richard Wright's *Black Boy*. Both poems subsequently appeared in *With the River on Our Face* (Tucson: University of Arizona Press, 2016). Copyright © 2016 Arizona Board of Regents. Reprinted by permission granted by the University of Arizona Press.

Vivian Faith Prescott: "Living by a Tank Farm Cradle Song" and "Transients" are from *Slick* (Alabama: White Knuckle Press, 2010.). Copyright © 2010 by Vivian Faith Prescott. Permission granted by author.

Gretchen Primack: "The Dogs and I Walked Our Woods" from *Kind* (Woodstock, N.Y.: Post Traumatic Press, 2012). Subsequently appeared online at The Quarry: Split This Rock Online Poetry Database on July 14, 2014. Copyright © 2012, 2014 by Gretchen Primark. Permission granted by author.

Tala Abu Rahmeh: "Pomegranates" appeared online in *Foreign Policy in Focus* on July 7, 2011. Copyright © 2011 by Tala Abu Rahmeh. Permission granted by author.

Hila Ratzabi: "Diary of Sila the Sky God" appeared in *Tinderbox Poetry Journal* (February 2014). Copyright © 2014 by Hila Ratzabi. Permission granted by author.

Shane Rhodes: "Circle the Wagons: In Ink: Meditation on Treaty Two" from *X: Poems* (Gibsons, B.C.: Nightwood Editions, 2013). Copyright © 2013 by Shane Rhodes. Permission granted by author.

Adrienne Rich: "For the Record." Copyright © 2016 by the Adrienne Rich Literary Trust. Copyright © 1966 by Adrienne Rich, "Trying to Talk with a Man." Copyright © 2016 by the Adrienne Rich Literary Trust. Copyright © 1973 by W. W. Norton & Company, Inc. from *Collected Poems: 1950–2012* by Adrienne Rich. Used by Permission of W. W. Norton & Company, Inc.

Katy Richey: "Spider's Orb" and "Recovery." Copyright © 2016 by Katy Richey. Permission granted by author.